POSTCARDS FROM ED

Not For Sale

ALWAYS A GIFT, NEVER FOR SALE
LittleFreeLibrary.org®

ALSO BY EDWARD ABBEY

FICTION

Jonathan Troy
The Brave Cowboy
Fire on the Mountain
Black Sun
The Monkey Wrench Gang
Good News
The Fool's Progress
Hayduke Lives!
Earth Apples: The Poetry of Edward Abbey

NONFICTION

Desert Solitaire: A Season in the Wilderness
Appalachian Wilderness
Slickrock
Cactus Country
The Journey Home
The Hidden Canyon
Abbey's Road
Desert Images
Down the River
Beyond the Wall
One Life at a Time, Please
Confessions of a Barbarian

Postcards from Ed

DISPATCHES AND SALVOS FROM AN AMERICAN ICONOCLAST

EDITED AND WITH AN INTRODUCTION
BY DAVID PETERSEN

MILKWEED EDITIONS

© 2006, Clarke Cartwright Abbey
© 2006, Foreword by Terry Tempest Williams
© 2006, Introduction, Selection, and Arrangement by David Petersen
All rights reserved. Except for brief quotations in critical articles or reviews, no part of this book may be reproduced in any manner without prior written permission from the publisher: Milkweed Editions, 1011 Washington Avenue South, Suite 300, Minneapolis, Minnesota 55415. (800) 520-6455 www.milkweed.org

Cover and interior photographs and documents courtesy Clarke Cartwright Abbey
Photograph of Edward Abbey and David Petersen courtesy of Caroline Petersen

Published 2006 by Milkweed Editions
Printed in Canada
Cover design by Christian Fuenfhausen
Interior design by Percolator
The text of this book is set in Whitman.
07 08 09 10 11 5 4 3 2 1
First Paperback Edition

Milkweed Editions, a nonprofit publisher, gratefully acknowledges sustaining support from Emilie and Henry Buchwald; Bush Foundation; Patrick and Aimee Butler Family Foundation; Cargill Value Investment; Timothy and Tara Clark Family Charitable Fund; Dougherty Family Foundation; Ecolab Foundation; General Mills Foundation; Greystone Foundation; Institute for Scholarship in the Liberal Arts, College of Arts and Sciences, University of Notre Dame; Constance B. Kunin; Marshall Field's Gives; McKnight Foundation; a grant from the Minnesota State Arts Board, through an appropriation by the Minnesota State Legislature, a grant from the National Endowment for the Arts, and private funders; an award from the National Endowment for the Arts, which believes that a great nation deserves great art; Navarre Corporation; Debbie Reynolds; St. Paul Travelers Foundation; Ellen and Sheldon Sturgis; Target Foundation; Gertrude Sexton Thompson Charitable Trust (George R. A. Johnson, Trustee); James R. Thorpe Foundation; Toro Foundation; Serene and Christopher Warren; W. M. Foundation; and Xcel Energy Foundation.

The Library of Congress has cataloged the hardcover edition as follows:
Library of Congress
Cataloging-in-Publication Data
Abbey, Edward, 1927–
Postcards from Ed : the collected correspondence of Edward Abbey, 1949/1989 / edited by David Petersen.— 1st ed.
p. cm.
ISBN-13: 978-1-57131-284-6
(hardcover : acid-free paper)
ISBN-10: 1-57131-284-6
(hardcover : acid-free paper)
1. Abbey, Edward, 1927—Correspondence.
2. Authors, American—20th century—Correspondence.
I. Petersen, David, 1946– II. Title.
PS3551.B2Z48 2006
813'.54—dc22

2006002354

This book is printed on acid-free, recycled (100% post-consumer waste) paper.

NATIONAL
ENDOWMENT
FOR THE ARTS
A great nation
deserves great art.

MINNESOTA
STATE ARTS BOARD

POSTCARDS FROM ED

But hell, I do like to write letters.
Much easier than writing books.

—E. A.

FOREWORD

TERRY TEMPEST WILLIAMS

February 14, 2006

Dearest Ed:

I miss you. We all do. I am sending you a cartoon that appeared recently in the *Salt Lake Tribune*: A grandfather and his granddaughter are standing on the rim of Dead Horse Point, overlooking Canyonlands and much of the Colorado Plateau. With his arm around her, he says, "One day, none of these public lands will be yours."

Right now, Ed, the cartoonists are the bravest among us. They are the truth tellers, the ones fearlessly drawing the lines between a free society and a society for sale. Evidently, selling off America's public lands is not only good for democracy, but good for the economy. It will pay the bills for building more roads and make up for the losses in the decline of timber sales. It will also help pay for the war in Iraq, a war predicated on lies. The outcry is faint. The streets are empty. We are comfortable here in the United States of America. We the People seem to be asleep, numb, and dead to the liberties being lost.

I wonder what you would be saying right now, and, more importantly, what you would be writing. *Desert Solitaire* was published in 1968—an antiwar credo written straight up, no fiction. It is a book of civil disobedience, or, more to the point, wild obedience—a guide to finding one's whole self in relationship to wildness, not one's fragmented self through war. You celebrate Arches National Park, one of the essential "democratic vistas" that your brother Walt Whitman urges us to embrace.

It's not hard to imagine what you would think of America's current "War on Terror." Your views on Vietnam are well documented. In a letter to your hometown paper, the *Arizona Daily Star*, you wrote on December 29, 1972:

> After winning the election with the fraudulent promise that "peace is at hand," the Nixon-Kissinger team have now revealed the true depth of their intellectual dishonesty and moral corruption. Through the tangled cobweb of official lies comes the thunder of bombs falling on the people of Vietnam. After eight years of defoliating forests, poisoning rice fields, burning villages, napalming civilians and torturing prisoners, our Government is now engaged in an apparent effort to obliterate the cities and destroy the population of the northern half of the little peasant nation of Vietnam. Nothing in American history, not even the wars against the Indians, can equal the shame and brutality and cowardice of this war.

But this war is different. We started it. And now we don't know how to end it. "Insurgents" (I can hear your voice interrupting, "Wasn't George Washington an insurgent to the British?") are blowing up trucks, tanks, and buildings daily. Our colony of Iraq has seen several thousand American soldiers killed and close to twenty thousand wounded—with tens of thousands of Iraqis dead. But we never hear about the Iraqi civilians. Nor do we see the flag-draped coffins of our own coming home weekly. And if mothers of the fallen speak out, we call them fanatics, hysterical liberals, "pawns of the failed femi-Nazis," and we arrest them at the State of the Union for wearing black T-shirts with the body count painted in white.

The projected cost of the Iraq War is said to top $2 trillion, given the health care costs for the wounded. To date, we have spent $173 billion, roughly $4.5 billion a month.

These figures provide some context for understanding the madness of the George W. Bush regime that has grandparents lamenting to their grandchildren that our public lands are now for sale.

At this moment, the Bush Administration plans to sell more than three hundred thousand acres of national forests, our public commons, to help pay for rural schools in forty-one states. Who could be against educating our children? The stories are spinning. The government certainly doesn't want to admit to selling off pieces of America's natural heritage to pay for a bloody war.

Gale Norton, the Secretary of Oil and Gas Development, says the land sales could yield more than $1 billion. The BLM, which you lovingly referred to as "the Bureau of Livestock and Mining" also plans to pawn their lands to raise a pitiful $250 million.

And if this is not fantastic enough, a charismatic congressman named Pombo, a character akin to those you created in your fiction, has come up with the idea of selling fifteen of our national parks. He lives in California near Disneyland.

Forgive my rant, Ed, but you encouraged this, you taught us the difference between anger and rage—how anger turns in on ourselves while sacred rage creates something useful and at times even beautiful—the art of healthy discourse with humor, always with humor. I can hear your words,

> Anger! I'm foaming at the typewriter again. But of the seven deadly sins, wrath is the healthiest—next only to lust. *Pop!* goes the pop-top. A can of Coors will calm me down.

So here's a story you will love—something you inspired but didn't live long enough to witness: The Glen Canyon Institute. They took your dare. Under the leadership of a Mormon physicist named Richard Ingebretsen, these conservative conservationists have created a legitimate movement to restore Glen Canyon by draining Lake Powell. In *The Monkey Wrench Gang* you envisioned taking down the dam, and they have taken this notion to be more than a metaphor. They see it as a mandate. They have stated their case, found figures that project the silting of Lake Powell in the next fifty years, and now are asking why this man-made pond is necessary and at what cost. Congress has taken them seriously enough to hold hearings. Earth First! may have held up the monkey wrench in defiance, but the Glen Canyon Institute has turned the wrench into a microphone, giving voice to all that has been destroyed and what must be restored.

A young Mormon activist named Chris Peterson, with glacial blue eyes, has been talking with Navajo medicine men, and just last summer filled a houseboat with elders so they could witness Lake Powell for themselves. The Rainbow Bridge Religion, which appeared to have drowned, surfaced once again in that revolutionary patience only native people can know— and a lawsuit is underway declaring these tribal lands sacred.

The irony of Nature is already in play. Lake Powell is being drained by drought. Elves' Chasm is exposed once again and Cathedral in the Desert is awash with light. Again, I hear your words:

> Action, there's the thing. Action! When I grow sick with the buzzing of the brain,
> I like to go climb a rock. Cut down a billboard. Disable a bulldozer . . . Climb a
> mountain. Run a rapid . . . "Be true to the earth," says Nietzsche. I like that.

The Earth is true to itself. This is what we are learning. Two new phrases for you, Ed, *global warming* and *climate change*—concepts just beginning to make their appearance in our vernacular before you left this world.

When the scientist James Lovelock brought the image of Gaia to the public's consciousness, he invited us to see the Earth as a living, breathing, self-sustaining, self-correcting organism. Now we see our beautiful blue-green planet heating up. Lovelock writes:

> The scientists delivered the grim message that some time during the coming
> century the Earth System, Gaia, will pass a threshold beyond which it is com-
> mitted to irreversible and mostly adverse change. Once we pass this threshold,
> set by the level of carbon dioxide in the air of somewhere between 400 and 500
> parts per million, nothing the nations of the world do will alter the outcome.
> We are in a sense like passengers on a small pleasure boat sailing quietly down
> the St. Lawrence River towards the Niagara Falls, not knowing that the engines
> are about to fail.

The warning is now a global alert. In this country of optimists, we are loath to hear it. We are currently told by those in power that the facts are fiction, and that "the American lifestyle is not up for negotiation." Congress has failed to enact legislation to lower fuel emissions or to slap a user-tax on gas guzzling sport utility vehicles, which are carving up the desert like a cadaver. And the United States continues to shun international efforts to lower global greenhouse gas emissions. We are not ignorant to this problem. We are arrogant. With temperatures rising the evidence is clear: we are responsible as a species for creating the single most worrisome crisis facing the planet.

So, here is my question to you, Ed. In this era where the war on terror is used as an excuse to exploit and plunder, and even to sell off our public lands; in this new world where the World Bank and World Trade Organization honor corporate rule over local enterprises, and where environmental issues are being usurped in the name of big business and free trade; in this time when the heat is on and Africa is burning up with tropical diseases such as malaria, tuberculosis, and AIDS; and where the word "bird" is now maligned with "bird flu" as the next pandemic suggests once again that we run into our houses and duct tape our windows shut as a collective fear threatens to overtake us: *Where is the place for wilderness?*

Writers like you and me, Ed, are viewed by some as akin to colonialists, part of an American-made system that continues to see wilderness as a frontier apart from the human community—something separate, outside ourselves. We have not conveyed our view of a larger community in the Leopoldian sense well enough—a community that includes plants and animals, whole communities, not fragmented ones—a community of other species that is indifferent to us but that we are not indifferent to. Wilderness is not a place of privilege, but rather a place of integrity, where the evolutionary processes of life are free to continue.

Your friend, the British philosopher Mary Midgley, understands your credo for the wild:

> Man is not adapted to live in a mirror-lined box, generating his own electric light and sending for selected images from outside when he happens to need them. Darkness and a bad smell are all that can come of that. We need the vast world, and it must be a world that does not need us; a world constantly capable of surprising us, a world we did not program, since only such a world is the proper object of wonder.

I wonder what will become of us as a species, Ed, if we lose this ecological balance within "the vast world."

The Hopi know. Vernon Masayesva, a Hopi elder, realized that every day for the past thirty-five years, 3.3 million gallons of sacred groundwater had been mined by Peabody Coal to run their slurry line, adding up to over 1 billion gallons. The aquifer was being drained. He saw that within a decade or so, the aquifer would be empty. Sacred springs were already drying up.

So Vernon Masayesva organized the Black Mesa Trust to protect the Hopi aquifer and expose this injustice. Spiritual values have become pragmatic ones. In the Hopi language, "Paatuwaqatsi" means "water is life."

Through the tribe's vigilance and in partnership with other organizations, the Mohave Power Plant was shut down in January of 2006, stopping Peabody Coal from operating on Black Mesa. The slurry line has been terminated. This action was not taken lightly and it was at great expense to the tribe. But in the end, water was found to be more valuable than the short-term subsidies the coal revenues provided. Daryl Melvin, a Hopi youth and part of the Black Mesa Trust, said, "We are nothing without water—the Hopi are water."

Water creates civilization. I see wilderness as water, our aquifer as human beings that ties us to the whole of this planet, the water that allows us to drink deeply from the source of community, a community that comprises all life, not just the culture of our own species.

I wonder, Ed, at this point in time, especially in the United States of America, if we are creating civilization or culture? I suspect the true answer is that we are creating both, and our task is to learn the difference.

And so, dear Ed, I thank you. Thank you for leading us to the Maze, where "the heart of it remains unknown," where both "ecstasy and danger" exist side by side in the Canyonlands of southern Utah. This is a landscape that cannot be sold. Nor can this strange, difficult, complicated maze of human thought and action regarding the wild be quelled.

Your photograph is on my desk. Your books are on my shelf. Your presence has entered our bloodstream as a patriot with vision. We will carry your example of sacred rage with joy and perseverance, and remember your words, speak your words:

> I will not. I will never surrender. I will fight through to the finish, whatever the outcome. I will not quit, I will not betray and desert the best thing in my life. No, no, I will not surrender . . . Earth is the place for love.

This past summer, a group of ten students from the Environmental Humanities Program at the University of Utah participated in a class called "The Ecology of Residency." Community mentors became the instructors. On a hot Sunday afternoon, the students met with Ken Sleight at the Pack Creek Ranch. They sat in a circle beneath the shade of cottonwood trees and listened to stories about you and the Monkey Wrench Gang.

As Ken was speaking, one of the students interrupted him and asked what it meant to be an environmentalist. Ken paused and looked directly at the young woman. "To be an environmentalist," he said, "is to be engaged in life—to commit to the protection of wilderness." And then he told them stories of floating down Glen Canyon before it was dammed. He exhorted them to help him take the dam down with their monkey wrenches. The students smiled. They were witnessing "Seldom Seen Smith" in the flesh.

And then Ken said, "I'm almost eighty years old. I've got a lot of secrets. I don't want to die with them." He looked down at his dusty work boots and was quiet for a long time. "The monkey wrench is not a symbol of destruction. Ed told me right here on this ranch, the monkey wrench is a symbol of restoration. It's symbolic of your own talents. That's how you are going to fix the world—with your own gifts and talents." This was a revelation for all of us, Ed, to see the monkey wrench as a tool of restoration.

Shortly before my brother Steve died on January 21, 2005, he gave me an old monkey wrench that he found in an antique shop. My brother was a pipeline contractor who worked the kind of backhoes, bulldozers, and trucks that the Monkey Wrench Gang sugared. But he was also an environmentalist, albeit a reserved one, who loved *Desert Solitaire* and the redrock desert of southern Utah. He also loved me, his sister, an activist writer. This gift was his acknowledgment that although we went about our lives differently, our hearts were in the same place, a shared love for all that is wild.

I tell you these last two stories, Ed, because your influence is profound and profoundly personal. It is an ongoing correspondence.

People often say you were larger than life. I disagree. You are life, fully and completely, wildly engaged in life—even in death. Every time I see Turkey Vulture soaring on thermals above the redrock desert, I know you are present, circling, watching, keeping an eye on the lonely lands you love. That your words can be read and reread and read again by each generation is more than hopeful. It is revolutionary.

With love,

POSTCARDS FROM ED

INTRODUCTION

AS OUR TITLE SUGGESTS, Edward Abbey had a special fondness for the economy of postcards. And often, even less. His first "letter" to me, in 1983, was half a dozen syllables scratched across the torn-off back of the *Mother Earth News* letterhead envelope in which, as western editor, I'd sent him a long, belabored plea for an interview. His response in whole: "Can't we do it by phone?"

No, I insisted in a second, far shorter letter. The magazine wants me to sit down and visit with you in person, at length, and I want to shake your hand. In due time the recluse relented and we met at the Arizona Inn in Tucson. And good thing too, since I would soon discover that conversing by telephone with Ed Abbey meant trying to decipher spasms of terse rumblings punctuated with deep voids of silence. Later, when we'd become firm friends, Abbey's calls would typically begin in silence, followed eventually by a deep-throated "Hello, Dave, this is Ed," then more silence. My wife and I found it amusing that a writer and public speaker of such confidence and force seemed so overtly uncomfortable on the telephone. And so it was that most of the time even a few words scratched hurriedly on postcards provided a superior form of communication to the phone. And at his best, in a gregarious or philosophical mood, he wrote letters like essays—long and eloquent, and, in his way, deeply personal. Both extremes are amply represented in the following pages.

"But hell," Abbey confessed to his journals and in missives to friends, "I do like to write letters. Much easier than writing books."

In fact, writing letters and postcards was an almost-daily ritual for Ed. As Terry Tempest Williams observed in the heartful eulogy she delivered at Abbey's Moab memorial service in May of 1989, addressing an audience filled with friends:

> I believe Ed knew and understood the art, the practice, of keeping in touch. The simple act of correspondence. Familiar? One white, generic postcard from Wolf Hole, from Oracle, from Moab, Utah. Signed always, "Love, Ed." Think about the thousands of postcards with Abbey's words, his scribblings that have crossed these sacred lands like a blizzard, like migrating birds, like shooting stars, U.S. Mail, Abbey's courier, keeping in touch.

Typically, Ed warmed up for a day of writing by lighting his corncob pipe and scribbling off a few notes to family or friends. And when the mood was on him, as it increasingly was in the final years, he composed long, thoughtful letters on his old Corona manual, addressed to publishers and editors, newspapers and magazines, writers and critics, politicians and bureaucrats, celebrities and fans.

As evidence of the value Abbey placed on his correspondence, and suggesting his intention someday to publish the best of the batch, he took the trouble to copy many early letters into his journals by hand (or vice versa, drafting letters in the journals, then recopying them for mailing), and to keep carbons of much or most of his typed correspondence. In addition to having open access to these rich resources—the journals and carbons are at the University of Arizona Special Collections Library—many of the cards and letters collected here were contributed by their recipients.

Doubtless, more Abbey missives remain out there on the wing, or have been lost for all time. My own culling deleted at least half. Former lovers, understandably, were chary to share their own private Ed with the world. John DePuy, among Abbey's dearest old friends, lost his entire stash in a basement flood (coincidentally replicating the soggy fate of Ed's four earliest personal journals). Jack Loeffler, another close friend, threw most of his postcards and letters away while "being Zenlike" not long after Ed died. Happily, Jack overlooked several good ones in that misguided moment of mourning, the best of which are included here. And so on.

Since this collection, of necessity, is a one-sided record of a lifetime of correspondence, I want to note that many recipients—New Mexico novelist John Nichols comes foremost to mind—gave as good as they got in ongoing discussions and (generally) friendly debate.

In the end, shortfalls notwithstanding, this collection comprises a treasure of outgoing Abbey correspondence spanning from 1949 to just days before the author's death on March 14, 1989. The photocopies from which these "postcards" were winnowed fill a bushel-sized Washington State Apples box. Years of relaxed, part-time effort went into tracking, reading, sorting, culling, and categorizing. The final selection provides a balanced sampling of recipients, subjects, moods (humorous to loving to red-hot angry), and styles (clownishly informal to classic classy Ed; tender to rude and offensive), while minimizing redundancies.

Concerning the latter, while most entries are presented here in their entirety, in the rare instances where editing was called for, the standard formality of ellipses is eschewed. My intent in preparing *Postcards*, in concurrence with the preferences of the Abbey family, was not to produce an i-dotted workbook for academic pedants, but to offer a smooth gift of words, ideas, and entertaining reading for fans, biographers, the public, and posterity.

But deletions are exceptions and, overwhelmingly, what Ed wrote is what you get, including personal quirks and inconsistencies of punctuation, spelling, and contraction—such as Ed's beloved "probly." Only in a scant few extremes, where meaning is at serious risk of being lost or confused, have I inserted bracketed clarifications. Additionally, where reliable information was available, I have provided bits of orienting background on people and institutions Abbey writes to or about, likewise contained in editorial brackets. At the back of this volume an extended notes section provides even more detail. An index follows, listing page numbers for the wide and varied topics of Abbey's letters. I have added brief chapter introductions to help place Abbey's correspondence within the larger context of his life and times. Otherwise, continuing a tradition begun when editing *Confessions of a Barbarian: Selections from the Journals of Edward Abbey*, I have followed Ed's outspoken editorial preference for "the lesser, the better."

Regarding the contemporary and future worth of this collection, I trust the perceptive reader to share my amazement at the overall timelessness—as well as the current timeliness—of these *Postcards*. Certainly, some prominent names and themes have slipped into history in the decade and a half since Ed last wrote to or about them. Yet they (Nixon, Vietnam, Jimmy Carter, et al.) remain very much alive in the national consciousness and conscience. More significantly, Ed's primary concerns in the latter half of the twentieth century remain among America's primary concerns today. Such vital issues as war, politics, environment, illegal immigration and overpopulation, racism and social justice, celebrity, art, music and literature, love, sex, nature, and death never atrophy, much less go away. Even readers who have not previously met Abbey in print (I hear there are a few, somewhere east of the West) will find this lively and personable collection, as Ed himself might put it, "stimulating."

For simplicity, readability, and relativity, the collection is presented chronologically. In addition to the logical appeal and ease of reading an adult lifetime of letters in the order in which they were written, personal concerns and cultural themes tend to sort themselves into sensible order as we go along. Thus, a chronological presentation is simultaneously a categorical presentation. Additionally, a chronological arrangement provides the collection with an unfolding autobiographical subtheme, shadowing the author's personal and philosophical evolutions and relationships, his ongoing self-education and career, the making of his books, and his life and approaching death, as they evolved through time.

In gathering and shaping *Postcards from Ed*, I've enjoyed the invaluable assistance and support of Ed's wife, Clarke, his eldest daughter, Susie, his younger sister, Nancy, and numerous friends. The enthusiasm for this project evidenced by editor H. Emerson "Chip" Blake and the Milkweed staff has been a joy throughout. That Terry Williams was not only willing but eager to contribute an at-once far-ranging and deeply personal foreword, even under the pressure of an approaching pilgrimage to Rwanda, demonstrates her lasting love, respect, and appreciation for Ed. Among the numerous individuals who contributed letters and cards to this collection—a few of whom invested heroic amounts of time and energy digging through dusty boxes and files of unsorted correspondence—we gratefully thank you, unnamed though you must democratically remain given this limited space, one and all. As Ed would say, "You know who you are, and so do I."

1949–1969

FOR VARIOUS REASONS—including a basement flood at his parents' home in rural Pennsylvania, which destroyed journals and other personal papers—letters from the early years of Abbey's adulthood are exceedingly scarce. Consequently, this opening chapter skims lightly across two decades of his life. During this period, having been honorably discharged from the U.S. Army in 1947 (minus a good conduct medal), Ed attended the University of New Mexico, Albuquerque, where he studied philosophy and literature, graduating in 1951 . . . toured Europe on a Fulbright Fellowship . . . hungrily indulged his long-simmering passions for the American Southwest, literature, writing, and women . . . married three times and divorced twice . . . fathered two sons, Josh and Aaron . . . published three novels (*Jonathan Troy*, *The Brave Cowboy*, and *Fire on the Mountain*) and, most significantly, wrote his classic man-in-nature memoir, *Desert Solitaire*.

Family, Home, Pennsylvania   (8 NOVEMBER 1949)

Friends—

I was wondering—could you lend me three or four hundred dollars? I have not yet bought either a horse or a motorcycle and am thinking of buying a car; not any car, but a '47 Ford one of my fellow students is trying to sell. It would really be a good buy; the thing is practically new. The money would not have to be in a lump—fifty a month would be enough.

But no doubt you are looking forward to the payday when your paycheck is all yours—and certainly I don't have to buy a car. But I should buy something; otherwise I'll continue to fritter my money away on records and books and wild parties. It's painful to remember that a mere six months ago I had twice as much money as now—where did it all go? I can't imagine. Of course, that money should have been saved for my Oxford tuition, but the truth is that I can't save money—certainly not for the sake of saving. If I have money I feel compelled to spend it on something. (The future be damned. Tomorrow I may be dead.) Typical hedonistic epicureanism.

· I intend to make some money next summer—if I can find a job. Either here or back east. Why not wait until then to buy a car? By that time I'll be broke.

If you can't lend me several hundred dollars, you are quite welcome to reduce or cut off the monthly stipend as much and whenever you please. I don't need the money—I'll just waste it.

I'm doing some writing but it's all of a highly technical nature—"the planes of reality," "Pythagorean philharmonica," "the polarities of experience," "*Principia Aesthetica*," "the isolation of data," "Democritian atomism," "Attic Romanticism," and such-like pretentious frivolity.

How am I doing, scholastically? Fairly well, I think, but the competition in these advanced philosophy courses is rather good. My days of coasting to distinction with my innate brilliance are over; from now on I'm afraid I'll have to study like everyone else.

The situation is difficult for me because my nearly universal range of interests continues—riding, girls, mountain climbing, exploring, machines, mysticism, music, vodka, politics, astronautics, poker—all of which interferes considerably with my half-hearted attempt to become a scholar. (Really not possible, I think, for me—the scholarly life, I mean. I'm too fond, much too fond, of fresh air and mundane pleasures.)

Of course, you'll congratulate me on this—saying that the general, the whole, the universal, is much better than narrow specialization, with its consequent dehumanization, isolation, blindness, and turtle-shell spectacles.

And so I persuade myself. But is it true? Entirely true? I think the matter falls definitely in an area of controversy, necessitating suspension of decision.

So Billy killed two squirrels and a rabbit?

According to Aristotelian metaphysics the rodents possess souls of sort, certainly inferior to human souls, but souls nevertheless and deserving of love and pity. Forgot about that, didn't you?

Reminds me—Bud and I went antelope hunting last weekend with one other fellow. Bud's friend got one. Having neither license nor rifle I drove the jeep while the others did the shooting. Quite exciting—driving off the road into the sagebrush over hills and down arroyos, rounding up the antelope like cattle. My but they're fast—we clocked one bunch at 40 miles an hour.

Merci beacoup for the $150. No, I don't know how much you still owe me.

Sorry to hear about the Oldsmobile's further sufferings.

It is now the hour of one and twenty in the morning, mountain time. The radio is on and I'm hearing a song called "Mule Train" for about the seventh time this evening. Quite a fad, this pseudo-Western culture. First "Riders in the Sky" and now this. But I must not let my aesthetic snobbery blind me to the fact that these two songs are immensely superior to the usual run of popular music.

Mid-term exams this week. That's why we're home so early and not in bed. Cramming. Debauchery will be resumed this coming Saturday night and will reach a high point next week for the annual Homecoming festival.

Love (platonic) to all and sundered.

Ned

Gilbert Neiman, Professor, Clarion State College,
Pennsylvania   (15 AUGUST 1959)

Dear Gilbert—

I don't know why I keep writing letters to you. You never answer them. You react but you don't answer. Trying to start a dialogue with you is like trying to cross-examine Zarathustra. Or, two monologues don't make a dialogue. Neiman the insoluble solipsist. Who are you? said Polyphemus. No-man, he replied. At least he . . .

Nevertheless . . . I'll try once more. There must be some way to provoke you. Perhaps you admire Beckett. I hope you do. Because I don't, I think the Beckett racket is no more justified than the fad for—you guessed it— Kerouac. Now Beckett is a great stylist, of course. Every line a delight to the nerves. And a wit, tho' not often a very subtle one. And his little nuvvles, in their highly specialized way, are perfectly shaped, perfectly coherent, fully realized. Perfect—like a nut in a shell. Like a hand grenade, etc.

Now this may sound like ample praise for anybody, but coming from me it ain't. I can appreciate with as much pleasure as any [?] the aesthetic virtues mentioned above, but for me they are not sufficient—I also demand, when claims to greatness are made, that the author have something to say about life in this world which is interesting, original, important, and true. By this final, perhaps unreasonable demand it seems to me that Beckett has failed. How? In what way?

(Oh christ, why did I start this? I don't feel like talking Literature tonight. I'd rather go out on the mesa and bay at the moon, with Newcomb, wine, and guitar.)

But back to Beckett and be damned. What does Beckett say? That the world is a great gray empty place, a vale of misery. Misery, what's more, without the dignity of tragedy—slapstick misery. Ugly misery. And why? Why is it like this? Beckett doesn't say, right out, but his implication is lurking in the background: We have lost Gawd. We should get down on our hands and knees and crawl back into the womb of the Holy Mother Church.

In other words, Beckett's work is merely one more example of the Great Christian Hangover. I'm willing to bet real money that within ten years Beckett will be writing orthodox morality plays in the manner of Eliot, Greene, Claudel, Waugh, Mauriac, and the rest of the yellow-bellied renegades that clutter up the literary scene today. (Powerful words, eh? Yes, I'm a dangerous man.)

Now I'm willing to grant that the element, the extreme susceptibility to re-conversion, is hard to see in Beckett. Why, even the author may not be aware of it, it's so far back in the stage wings. But it's there. That Jesuitical Dominican stink, I can smell it from here. The smell of the olde miasmal mist, the dank dim odor of rotten cathedrals. (As Amis says: "Thank God for the hydrogen bomb and the 20th century!" Amen, Allmen.) (And in my background, at the moment—Shostakovich, of all persons, on the FM. Stalin's theme song, dream song . . .)

Now—how do I know that Beckett's got a guided missal hidden in his shoulder holster? Bear with me, comrade:

I know it, or at least suspect it, because his disgust and misery, his alleged "pessimism," is exaggerated, blown-up, generalized, abstract (despite the comical detail), and hollow, very like a balloon. In short, his vision of the world offers us the kind of fractional truth (½?) which, when presented as a total truth, is in fact a total untruth. A fakehood. A lie. Not a deliberate lie, of course, in Beckett's case, but the kind of lie which emerges involuntarily from some bias buried in the writer's gut.

Beckett wants to see the world this way and in order to do so he's obliged to disregard or suppress awareness of such things as: love in the subways, love in Hoboken, love in the foxholes, Spring in Vermont, the emerald waters of Big Sur River, the buzzards soaring over Utah, flash floods, Princes Street in Edinburgh on a mild September evening, hurricanes over Key West, the shoeshine boys of Napoli (talk about human buoyancy!), skiing down the slopes of the Arlberg on a sunny afternoon, the golden maids of Skandia, Austrian beer, the sound of Spanish voices at the Pyrenees, bicycling thru the Hee-lands with a good-lookin' woman, climbing balconies in Vienna, the wild steppenwulf roar of Russian soldiers singing their barbarous songs, Professor Pidcock sipping his iced coke in the Student Union Building, the mountains of New Mexico, the little fishing boats in Half Moon Bay, the black stockings and ponytails of North Beach; poetry and ideas, the cottonwoods along the Rio Grande in late October, the good old USA where a man is still a man (compared to England anyway), and everything else that delights the eyes, ears, nose, taste, touch, mind, and heart—like overturned streetcars in Barcelona! Burning!

And buzzards soaring over Utah . . .

That's why Beckett has to tell his stories in that specialized manner of his: the abstract Kafkan landscape, the abstractified situation, the faceless past-less future-less aliens that serve him for types of the human, the monomania for logical exactitude—nothing being more remote than logic from human life—and finally the style, that chilling concatenation of inverted clichés, all this is necessary in order to give his work the illusion of being a generalization about the world. In order to make his generalization valid, he has to write in fantasy. Because his vision is futuristic—meaning grossly oversimplified, half-true, half-assed, half-baked—the outlook (hardly a philosophy!) of a crank and a crackpot.

If Beckett once dared to write in a more or less realistic style, dealing with plausible people in credible difficulties, his idea of things, his private ideology, would suddenly be exposed for what it is—hoked-up fakery. But Beckett is determined to make human life appear contemptible—therefore he has to abstractify, mystify, oversimplify, falsify—instead of a work of imagination he gives us the product of fantasy.

But I still haven't made my point or reached the conclusion of this here sillygyzm. Why does Beckett want the world to appear worthless? The easier to reject it, that's why. And then—there's nothing left. Nothing. Thus pessimism. Unless—faith strikes! God! Heaven! Salvation! (Thru the sacraments of the true church, of course.) And the rest of the old familiar shit.

Perhaps I shouldn't call it shit. That's a bit crude. I don't really despise Christianity or even the Roman Church, and certainly not the incontrovertible glory of the Middle Ages. What I do despise is the contemporary inclination to flop to the knees and crawl back into the past, to shy from what seem like impossible problems in order to bury the head, asshole aloft and twitching, in the Sands of Time. Cowardice, I calls it. Illusion-seeking. Womb-crawling. And treason. Desertion in the face of the enemy.

Strong words indeed. But I've always been rather a blunt, tough, plain-spoken type . . .

As I said before, I don't accuse Beckett of having committed himself to the final step. At present he's still the total pessimist, the sad and desperate man completely free—as he fancies—of all illusions. All worldly illusions. Doesn't it remind you of the Hollow Man? Of the Wasteland? Of course it does—Beckett is following in the Master's footsteps. That's why, unless he makes a sudden divergence, he's likely to end up in the same attitude as the

Old Guy—eschatological as hell, eyes riveted on the Unmoved Mover, the still center of the world, while he masturbates his ego here below.

"History is a nightmare from which I am trying to awake!" Yes, Joyce had the same Christian streak in his guts. Remember the final page of [*Finnegans Wake*]— "If I seen him bearing down on me now, etc. etc . . ." But Joyce was a great man, a prince among minds, the artist-saint; he couldn't Fall for a simple tale like that that's enthralled our man Beckett, who's just a little punk compared to his Boss. Or is Beckett just a pocketsize Céline?

But you see my point. Beckett, now busily publicizing his Dark Night (of the Sole?), persuading himself and fans that he has seen the Truth about This World in the form of a banal and exaggerated and therefore unlikely pessimism, has prepared a position—perhaps unawares—where he now faces a dilemma: suicide or—a return to the faith? We know what usually happens in such cases: the miserable old world seems worth clinging to after all, no matter how esoteric the metaphysic or desperate the well-ground axiology. All the easier if you think you've got a finger in another world. So Beckett writes his little fantasies. And inevitably one form of fantasy leads to another.

Yes, I know, the Christ-boys may be correct. Maybe the earth is only a testing-ground, merely the purgatorial gateway to Hollywood-Heaven or Hoboken-Hell. But permit me to doubt it. Yes, I'm an atheist. Tho' earthiest might be a better term. I believe in the Earth. Let Heaven go to Hell! I am comforted in this dogmatic intuition by the everpresent recollection that two of the finest brightest cleanest civilizations yet to appear on this planet—the Greek and the old Chinese—were essentially non-theistic. Until Plato and Mao Tse-tung came along to poison it all.

Are you with me in this, Komrad? Eh? Reservations? Speak—! Don't just stand there holding your piece!

People who write letters like this are insufferable. Yet think, Gilberto, what an elegant conversation we could carry on by mail—if only you were willing. Or able. Or interested.

Good luck with your musical chamber pot. Let me know when anything good happens.

Regards, Ed
Albuquerque, New Mexico

Judy Pepper (8 SEPTEMBER 1965)

The land is lovely now, more beautiful every day. The golden light of autumn is beginning to appear, not in the sky but in the flowers: match-weed, rabbitbrush, princess plume, beeweed, mule-ear sunflowers, all are flaming forth in yellow. A cold October wind blows down from the mountains, tho' it's still September here below. I must climb Tukuhnikivats once more before I leave. Most of the tourists are gone and I roam thru the Devil's Campground in the purple evening thinking of you, treasuring our trysting places, stopping each night at that place on the sandstone near the juniper where we built a little fire and last made love. . . . I kiss it where you lay.

—Arches National Monument, Utah

The Nation, New York City (12 OCTOBER 1966)

Editors:

Re the reviews and reappraisals of Wm Faulkner:

Before the critics are allowed to enshrine F. permanently among the greats of Am. lit., would it be unseemly to bring up the question of whether or not this writer told us the truth about the world he lived in? E.g., How much correspondence is there between the South rep[resented] in F's novels and the South as revealed by the public events of the last ten yrs? Where in F's work, e.g., can we find anything that would have led us to anticipate the character of the civil rights struggle . . . and the quality of such people as Barnett, Meredith, Clark, Connor, Wallace, and King? And if F's portrayal of the South was so strangely incomplete, or misleading, or even false, what then is the true value—literary or otherwise—of his art?

Yours,

E. A.

Al Sarvis (13 DECEMBER 1966)

". . . frittering my life away"? Perhaps. I don't know. What should a man do? Assailed at times by a sense of desperation—in seven weeks I'll be forty years old and still don't know with any precision who or what I am. Or why.

Booze but a [?] and even my one experiment with LSD an uncomfortable and inconclusive failure: the stars quivered in a cloudy cobweb but the big spider God failed to appear. Am resolved therefore to continue on my present course: to compose somehow the one good novel; to try to be good to my wife; to run Cataract Canyon in a kayak; to raze more billboards; to build that solid house of rock and wood far out somewhere where my sons and grandsons can find at least a temporary refuge from the nightmare world of 2000 A.D.; and to be ready, with rifle or [?], for the apocalyptic showdown which yet may come—I hope—in our lifetimes. . . .

Death Valley, California

Mr. Keith Green, c/o Taos "News,"
New Mexico (1 FEBRUARY 1967)

Mr. Green:

A Taos friend has sent me a copy of your column in which you give objections to my *Harper's* article, "Land of Surprises." Since some of your statements are more surprising than mine, however, I would like to make the following comments:

You state that the SW has been the last part of U.S. to be developed. This will be startling news to your Indian and Mexican neighbors, who will remember that the pueblos of NM with their rich and integrated culture, and the city of Santa Fe, a blend of Pueblo and Hispanic, were founded long before Captain Smith and his sot-weed promoters first prowled up Chesapeake Bay. The SW was not the last but the first part of America to be developed.

And just what do you mean by "development"? Something which resembles NY—or LA—or Phoenix and Albuquerque? Would you really want to see northern New Mexico become more like those places and less like what it still remains?

You [?] accuse me of wishing to keep the Southwest "empty." But it is not empty; it is full to its limits with beauty and terror, life and death, loneliness and joy, grandeur and heroism. The point is to keep it this way and not let it be reduced to the same dead level of totalitarian monotony which we find e.g. in Albuquerque's "Princess Jeanne Park" (who the fuck was

Princess Jeanne?). And if you want to see something truly empty, take a look at the main drag of Phoenix on Saturday afternoon.

And oh yes, I've heard of the Rio Grande. In fact, I waded across it several times when I first went to school in Albuquerque twenty years ago. But of course there was more water in those days.

Yours truly,
Ed Abbey

Arizona Daily Star, Tucson   (10 AUGUST 1969)

Dear Sir:

A friend recently sent me a clipping from your alleged newspaper. It's an editorial aptly entitled "Baloney" from your June 29th issue, in which you seem to accuse both Wallace Stegner and myself of writing about the West without adequate knowledge of the region. But on this point Wallace Stegner requires no defense, as anyone even slightly acquainted with his career should know; and for myself, though I have lived only twenty-two years in the Southwest (so far), I am willing to bet my bottom dollar that I have seen at least as much of it as the writer of your editorial.

When I wrote in my review of Stegner's book that "there is no West anymore," I meant the West as a distinct cultural region. Of course our unique landscape still remains (or those portions of it which have not yet been flooded by dams, disemboweled by copper mines, buried under asphalt, and obscured by fungus-bearing smog), but the general way of life, as typified by our overgrown cities, is patterned after that of Los Angeles. Can you deny it?

You claim the Old West still exists in much of its "primitiveness and squalor" (your words). Here I agree with you; it still exists, all right, in the primitive minds and squalid greed of those promoters and expansionists whose highest ambition appears to be the debasement of Arizona, New Mexico, and Utah to the level of southern California's ant-hill existence.

Edward Abbey,
North Rim [Grand Canyon, Arizona]

Evergreen Review, **New York City**   (25 AUGUST 1969)

Sirs:

Nat Hentoff's article on "The Dispensables" (*ER* 9/69) is not bad, so far as it goes. But altho I can agree with most of what he writes, I am shocked by what he omits: that at least half the trouble between the races is caused by overcrowding, by overpopulation. Or to use terminology more familiar to *ER* readers, by too fucking many people—and too many people fucking.

Case in point: Hentoff cites Negro suicide rates and infant mortality rates as being twice the national average. He also mentions the fact that blacks now make up 12 percent of the population—they used to be 10 percent. In other words, the black sector is growing (despite higher death rates) not only absolutely, but relatively. The connection of this little statistic to poverty, crime, drugs, police criminality, and racial hatred should be obvious, without further explication, to even an *Evergreen* reader.

Lest some supersensitive black chauvinist now rear up on his hind legs and start howling that I'm a racist, let me add that I think the whites are contributing their share to this basic problem. Put it this way: every couple who have more than two kids are being socially irresponsible. This applies to all: black, white, brown, red; to the rich as well as the poor; to the hip and freak and longhair as well as the straight, square, and cueball.

Solution? The taxation system should be revised so as to penalize, not reward, those who lay unfair burdens on their neighbors and on posterity by breeding us all into the madhouse.

Most people have no business having children anyway. Look around you. Look at them.

Edward Abbey
North Rim

(copies to: *Catholic Worker, National Review, National Guardian,* etc.)

1970–1974

DURING THESE FIVE YEARS, Abbey resided serially at North Rim Grand Canyon, Aravaipa Canyon (Arizona), Tucson, and Moab . . . published one novel (*Black Sun,* which was among his personal favorites) and three photo books (*Appalachian Wilderness* with Eliot Porter, *Slickrock* with Philip Hyde, and *Cactus Country*) . . . fathered Susanna . . . lost Susie's mother, Judy, to leukemia . . . and met Renee Downing, whom he married on February 10, 1974.

Warren Page, Shooting Editor, *Field & Stream*,
New York City (6 APRIL 1970)

Dear Warren,

Thanks very much for your long letter of March 30th. I'll keep it on file, to be answered in detail if you will agree to the publication, in your magazine, of an exchange of letters on the general subject of wildlife conservation and trophy hunting.

Whaddeya say?

Now that I've started this letter, though, there are some things I must say:

1. Don't lump me with that crook Senator Dodd, please. As you will recall from reading that DESERT book [*Desert Solitaire*], I am very much against gun control laws. In fact, I am in favor of replacing the draft and/or an all-volunteer army, with a citizens' militia, *a la Suisse*, with every household armed and loaded with guns and ammo supplied to each free of charge by the Government. This won't reduce the murder rate, but we've got about 150 million too many people in this country anyhow. I am very much afraid of a monopoly of the means of violence by the police and the military— much more afraid of them than of ordinary criminals.

2. I agree that organized hunters and fishermen are often the best of allies in various conservation battles. But we're not getting much help from them here in Arizona in trying to save the mountain lion from extermination. Most hunters around here still seem to think that by ridding the state of lions we'll have more deer to shoot at.

3. I have several serious objections to trophy hunting—moral, esthetic, biological, and ecological—which I'll explain later. But I am not prepared to outlaw the sport, provided that it does not threaten the quality and abundance of the animals concerned. Let me assure you of that much.

Sincerely, Ed Abbey—Ajo, Arizona

(NO REPLY)

Tucson Daily Citizen (20 SEPTEMBER 1972)

Dear Sir:

The police helicopter is an unnecessary evil. The money being wasted on that infernal and idiotic machine would be sufficient to add another fifteen or twenty men to the force. The helicopter cannot be justified as a crime preventive; noise pollution is a crime and should be recognized as such, and in all the stink and smog and clatter of downtown Tucson, no individual machine is more obnoxious than that helicopter.

Even if the helicopter could glide about quiet as an owl, it remains still objectionable on even more serious grounds: aerial surveillance of a sup-posedly free citizenry is an affront to us all, and one more significant step toward an authoritarian police state. There are far better ways to prevent crime than by sending Big Brother aloft to keep his beady 450-watt eye on us dues-paying citizens.

I would suggest, for example, that a few good men on bicycles (*a la francaise*), properly uniformed and equipped, patrolling swiftly and silently through their own neighborhoods, friends not enemies of the people they work among, could do far more to prevent crime than two official Peeping Toms roaring over our rooftops in their fifty-dollar-an-hour plastic bubble.

Let's think about this, people. You too, City Officials.

Yours sincerely, Edward Abbey—Tucson

Harper's, New York City (20 SEPTEMBER 1972)

Dear Sir:

There's no getting around it. Paolo Soleri's arcologies, like B. F. Skinner's boxes and Buckminster Fuller's domes, point the way toward the ultimate technological tyranny. These men are archaic lunatics who haven't had a new idea since the New York World's Fair of 1939; in their obsession with cement, iron, glass, and electronic gadgetry, they belong to the age of Henry Ford and Thomas Edison; in their devotion to planetary planning, they are the ideologies of a universal technocracy, which the militarists and industrialists behind them are already striving to impose upon this long-suffering Earth.

Those who see in Soleri's arcologies a resemblance to anthills are absolutely correct; they are indeed similar to the dome-heaps of the harvester ants, which crowd upon one another in festering swarms, one and all subject to the blind telepathic instincts of the race, and leave the land surrounding each "city" totally stripped of all vegetation and all life. That is the kind of "nature" which these human anthills would offer us. Such a form of change is not evolution but devolution—a regression to pre-human modes of existence. Soleri's inability to perceive the essential connections between man and the rest of nature is typical of the Judeo-Christian tradition, which attempts to divorce humanity from earth and is therefore responsible for most of the ills, such as industrialism, militarism, and nationalism, which plague us now in this most unpopular of all centuries.

May some power save us from the Planners. They are totalitarian in their means and ends; they have created a Machine which will destroy us all unless we find a way to stop it.

Edward Abbey—Oracle, Arizona

PS: A word on Thompson's word about the novel: The only reason that the antics of men like Mailer and Kesey ever attracted the attention of the news media is because, once upon a time and long ago, Kesey and Mailer wrote some interesting novels.

Arizona Daily Star, Tucson (29 DECEMBER 1972)

Editor, the *Star:*

After winning the election with the fraudulent promise that "peace is at hand," the Nixon-Kissinger team have now revealed the true depth of their intellectual dishonesty and moral corruption. Through the tangled cobweb of official lies comes the thunder of the bombs falling on the people of Vietnam. After eight years of defoliating forests, poisoning rice fields, burning villages, napalming civilians, and torturing prisoners, our Government is now engaged in an apparent effort to obliterate the cities and destroy the population of the northern half of the little peasant nation of Vietnam.

Nothing in American history, not even the wars against the Indians, can equal the shame and brutality and cowardice of this war. It makes an obscenity of our Christmas holidays and sinks our own Government and all who passively consent to its atrocities down to the moral level of Stalinist Russia and Hitler's Germany.

Our so-called leaders speak of an "honorable" withdrawal from Vietnam, but there can be no honorable conclusion to such a dishonorable war. The only decent thing we can do now is to somehow compel those moral degenerates in the White House and Pentagon to stop their cowardly attack on Vietnam and then begin at once, as best we can, to help the survivors in that devastated land rebuild their farms, homes, villages, and cities, and reconstruct their shattered culture. If, that is, they would even be willing to accept aid from our bloody hands.

Edward Abbey

Arizona Daily Star, Tucson   (22 FEBRUARY 1973)

Editor:

I see by the papers that some vandals have been cutting down billboards in the Tucson area. A local developer refers to these vandals as "criminals." Legally speaking that may be so. But surely the worst criminals are these same developers who are devastating the beautiful desert in order to slap together their squalid housing projects, most of which will be slums ten years from now. (If the roofs don't blow off before then.) Equally guilty are the landowners making enormous windfall profits through rezoning and the city and county politicians who have apparently sold out (most of them) to the developers.

Isn't it time that we all recognize that Tucson is big enough? This will not become a better city by becoming bigger. How many Tucsonans would rather live in Phoenix or L.A. than here? The same goes for Arizona as a whole. Arizona has been developed enough. The population is big enough. We do not need more people or more industry in this state. We should take a clue from Oregon and adopt measures that would discourage any more immigration.

Arizona is still a good place to live. But it won't be much longer if the local developers, bankers, landowners, and politicians are allowed to have everything their own way.

Janet Moench [E.A.], Tucson

Tucson Daily Citizen   (1 MARCH 1973)

Editor:

The lecture by R. Buckminster Fuller last week at McKale Stadium was one of the funniest things I've ever witnessed. While he droned on for 2½ hours in praise of technology, few people present could hear what he was saying. The reason: technology. A badly designed building and a useless p.a. system. Not that it mattered much: What Fuller had to say, as we learned from the papers the next day, was the same thing he's been saying for about sixty years. And that is, if only we give the technocrats a free hand, they will solve all human problems (by 1980!) by means of more and more technology . . . simply ignoring the fact that our most desperate problems, such as overpopulation, industrial pollution, and the waste of natural resources are themselves the product of blind faith in technology.

The sad truth about Fuller is that he has outlived his time. He is obsolete. He belongs to the age of Henry Ford and Thomas Edison. He was the Poet Laureate of the New York World's Fair of 1939, and his only actual achievement—the invention of the geodesic dome—has itself become another nuisance in an age of junk: pale polyurethane warts springing up like funguses all over the American landscape, symbols and symptoms of the Plastic Plague.

Edward Abbey, Tucson

Wendell Berry, Port Royal, Kentucky   (17 MARCH 1973)

Dear Wendell—

Thanks very much for having your publishers send me the new book of poems. I like the book, and envy your dedication.

Something you write in *A Continuous Harmony* [*Essays Cultural and Agricultural*] still bothers me. You choose to cast doubt on what is called the "linear view" of human history. But—suppose Darwin was right? Suppose evolution is true? Then, if so, not only human history but the history of all planetary life must be seen as a kind of grand "progress," (as in a march) from the simple to the complex toward the unknown. A mystery.

The trouble with the cyclical view of life, of existence, is simply that there is no evidence for believing it true. No?

All the best, Ed Abbey—Tucson

Senator Frank E. Moss, Washington, D.C. (26 MARCH 1973)

Dear Senator Moss:

Thank you for your letter of March 21st in response to my letter regarding the Lake Powell–Rainbow Bridge issue. I am writing again on this same matter because you did not reply to the specific points which I raised in my letter.

E.g., you say that if Judge Ritter's order is allowed to stand, the four upper-basin states will lose 4 million acre-feet of water immediately and one million acre-feet of water annually thereafter. Anticipating this argument I asked you why the water cannot be stored just as well in "Lake" Mead (now about 60 percent full) and credited to the upper basin states. Why should Bridge Creek below Rainbow Bridge, as well as a hundred other lovely and world-unique side canyons in the Glen Canyon system, why should they all be flooded, destroyed, generally mucked-up when a simple change in book-keeping procedure could avoid the whole mess?

I also raised the larger question, which you also failed to answer, as to what difference it makes anyway, to 99.9 percent of us Americans, whether the limited and badly abused and over-used Colorado River is exploited in the upper basin states or the lower basin states? Really, what difference does it make, when there is not nearly enough water in that poor old river to satisfy all the millionaire agri-businessmen of the Southwest? As you well know, not a drop is allowed to run its natural course to the sea anymore, and as you also know, Mexico is not receiving its agreed-upon share.

Furthermore, from the strictly economic-production point of view, the waters of the Colorado will return more in the way of agricultural produce down in the Imperial Valley of California than they will in the shorter growing-seasons of the upper basin states.

You describe correctly the muddy mess which a barrier dam would create below Rainbow Bridge, when the water level is low. But you fail to mention that the same effect will follow the rise and fall of Lake Powell's waters, if the reservoir is allowed to intrude within the boundaries of the Monument. In other words, if the reservoir is filled to full capacity at any time, the inevitable draw-down later will leave behind the usual "bathtub rings" on the canyon walls and stinking mud flats in the canyon bottoms. Of course this is already happening throughout Glen Canyon NRA every time the water level is lowered.

This letter is already too long but I cannot resist commenting on one other thing: You state that forty thousand people saw Rainbow Bridge last year whereas only a "handful" saw it before the inundation of Glen Canyon, when it was necessary to walk 6½ miles up from the river. You regard this as a clear-cut improvement in the nature of things. That is a form of quantitative logic, all too sadly typical of the growth-is-progress syndrome, which more and more Americans are coming to question these days.

Why, Senator Moss, why, I ask you, do you believe that "more" is the same as "better"? The 6½-mile walk to the Bridge was not difficult; as one who actually did it, I can say that it was quite an easy walk, on a perfectly adequate trail, with water—clear beautiful drinkable running water, available most of the way—and shade enough to make even the June heat tolerable. The walk to the Bridge and back could easily be made in a single day, by anyone in average health, of any age from eight to eighty. And it was a beautiful canyon, and getting to the Bridge and back was a mild but beautiful adventure, the kind of experience one treasures for a lifetime afterwards.

Rainbow Bridge is much more than a geological oddity: its whole setting, its comparative remoteness, its character as part of a greater whole, is what made it and getting there such a wonderful and unforgettable pleasure. Those six miles were all too short; I now envy those who first saw the Bridge by the fourteen-mile approach from Rainbow Lodge, around the mountain.

How can that experience be equated with forty thousand annual quick visits by people roaring in and out on motorboats who generally see nothing but the wake of the boat ahead, hear nothing but the roar of motors, feel nothing but the impatience characteristic of motorized travel to get on to the next "sight"? The fact that all these multitudes never bothered to go see Rainbow Bridge before access was made easy proves only one thing: they simply were not interested.

And ease of access does not create interest. Quite the contrary: it has reduced interest. That "blue finger" of Lake Powell has transformed what was once a delightful adventure into what is now merely a routine motorized sight-seeing excursion. The loss is great, and immeasurable, and cannot be compensated for by any amount of industrialized mass tourism. You cannot creep from quantity to quality. The two are not commensurable. I have also made the visit to Rainbow Bridge by motorboat and can personally testify that it is a meager, shallow and trivial experience when compared to the hike up the canyon. In fact, as they say, there is "no comparison."

Something priceless was destroyed by the flooding of Glen Canyon, which no amount of motorized "visitor use" can ever equal in human values. Our duty now is to save what still remains of that great canyon system—especially Rainbow Bridge—and to begin the long and arduous effort to restore it all, eventually, to its original and natural condition.

It would be nice if you would help, Senator. Forget Art Greene and his tour-boat business; to hell with those sugar-beet growers up around Vernal. There are far better things to do and be and save in the glorious and absolutely unmatched state of Utah.

New York Review of Books, New York City (30 MARCH 1973)

Editors:

In his review of the book *Retreat From Riches* [*Affluence and Its Enemies*, by Peter Passell] Jason Epstein mentions the Earth Day slogan "Growth for the sake of growth is the ideology of the cancer cell." He dismisses the analogy as an argument against ever-expanding industrialism. Nature as a whole, he asserts, operates on the same principle as cancer. All living things, he seems to believe, subscribe to the "ideology" of growth for growth's sake. Therefore, he implies, we have nothing to fear from expansionist industrialism.

Not so. Most species within nature aim not at unlimited growth but rather at optimum growth; that is, a condition of stability, fulfilling but not destroying the species' appropriate niche within the larger life-system. Likewise, the individual organism, if it is healthy, seeks not endless growth—which is monstrous and suicidal—but rather maturation and reproduction, which also coincides with the "ideal" of the species. Both tend to serve and sustain the ends—whatever those may be—of evolutionary change as a whole.

Cancer is distinctive and pathological precisely because it does not conform to this pattern, or recognize any limitations; the disease with—as well as of—hubris. Delighting in nothing but multiplication, cancer ends by destroying both its host and itself. The analogy to our modern planetary growth-devoted techno-industrial society (whether capitalist or socialist makes no difference) is complete and exact. Like cancer, expansionist industrialism believes in nothing but more expansionism. Growth equals power: power equals growth. Again like cancer, the process will self-destruct. Not, however, without human suffering, which will be great until a different kind of society based on a more stable adaptation to the earth's thin skin is somewhat achieved.

Unlike Jason Epstein, I find the idea of placing a limit on industrial growth quite thinkable. Not only thinkable, not only desirable, but essential. Affluence consists of far more than the endless production of junk, under the ever-growing mountain of which many good things (like healthy human-type people) are benignly suffocated.

For example, many of us would gladly forego La Tache (whatever that is) served in Baccarat glasses (who needs them?) in exchange for breathable air and edible bread. That, and freedom from more and more technological tyranny—police helicopters, for example—is part of my notion of what affluence really means.

A sound argument could be made for the case that growing industrialism not only does not eliminate poverty (there are as many poor people today as there were in the depths of the New Deal—40 million), it increases poverty. Industrialism, beyond the optimum point, which we passed about seventy years ago, tends to impoverish, not enrich, our lives. Ask any Indian. Ask any Appalachian.

Phoenix New Times   (18 APRIL 1973)

You people put out a nice little newspaper and I have great hopes for it. But I must record a few carps. Why else write to the editors? To wit:

The interviews. Can't you ever think of anybody to interview but those rock-music ephemerids who alight briefly in Tucson or Phoenix before fluttering on into oblivion? I mean Leadbelly was all right. I mean Big Bill Broonzy was right up there with Satchel Paige. But these current white imitation-Negro musicians with their imitation-Negro music talking about themselves in the technical jargon invented by real black men on the streets of Memphis thirty years ago . . . too much.

So much for teeny-bopper music. Then there's teeny-bopper religion. When Prof Richard "Baba Ram Dass" Alpert, masquerading as a mystical Hindoo, expounds his new doctrine, he still sounds like Prof Alpert. With this difference: Whereas before he taught within a tradition honestly come by, his own, he now pretends to be what he is not. As anyone who has read his manual (hardly a book) called *Be Here Now* knows, every idea in it was stolen direct from Advaita-Vedantism, the Hindu equivalent of say our own Christian Episcopalianism. Both are ancient and honorable worldviews, in their way, but when the former is reduced and traduced by Alpert into the condescending street-folk style of *Be Here Now*, it becomes fakery, hokum and a fraud—what Alan Watts would call the philosophy of goo. (When you draw your daily milk from the great cow of the Living Earth it is a grave discourtesy to speak of that cow as merely "illusion." Show a little respect, Baba.)

Myself, I prefer somebody like Oral Roberts. At least he's an honest humbug. A genuine American con-artist. Dependable. (Come here Oral, I got a job for you.) He doesn't trim his sails to all the wild winds of pop-culture fads. He still has hair on his head. Where he got the hair is his business. He doesn't blind your eyes with Klieg lights bouncing off an oily dome.

You ask for constructive suggestions? Happy to oblige. We were visited doubly last year by that humorless old crackpot R. B. Fuller. He is another Sacred Kow of Pop Kulchur whose "cosmic thinking" is long overdue for rigorous examination. Why didn't you do a critical, not genuflecting, interview on him? Of course I realize he never answers questions. Questions interfere with the tractorlike clanking of the Cast-iron Monolog. But you could've tried to throw a few interrogative monkey wrenches into the Rube Goldbergian machinery of Fullers receptor node. . . .

The world is real. Tell Baba Ram Dass to love it or leave it. Tell all them gurus from the sickliest nation of earth to go home and regroup before coming over here telling us how to live. Physician heal thyself. Maharishi go OM. Life realized in action etc., from cattle-growing to poetry. Nirvana is for Nodes, for the limp, passive and maimed, not for working human-type people etc. etc.

Ed Abbey—Tucson

Victoria McCabe (19 MAY 1973)

Dear Victoria,

Herewith my bit for your cookbook. This recipe is not original but a variation on an old (perhaps ancient) Southwestern dish. It has also been a favorite of mine and was for many years the staple, the sole staple, of my personal nutritional program. (I am six feet three and weigh 190 pounds, sober.)

I call it Hardcase Survival Pinto Bean Sludge.

1. Take one fifty-pound sack Colorado pinto beans. Remove stones, cockleburs, horseshit, ants, lizards, etc. Wash in clear cold crick water. Soak for twenty-four hours in iron kettle or earthenware cooking pot. (DO NOT USE TEFLON, ALUMINUM OR PYREX CONTAINER. THIS WARNING CANNOT BE OVERSTRESSED.)

2. Place kettle or pot with entire fifty lbs. of pinto beans on low fire and simmer for twenty-four hours. (DO NOT POUR OFF WATER IN WHICH BEANS HAVE BEEN IMMERSED. THIS IS IMPORTANT.) Fire must be of juniper, pinyon pine, mesquite or ironwood; other fuels tend to modify the subtle flavor and delicate aroma of Pinto Bean Sludge.

3. DO NOT BOIL.

4. STIR VIGOROUSLY FROM TIME TO TIME WITH WOODEN SPOON OR IRON LADLE. (Do not disregard these instructions.)

5. After simmering on low fire for twenty-four hours, add one gallon green chile peppers. Stir vigorously. Add one quart natural (non-iodized) pure sea salt. Add black pepper. Stir some more and throw in additional flavoring materials, as desired, such as old bacon rinds, corncobs, salt pork, hog jowls, kidney stones, ham hocks, sowbelly, saddle blankets, jungle boots, worn-out tennis shoes, cinch straps, whatnot, use your own judgment. Simmer an additional twenty-four hours.

6. Now ladle as many servings as desired from pot but do not remove pot from fire. Allow to simmer continuously for hours, days or weeks if

necessary, until all contents have been thoroughly consumed. Continue to stir vigorously, whenever in vicinity or whenever you think of it.

7. Serve Pinto Bean Sludge on large flat stones or on any convenient fairly level surface. Garnish liberally with parsley flakes. Slather generously with raw ketchup. Sprinkle with endive, anchovy crumbs and boiled cruets and eat hearty.

8. One potful Pinto Bean Sludge, as above specified, will feed one poet for two full weeks at a cost of about $11.45 at current prices. Annual costs less than $300.

9. The philosopher Pythagoras found flatulence incompatible with meditation and therefore urged his followers not to eat beans. I have found, however, that custom and thorough cooking will alleviate this problem.

Yrs, Edward Abbey—Tucson

John Davis and William J. Briggle, Glacier National Park, Montana (6 NOVEMBER 1973)

Dear Sirs:

People down here have heard about the wilderness and development proposals for Glacier N.P., and like most of your own local citizens who are seriously interested in Glacier, and the national park system in general, we too believe that the park should be preserved in its natural, wild state to the maximum extent possible. That, after all, is what the parks are for. This means that all of the park not already "built-up" with permanent developments should be given official wilderness status.

As for transportation into and within the park, it must be plain to all by now that the private automobile (and other motorized forms of access) is both destructive to park values and wasteful of what is supposed to be a dwindling resource—oil. Cars, motorbikes, powerboats, should be banned completely from all national parks. For those too old, infirm or obese to walk, the Park Service should provide shuttle-bus service to principal points of interest. That way the park would remain open to all, with special privileges for none. Please include this letter in the hearing records.

Yrs truly, Edw. Abbett—Oracle, Arizona

Copy to Director, N.P.S.

Ian Ballantine, President, Ballantine Books,
New York City   (19 NOVEMBER 1973)

Dear Mr. Ballantine:

Sorry to trouble you with author's troubles but I have what I feel are some legitimate complaints:

You have published four of my books now, in paperback editions, in the last three years. I mean *Desert Solitaire, The Brave Cowboy, Fire on the Mountain* and now *Appalachian Wilderness* (with Eliot Porter's photographs). My complaint is that apparently these books are hard to find in bookstores right here in the Southwest, where presumably they should be most likely to sell.   .

I keep getting inquiries from friends and strangers asking where they can buy these books in paperback; I refer them to the bookstores, naturally, and they then tell me the bookstores don't seem to have them in stock.

Why not? Don't you have any salesman in the Arizona–New Mexico area?

My other complaint: I am annoyed and disappointed that none of the corrections I wanted made in your edition of *Desert Solitaire* or in your edition of *Appalachia* were ever made. Why not? I sent your editor-in-chief at least two letters spelling out in detail the changes that should have been made, as well as letters to Jack Macrae at Dutton on the same subject (he published the original edition of *Appalachia*), which he says he forwarded to your offices. What the hell's going on anyhow?

What else? There's something else I was mad about but now I've forgotten. Oh yes, still haven't received any copies of your *Appalachia.*

And one final note: I do appreciate your publishing these books of mine; I realize perfectly well that they are dubious propositions commercially. But having taken that risk, for which I am grateful, why don't you make certain the books are at least available to prospective purchasers?

Regards, Edward Abbey—Oracle

Mizz [Ms.] **Magazine**   (15 DECEMBER 1973)

Dear Sirs:

Some us menfolks here in Winkelman ain't too happy with this here magazine of yourn. Are old wimmin is trouble enuf to manage as is without you goldam New Yorkers shooting a lot of downright sub-versive ideas into their hard heads. Out here a woman's place is in the kitchen, the barnyard and the bedroom in that exack order and we dont need no changes. We got a place for men and we got a place for wimmin and there aint no call to get them mixed up. Like my neighbor Cliff Wood says, he says, "I seen men, I seen women, aint never seen one of them there persons." Thems my sentiments exackly. You folks best stick to tatting doilies. Much obliged for yr kind consideration, I am

Yrs truly, Edward "Cactus Ed" Abbey—Winkelman, Arizona

Scientific American, New York City   (20 MAY 1974)

Sirs:

It seems to me the time has come for *Scientific American* to make some effort to participate in the world that most of us actually inhabit. The highly abstract and technical articles which comprise almost all of the magazine's content from month to month are all very well, in their fashion, but can be found in the specialist journals which fill up so many shelves in any library of science.

What we really need from a magazine like yours is professional exploration of the problems and issues which have so largely been the result of technology and science. For example, here in southern Arizona we are plagued by something called smelter pollution. All can see the befouling of the air and many feel that the health of plants, animals and humans is threatened by these obnoxious vapors. Yet it is difficult to find the technical expertise to substantiate these fears, while the great copper mining and smelting corporations, with their huge resources in money, are able to buy up our state legislators and smother the population in not only smog but self-serving advertisements in the state newspapers.

The people need help here: when is science and when are scientists going to begin serving the public interest? When is *Scientific American* going to begin to deal with the sort of questions raised explicitly (but not properly answered) by the simple-minded, condescending, self-glorifying, eco-pornographic, fraudulent (and tax deductible) advertisements, such as those by UOP, Gould and ITT, in the pages of your own magazine?

Yours truly, Edward Abbey—Oracle

Sam Taylor, Editor, *Moab Times-Independent* (15 SEPTEMBER 1974)

Dear Sam,

Slim Mabery complains that the Park Service won't let him drive his four-wheel-drive down the old Halls Creek trail in Waterpocket Fold any-more. Makes you wonder how the Halls family ever got down in there, doesn't it? Do you suppose they drove a team and wagon? Or rode horses? Or maybe even walked? On their feet? Their own feet?

Makes you think about this whole business of the Winning of the West. I've been doing some research on the subject and so far have not been able to find any evidence that Coronado or Escalante, D. Julien or Jed Smith or even the cowboys and pioneers went tearing around the West in Blazers, Broncos and CJ5's. And poor old Wesley Powell, a scientist, and a major, and a one-armed veteran, he went clear down the Colorado River without a cabin cruiser, without even an outboard motor!

All those people wandering all over the desert and up the mountains and through the canyons without motors. Pretty weird. And not a comfort station west of the 100th meridian. Far out.

Ed Abbey

John Macrae, New York City (7 OCTOBER 1974)

Dear Jack,

Am up here on high plains inspecting strip mines for article on rape for *Playboy* Mag.

Thanks very much for your hospitality. A great house, and I really enjoyed the chance to meet Gaddis.

Come visit us in Feb. or March, and if you still want me to write the words for the America Book, bring fucking contract. But visit, in any case. Hope your personal situation is resolved soon, one way or the other. Remember Ovid's sure cure for heart trouble: "NEXT!"

Best regards, Ed—Moab

Thomas Brumley, Moab, Utah   (20 OCTOBER 1974)

RE: "Brumley's Bromides" column in *Moab Times*

Dear "Thomas Brumley"—

The national forests, like other public lands, are the property of all Americans. They do not belong to the beef industry, the logging industry or the mining industry. All such commercial uses of our national forests are subject to whatever limits and constraints we the public, acting through our public servant the Forest Service, believe to be desirable at any given time. The question of cattle grazing in our forests, therefore, does not involve any issues of personal rights or "liberty." Why should a few have rights denied the rest of us? If cattle grazing were a right, then each of us would have the equal right to run a few head—or a few thousand head—up on the mountain whenever we felt like it. We would have the right to hack down a swath of timber or bulldoze a cabin site or strip-mine Brumley Ridge at our own discretion, anytime. Is that really what you wish to advocate, "Brumley"? Think carefully now.

Furthermore, the live human beings who serve us in the Forest Service are neither "anonymous" nor "faceless." Nor are they hard to find or to argue with. They all have names and faces, telephone numbers and addresses. For instance, "Brumley," you'll find a U.S. Forest Service office right beside the main highway at the south end of Moab. Anyone there would be happy to give you the whole roster, I'm sure, right up to Chief McGuire and his office number in Washington, D.C.

Of course the Forest Service is part of a monstrously overgrown and cumbersome bureaucracy, no doubt about it. But then we all live in a monstrously overgrown and cumbersome industrial society, dependent slaves of a gigantic machine which we can neither control nor even understand, as contemporary events make clear.

What's the solution? Damned if I know—but one small step, which might help, would be to keep as much of that machine out of Utah as we can, before it tears up, paves over, plagues, blights and rapes this state as it has already raped so many of the forty-nine others.

Ed Abbey—Moab

Rolling Stone Magazine, San Francisco, California   (24 OCTOBER 1974)

Editors:

This here letter's kind of late, I suppose, but it takes us a long time to get around to anything out here and what I wanted to tell you is how you finally did something right by running those interviews with my personal hero Glenn Gould. After all the pages and pages of expensive newsprint you waste on tedious mediocrities, it was a genuine pleasure to encounter in your otherwise predictable pages the mind, wit, intelligence and rational speech of a verifiable musical artist and actual grown-up human being. Good work, men.

So. Now: let's have more interviews with people like Glenn Gould (if any), and rather less attention paid to the day-by-day perturbations of Teeny-bopper Kulchur, which is really the same sick slick commercial swindle today that it was back in the brass-age times of Perry Como, Bing Crosby, Rudy Vallee and—what's his name?—that other one.

Also, more Docktor Hunter Thompson for chrissake! Why the fuck do you think we subscribe to your bleeding rag anyhow.

For Christ's Sake?

Edward Abbey—Wolf Hole, AZ

Alan Harrington, Tucson, Arizona   (ALL HALLOWS' EVE 1974)

Dear Alan,

We're having a party Saturday night to which you & Peggy & Steve are invited. (And nobody else.) "Be there or be square." Seriously, life is kind of dull and solemn up here in the redrocks. Which is the way I like it.

So you know Gaddis too? Much better than I do, obviously. Although I am one of the few to have read *The Recognitions* all the way through. Did I mention that he told me he has completed a second novel, called *JB* [*JR*] or something like that, to be published soon, I guess.

Gaddis struck me as a rather gnome-like fellow, much older than I imagined him (my impression having been fixed twenty years ago), very droll and witty (which I did expect), full of stories out of his Harvard days (says he was thrown out his senior year for "secreting" a girl in his room), and yes, he did mention a drunken brawl in some Irish bar in New Haven. Had many nasty things to say about his publisher—Harcourt, Brace and Jovanovich—particularly Jovanovich. . . .

Anyway, I did like him: he is a man of much charm and of course an entertaining talker—much like you, Harrington.

When the hell you gonna send me that book you promised? I'm still waiting. I'll send you mine if you send me yours.

Sorry about the *NY Times* contretemps or whatever you'd call it. I did not really want to review your book, since I don't believe in reviewing a friend's book, but I thought my letter might prod Leonard into getting someone to review *Love & Evil*. Anyway, as you say, it all turned out in about the worst possible way for you and I don't know what you can do about it except say fuckem and move on to the next, like Cassius Clay–Muhammed Ali. Wish me better luck with mine but don't consult any goddamn Chinese books in advance.

Mine is back on my lap, by the way, all 740 pounds of it, and they want it returned to NYC in a week! Crazy. In other words, they don't want me to re-write it, except for a few little bits here and there, and that's what I call disconcerting. I think they're in a hurry to print it before costs go up any more. A legitimate concern—which I share.

Furthermore, it may well be, as the editor-publisher seems to think (a guy named Ed Burlingame), that *The Monkey Wrench Gang* is the kind of nuvvle the less you fuck around with it the better. I hope he's right and I'm glad to seize on the escape: just the thought of somehow retyping most of all those weary pages was a nightmare to me. So we'll make it a fast sloppy production (leave the art & craft to the Nabokov-Barthelme-Heller crowd) and hope for the best. I always write in a kind of blind stupor anyway, with only the dimmest awareness of what I'm trying to say or do. The shotgun method, I call it: write many, many, many books, in all directions, without taking much aim, and maybe just maybe at least once—you'll hit something. It worked for Shakespeare. Mark Twain. Who else?

Knut Hamsun?

Is *Raintree County* any good? I never read it. If it's not, then Lockridge really blew it, didn't he?

And you never did tell me why you disliked *Zen & the [Art of] Motorcycle [Maintenance]*. When I read it, several months ago, I was at first quite impressed. I took it to be a novel of ideas and found it fascinating as a sort of recapitulation of my own undergraduate days, when I thought I was a philosopher with a whole new system to lay upon the world. After a while, though, doubts. (About the *Zen* book.) Now, while I still admire Pirsig for what seems like the dogged and stubborn integrity of his effort to understand himself and his personal history (apparently the book is primarily an autobiography), I am uneasy about some of his conclusions.

The adulation of technology, of course, for one thing—his attitude seems to me much too uncritical, too simple, too eager (now that the 20th century's worship of technology comes to appear, more and more, not as the flowering of reason and ratio—Pirsig's view—but as the most dangerous sort of irrational sick romanticism—e.g., Bucky Fuller, B. F. Skinner, the Atomic Energy Commission etc. etc. etc.).

But that's merely the more obvious objection: more important, maybe, is Pirsig's emphasis on personal salvation at whatever cost, and to hell with everything else. I have always found that emphasis disagreeable, whether Zen Buddhists, Hardshell Baptists, Roman Catholics, transcendentalists, psychedelics, mountain climbers or whatever the sect that spawns it. Of course, if you're as sick in the soul as Pirsig was, no doubt the drive is justified. Nevertheless, as an approach to life, it seems to me too narrow, too selfish, too egocentric, too greedy and desperate, lacking in common dignity, too much the character of the rats that leave a sinking ship—prematurely. (The ship may yet be saved, with a little common sense and mutual aid.)

Time-Life fired me from the Sierra Madre project. Too much stuff on Mexicans, they say, not enough on the birds and bushes. Fine by me. Now I can concentrate on my tennis. Tell me what you're doing now: the immortalist novel?

Renee, too, is making mutterings now about going back to school. But here, where? Maybe I'll have to ship her back to Tucson now and then, for a term or two, now and then. She wants to be a wildlife biologist, she thinks. I am inadequate.

Replace anxiety with fear? Why not? A positive step. See you soon, probably.

Love, Ed—Moab

Indiana [Pennsylvania] Gazette   (CIRCA EARLY 1970s)

Dear Editor:

I have read with pleasure two recent letters in your "Readers Write" column from a certain Paul Abbey of "Home" (is there really such a place? or is the writer putting us on?) Pa. In any case, Mr. Abbey demonstrates a rare talent for polemical satire—or satirical polemic—and I do not hesitate to predict that this young man, if he persists, will go far in his chosen field. Whatever it might be.

As for his advice, I find it practical and useful. I do a lot of coasting myself (out here we call it Mexican overdrive), especially when descending mountain grades; you can save a lot of gas that way.

I also drive slowly and "tranquilly" at all times except when approaching intersections. Based on mathematical reasoning, verified (so far) by experience, I believe it to be a fact that the faster you flash through an intersection the less your chance of colliding with the opposition. Do not be distracted by traffic lights, of whatever shade of blue or pink; their only function is to confuse the timorous.

Yours sincerely, Edward Abbey—Wolf Head, Ariz.

Alan Harrington   (18 NOVEMBER 1974)

Dear Alan,

Much thanks for the book *Love and Evil*. I have read it and I like it. I think it is entertaining, always interesting and in places fascinating. It should be a popular book and will catch on with a big readership sooner or later. I have considerable admiration for Dan Sakall and his patience and sympathy for his flock of what I would be inclined to dismiss as hopeless losers. If I may venture one critical comment, I would say that *Love and Evil*, though important to an understanding of the basement of our society, lacks the high intellectual excitement of *The Immortalist* and *Psychopaths*. That results, inevitably, from the fact that the book is a collaboration: too much case history and not enough Harrington.

I hope this does not seem like a put-down to you; I know from repeated personal experience how depressing and exasperating it is to be told that your latest book, while admirable, is not as good as some earlier work. (I am regarded, where I am regarded at all, as a one-book author and of course that knowledge fills me with rage.) Anyway, my comment is not a putdown nor meant to be; *Love and Evil*, though not as good as your next book, is an important and significant work and I imagine it will be read and pondered for many years. And once again, though I'm sure I've said this before, I want to tell you how pleased and honored I am that you chose some words by me for an epigraph.

I haven't been in Tucson since last August, when I moved our furniture out of the old stone house. I will be coming down in a few weeks, before Christmas, and will see you then.

Haven't heard from [William] Eastlake for two months.

Busy revising my Monkey Business novel. Wearisome work but necessary. Wake up at six in the morning fretting about it. Spend half my time erasing all the commas and semi-colons which some goddamned fucking fuss-fidget of a publisher's editor has inserted in the typescript. It will be, nevertheless, a jolly jubilant jocund and jazzy nuvvle and a smashing success. Probably.

What else is news? The leaves are falling off our trees and the mountains are covered *mit schnee*. There are times when I think we should've stayed in Tucson. Not many. Incidentally, we bought a little hay and watermelon farm, about sixty acres, on the banks of the Green River. Next year, hopefully, we'll be building a house and going irretrievably bucolic.

All our best to all of you, Ed

Ed Burlingame, New York City   (NOVEMBER 1974)

Dear Ed B.:

Air-mailed another two hundred pp. to Baker Friday morning. Hope she gets it Monday.

I suppose this is a trivial matter but I do want to object to the maddening fuss-fidget punctuation which one of your editors is attempting to impose on my story. I said it before but I'll say it again, that unless necessary for clarity of meaning I would prefer a minimum of goddamn commas, hyphens, apostrophes, quotation marks and fucking (most obscene of all punctuation marks) semi-colons. I've had to waste hours erasing that storm of flyshit on the typescript.

About the matter of spelling out numbers, I confess I am in doubt. Most important of course is consistency, no matter how foolish, but I do think exceptions should be made, as in the case of the police ranger radio dialogs: do not the simple numbers convey better the quality of that kind of semi-human coded talk? As for mileages and heights and money I will accept whatever is customary.

Other minor items: after mailing it back to her, I've decided that Miz Baker was right about Janis Joplin (Chapter 16, now entitled "Saturday Night," page 405 or thereabouts). Let's spell it correctly in the first reference—"one Janis Joplin of martyred memory"—but as Jalopy in Hayduke's hazy recollection of the scene a page or two later.

And in the same chapter, re Hayduke's height: does five foot eight seem tall enough? Too short for him? What is your impression? Or would he be about five foot ten? This is very important and I've already lost an hour's sleep over it.

Also, Bonnie Abbzug's age: is twenty-eight too old for her? How about twenty-four or twenty-five? A former girlfriend of mine, aged thirty-two at the time, had insisted that the world is sick of reading about women in their early twenties; out of male chauvinist deference I compromised and made Bonnie twenty-eight. Now a year later and much wiser, I wonder. Can a woman of twenty-eight be referred to as a girl? Can she look like a girl? Who cares? An irritating trifle.

What else is troubling me? I am still not sure but that the description of highway construction techniques is not too long and [I] will probably delete more of that during the next stage of refining the story.

In many cases, when in doubt, I have left in lines and paragraphs which I may later delete. Much easier to delete than add, right?

I believe I took care of this, but in the first Hayduke chapter delete any reference to "Ranger." There were no Army Ranger units in the Vietnam war. Not since Korea. Substitute simply Green Beret or Special Forces for Ranger. The gateway slogan is correct for Vietnam, however, and must remain.

About Hayduke's jeep: if a simple 4-cylinder engine (4x4), then 55 or 60 would indeed be max highway cruising speed. Later civilian models, however, with 6-cylinder engines, can cruise at 65 or 70 and of course up to 80 or 90 downhill. Since he succumbs easily to the temptation to speed, we must make sure that the description of Hayduke's jeep is compatible with this tendency.

Time scheme: I think I have straightened this out by having the major action begin in June. Perhaps we should also have that Lee's Ferry meeting and boat trip ([Seldom Seen] Smith's chapter) take place in April or May so as to shorten the overall time-period. Would you check those chapters, as revised, and see if that can be done without extensive alterations. I think there are references to October in Hayduke's first chapter also. Doc's is vague, and Bonnie's too.

Where you and your editors have suggested cuts, indicated by red or green brackets, I have sometimes erased the brackets, meaning that I want the line or lines to stand. In most cases I have agreed with your suggestions and crossed out, lined out, X-ed out, the offending passages. In other cases I have neither erased your brackets nor crossed out the matter so enclosed, and the meaning of that is this: delete. Delete the material so enclosed, I mean.

As for numbers enclosed in penciled circles, what does that mean? I usually let it stand. I'd better telephone you about some of this or we'll end up with a nightmare of varying styles of punctuation and spelling. (Christ but I'll be glad when this is finished. You should never have let me get my hands on that manuscript again. But I'm glad you did—it demands re-writing. The version of *Monkey Wrench* which you first read ((now it can be told)) was literally and actually the very first draft of the novel, as it originally poured out from a sick and disordered mind.)

I like the subtitle, *A Novel About* etc., because I think it should provoke and excite the casual browser's curiosity. I also like it for its own sake. I also like it as a stand-in for the conventional jacket blurb, which is usually more embarrassing than informative. That's why, if you feel the book must have a jacket blurb (I don't), that's why I wrote or rather had [Seldom Seen] Smith write, in his own style, an Official Jacket Blurb for the book.

I think Doc should remain age 49-1/2 in order to make his relationship with Bonnie more plausible. I have deleted, as you will notice, most of the references to "old" Doc and some other suggestions that he is older or somehow physically decrepit. If you think more such modifications are needed, go ahead and make them yourself, if there is not time enough to consult me about it. But I want you to do it, not that punctuation fiend who lurks somewhere in the mustier corners of Lippincott (founded in 1792? ah, quite so). Perhaps he relinquishes Bonnie to Hayduke too easily, or it may seem so, but Doc is supposed to be an amateur philosopher capable of priding himself on a talent for detachment which he thinks he possesses— but does not really. Is it not conceivable that he knows or anticipates that Bonnie will eventually return to him anyway?

Does Bonnie have enough moxie? Should I make her tougher? (Yes, very late in the day to bring up this.) I had always imagined I'd have an easy comfortable year to revise and rewrite this nuvvle to my satisfaction. Nevertheless, now that we're launched on this headlong effort, I am as eager as you to see the book come out next Spring. Or next summer. What's wrong with May, June or July? I am dimly aware that books and book publishers are subject to some kind of seasonal rut and foaling cycle, but must it be religiously observed? Glancing at my copy of McGuane's 92 in the Shade, for example (and a very fine novel it is), I noticed that it was published officially in July. And yet survived. I do not mean to make a big point of this, and all other things aside, the sooner you wrench this book out of my hands the better it will be not only for me but also the book.

Enough for now. Back to the final three hundred pages. Should be finished two weeks from yesterday. Regards.

Ed Abbey

Mountain Gazette, Denver, Colorado (NOVEMBER 1974)

Dear Editors:

I see in Issue 27 the female chauvinists are writing you letters again, complaining about those sexist ads by Ascente and Stephensons. Now I ask—what's wrong with a little sexism in a workingman's magazine? I guess maybe I'm queer, but I like to look at pictures of naked girls, especially beautiful naked girls, although I got nothing against ugly naked girls; they are interesting too.

Exploitation? Who's being exploited? The girls in the ads don't look like they're posing at gun-point. They look like they're doing it for fun, or else for money, or likely both, in which case nobody is exploited and the costs are passed on to the consumer. I don't mind. Exploitation, shit. How about sheep, Mizz Kayte Mann of Englewood, Colorado? Take all those pictures of sheep you see in mountain-type magazines: how do you think those ewes feel about being treated like mere "beautiful things," mere "objects"? Think about it. This whole *Mizz* Magazine business of androgens and sexism is getting mighty tiresome. Like I tell my friends Castenada and Guru Maharaji and Baby Ram's Ass, "Life is too short for bullshit."

More human polarity,
Ed Abbey—Wolf Hole, Arizona

1975–1976

AS 1975 BEGAN, Abbey was awarded a lucrative Guggenheim Fellowship. After Moab, his next home was the Numa Ridge fire lookout tower in the back-country of Glacier National Park, Montana, from where, after just a few months—complaining about "this wet dark clammy-cold Northwest" and dreaming "of Vermilion Cliffs, of White Rim, of Grand and Slickhorn gulches"—Cactus Ed returned to Moab. During these two years Abbey also visited his sons, Josh and Aaron, in Chicago . . . and published *The Monkey Wrench Gang*, his most infamous novel.

Alan Harrington (14 JANUARY 1975)

Dear Alan,

Thanks for the copy of *Bookletter*. I for one had no idea you were obscure; you have enlightened me: I first heard of you about fifteen or twenty years ago in a review of *Doctor Modesto*, and have seen reviews of every one of your books since, long before I ever met you personally. If you are obscure, what does that make me? But as you say, why complain; there are advantages.

Enclosed is a copy of the current issue of *Mountain Gazette*, which is, as you will see if you read it, a sort of nature-lovers' *Rolling Stone*. Which I also read regularly, if not faithfully. If you ever want to sell something and can't sell it anywhere else, try *Mountain Gazette*: they only pay $125 (at least that's what they pay me), but even that is better than the *Chicago Review*—and far more prestigious. And they will print almost anything, if only it has some connection, however attenuated, to the so-called out-of-doors.

"Out-of-doors"? We're also out of Feenamint today, Madame, sorry. And out of sorts. Out of pocket. Out of sight. Curious idioms.

Am pissing away my life, as you can see, up here in the backlands, when I should be out cutting wood, prospecting for lead and zinc, or fishing for chub through a hole in the ice. Am also returning your magazine but would be interested in reading reactions other than mine to your George Pectin piece; who for example are the other Pectins you mention? Clue me. Could I be one of them myself perhaps? The writers of "quite dull sociological tracts," maybe? You see, I am just as insecure as you, Alan, when somebody brings it to my attention. Most of the time I don't think about it; the same way I handle Death: don't think about it. Always putting off the necessary confrontation until tomorrow.

Sorry we couldn't get together more when I was in Tucson. Somehow we must find you & Peggy a babysitter. Did that bum Eastlake ever show up? He hasn't written to me for two months. When's his goddamn *Scalp-dancers* nuvvle coming out?—I still hope to beat it into print—but maybe not. How's your *Immortalist* novel coming along? Nicely, I trust. Painfully if necessary.

Right now I'm trying to finish a magazine article about rape (rape of the West, that is), another sociological tract, of course, before heading into something else, I don't know what. Maybe that agricultural novel, if Guggenheim [Memorial Foundation] comes through to prop me up for it.

Or maybe something entirely different: e.g., I am fascinated by the problem of—Israel. Because of my past Jewish wives and girlfriends? Because of the Negev? I don't know: but I keep thinking of making a trip over there, before the oil-fueled Arabian hordes come streaming across all borders. What do you think? Is there a new book in that old tragedy?

The best, Ed—Moab, Utah

Rolling Stone, San Francisco, California (25 FEBRUARY 1975)

Sirs:

To call Bob "Dylan" a poet, as Gleason, Cott and Landau are willing to do in your pages, is a debasement of our common language. Are the times really so hard that grown men must make a living by pandering to the juvenile tastes of Teenybopper Kulchur? Anyone who sets himself up as a critic of music or poetry must at least have the ability to distinguish between art and commercial garbage, between the true and the fake. Furthermore and equally important, the critic must have sufficient honesty and courage to name the latter for what it is.

Bob "Dylan," like George Harrison or Tanya Tucker or Eric Clapton or Barry Manilow or any one of the five hundred other imitation-Afro entertainers now cavorting on the public stage, is an entertainer, not an artist. Pop music today is the same sick slick commercial babyfood that it was back in the brass-age times of Bing Crosby, Perry Como, and—what's his name?—that other one, Nixon's pal. Bob "Dylan," like his predecessors, is distinguished chiefly by his ability to follow the trends. When folk music and social protest was the thing, he came on with his parody of Woody Guthrie. When the mass public turned to rock, "Dylan" went electric. As phony country supersedes simulated-Negro rock, we'll find "Dylan" still faithfully following the million-headed mob.

This is not a put-down of popular music. Pop music has its place: it's great for dancing, it makes perfect background noise for parties, and it's ideal for hammering out fenders or fixing flats too, which is why you hear it every day in every body shop and gas station in the land. But pop music is not art.

What is art? One can answer that question best by pointing to examples. The music of Glenn Gould, for example. Or the poetry of such contemporaries as Gary Snyder, Jim Harrison or Galway Kinnell. Anyone who can't see the difference between their work and the bubblegum lyrics of Bob "Dylan" needs glasses. What is a poet? Well, we recently had a real poet in our midst, the real Dylan, Dylan Thomas. Any would-be critic who can't tell the difference between a poem such as "And death shall have no dominion" and the relaxed outpourings of the perpetual adolescent who stole his name (at the age of thirty Bob "Dylan" still can't grow a man's beard, as the portrait on page forty-two of *Rolling Stone* so pathetically reveals) should find himself a more fitting trade. Writing album liners, maybe, for Led Zeppelin, Alice Cooper, Tammy Wynette, Foghat, Randy Newman, John Lennon, John Denver, et al., ad infinitum, ad nauseum. Yeah and don't forget the Almond Brothers. And Janette Jalopy. All those whose names are writ in lizard piss.

Fun is fun, men. But life is too short for bullshit.

Ed Abbey—Wolf Hole

Paul Revere Abbey, Home, Pennsylvania (14 MARCH 1975)

Dear Dad,

Got your long letter and feel very bad. I am terribly sorry if I hurt your feelings. I did not mean to; I was responding to a letter from Mother in which she said you seemed to be wasting away, in effect, by staying in bed all the time. At least that was my impression of what she said, though I'm not sure where I put her letter now.

You know damn well you have always been my hero, and I know damn well you have worked very hard most of your life, and maybe you did, as you say, overstrain your heart at some time. Nor did I know that you have been to see two more doctors in addition to Bee. Of course, if all three doctors agree that you should take it easy, then I agree with them: you should. I guess it is unrealistic of me to think that you could continue to do the extraordinary things you used to do right up to the end of your days.

Painful subject—but surely we can be open with each other. I know that you are going to have to die sometime, probably before I do, and I hope very much that it doesn't happen to you in a goddamned hospital bed. Having witnessed that kind of end for someone I love already, I don't want to see it happen that way to you. On the other hand, I do want you to hang around as long as possible, just as I plan to do myself.

I suppose each of us has his own fantasy of how he wants to die. I would like to go out in a blaze of glory, myself, or maybe simply disappear some-day, far out in the heart of the wilderness I love, all by myself, alone with the Universe and whatever God may happen to be looking on. Disappear—and never return. That's my fantasy. And I suppose, unconsciously, I have imagined that kind of death for you. But why should you want to fulfill my fantasy?

And furthermore, by the time I'm your age (if I live that long), I'll probably see things in a different, not quite so romantic, light. Anyway, I apologize, and do look forward to seeing you here in Moab this spring. Then we'll go out on Grand View Point and talk the whole matter out, to the very end. I love you, old man, never mind all the stupid things I may have said.

Ed—Moab

Don Congdon, New York City (29 MARCH 1975)

Dear Don:

I'm sorry I failed to send you a carbon of my letter to Burlingame re my proposal to publish a collection of my magazine stories. I usually do send you carbons, as you know, especially where matters of business are con-cerned. In any case, my letter to Burlingame was essentially the same as the one I'd sent to Hills at McGraw-Hill a year or so ago, with similar results. (Hill owes me a letter, incidentally, on the subject of the novel so-far called *The Good Life*; he had some good ideas about that book, which is the next piece of fiction I plan to do.)

I realize that a collection of magazine articles makes a difficult book to sell; still I think that some of my short pieces are as good as anything I've written, and could be tied together on some sort of unifying theme (per-haps with added "bridge" material) to make a companion volume to *Desert Solitaire*. I even have a title for such a book: *Desert Solecism, or Secrets of a Solitary Masturbator*. Vanity, vanity. . . .

This is supposed to be an official secret until April 4th but apparently I have been awarded a Guggenheim grant. Now that I don't need it. Some of the credit should go to Bill Eastlake, who wrote a nice letter for me. The project specified is, of course, the novel mentioned above.

I'm glad to hear that *Atlantic* wants to print "Telluride Blues," though it would have been more topical last fall. Certainly the article will require editing, particularly updating. E.g., Zoline's ski resort is now up for sale and the town marshal lost his job etc.

As Bill [Eastlake] says, I have been wandering a bit during the past two months, in Arizona and Sonora, but I come back here every two or three weeks to read the mail and will probably spend the summer here. Renee and I are thinking of a trip to Europe in September; the kid has never been east of 8th Street and 2nd Avenue. We are thinking of making a base for the winter in Vienna, with branch offices in Napoli, Edinburgh, Stockholm, Avignon—all my old haunts. Any suggestions? Then return to Moab in time for the Spring planting. (Alfalfa and watermelons.) What do you think of that plan? Must consult Bill too.

I told Burlingame that I would come to New York for an interview with *Publishers Weekly*, whenever that is arranged. Naturally I expect to visit with you then as well. I am also supposed to be interviewed by somebody from the *Smithsonian* Magazine sometime this spring on the subject of paleontology, old bones and other fossils, that sort of thing; as my agent I gather it is your duty to know about such matters. But if this business gets much heavier I shall withdraw into my inner self. I thought nobody would ever find me in Moab—or "Nomad"—Utah, but already there are bearded young strangers knocking on the door uninvited (one of the obvious disadvantages of not having a telephone), and long earnest letters from strange women, which my wife answers.

Moab is a very small town, pop. 4500. I have more privacy in Tucson. I have already written to Burlingame about this but please make sure my current place of residence does not appear anywhere on or in the *Monkey Wrench* book or in any publicity, if any, associated with it. My official address, for all purposes of public relations, is the well-known Wolf Hole, Arizona.

Incidentally, I don't think I was "fussy" about the book jacket, as Burlingame says; I merely pointed out to him that the artist had confused a monkey wrench with a pipe wrench. Also, I tried to get him to simplify the jacket copy, or blurb, which is embarrassing, as usual, but acceptable. I would have preferred no blurb at all but apparently that cannot be. I will enclose a copy of that letter if I can find it.

Sent in the *Playboy* article over a month ago; they are still trying to make up their editorial minds about it. The final product was seventy-one pp long or a bit more than twice what they asked for, which is no doubt creating difficulties. The Muse grabbed me by the shorthairs. I got carried away. What else is on my mind, such as it is? Oh yes: the librarian of the University of Arizona, David Laird, is trying to gather into his archives all the letters I've written (oh my Gawd!) to various people, and I told him he could ask you for copies of mine to you, if you still have them, or some of them. Probably not a good idea but it's too late for modesty now.

Well as you can see, Don, I am having a helluva good time and immensely pleased with myself and am doubtless headed for some unimaginable and disastrous denouement. Last week, for example, I hiked for four days and forty-five miles, alone, along what's called the White Rim of the inner canyon of the Green & Colorado Rivers in Canyonlands National Park, nearby, ending up in a blizzard—and survived. If this sort of good luck keeps up I am bound to become a roaring egomaniac, insufferable even to myself. I may even do some Grape Nuts commercials, when Euell "Ever Fuck A Pine Tree?" Gibbons croaks, as he soon will from eating all that organic garbage.

Enough, enough. . . .

Regards, Ed Abbey

William Eastlake (22 SEPTEMBER 1975)

Dear Bill,

Your book arrived a day after I sent you my last letter. Thanks very much for the book and its generous autograph. As for the inside of the book, I find it everything an Eastlake novel is supposed to be, viz: very funny, wise, sad, ridiculous, fantastic, beautiful, emotionally disturbing, etc. In short, vintage Eastlake and the best of wines for soul and brain. You're some kind of genius, old man, and that's the truth. God Help You.

My book's disappeared already, I guess, as always happens; probly the publishers can't even afford a postage stamp to send me a letter, but since I've already spent all their money it don't matter much. I did agree to go to something called Arizona Authors Day in Phoenix on November 20th—if you would come too. We can get drunk together and raise hell in Diamonds

Department Store, autographing books. (Like McGuane, I'll do anything for money these days: got no other source of income anymore.)

About ready for our third cutting of alfalfa up at the Green River gopher ranch. Despite a whole summer of benign neglect the place is actually putting out hay. Not much but some. Must replant next year. Splendid weather here. Went down thru Cataract Canyon last week, a five day boat trip, and will do another in Lodore Canyon next month.

Suzi and Renee well and happy; Suzi's second grade teacher is indoctrinating her kids with *Mizz* Magazine dogma, but I suppose that's alright. At least for the girls. I personally do not think it a good idea to tell little boys they can grow up to be nurses or cocktail waitresses. Equality, yes; but identity, no. That's my theory of the sexes. Equal but separate.

(Am becoming quite reactionary in my late middle age.)

What else is new? [Doug] Peacock's coming. I make a speech at NAU in Flagstaff October 22. Meet me there if you can—if not sooner. You've never heard me give a speech—a strange and moving experience. (Most of the audience gets up and moves.) (Their bowels?) Did you find a new agent? Reconcile with Congdon? Sell your *Bombed In Boston* book yet? [*The Long, Naked Descent into Boston*]

Inform. What're you writing now? All my best to you & Marilyn.

Ed—Moab

Jay Livingood, c/o *Deseret News*,
Salt Lake City   (23 SEPTEMBER 1975)

Dear Mr. Livingood:

Below is the "official jacket blurb" which I wrote for the novel, *Monkey Wrench Gang*. You may use it in your interview-story, if you like. Seldom Seen, of course, is a character in the book.

Yrs truly, Edward Abbey—Oracle, Arizona

Seldom Seen Smith Explains About This Here Book:
This here book it's about that monkey business took place down around Pakoon Spring and up at Tin Cup Mesa and over by Muley Twist and south of Hog Wash Seep and yonder past Lean-To Point and some them other places in betwixt you probly read about in the papers and that's about all I got time to say about any of

it right now and anyhow I dont see why that man Abbey cant explain about his own goddamned book except he'd lie about it and not tell you this book should be hid from children and other impressionable adults and now if you folks'll excuse me I really got no more time to talk about it because if I haint mistaken that's old Bishop J. Dudley Love a-comin' over Cockscomb Ridge there with his whole goddanged Search & Rescue Team and I ought to got the hell out of here about two hours ago, so long.

Dianitia, New York City   (3 OCTOBER 1975)

Dear Dianitia:

Idea: next time you write up an ad for *Monkey Wrench* (or any other book for that matter), it seems to me that it might be useful, make the ad more interesting, if you juxtapose the con with the pro. Rather than attempt to overwhelm the reader with a sea of encomia carefully culled from selected reviews, tease his/her mind (if any) with paired-off praise and censure. E.g., though I no longer have the reviews on hand I think I remember one writer comparing the end of *MWG* to "a cheap Hollywood trick"; another calls the attempts at humor "flat and arch"; another speaks of the style as "swollen with verbose verbiage"; and one says of my mild sex scenes that they are "the least arousing since Lord Wimsey's honeymoon." Etc. etc. This is great stuff, and if counterposed to opposite opinions might well titivate the biblio-freak's skeptical curiosity.

Incidentally, though I know his intentions were good and I am grateful for his interest, I cannot forgive our friend John Baker of *PW* for making me talk like an Englishman in that so-called interview. No matter how drunk or incoherent I may actually have been, I know that I do not—never could—talk like an Englishman. Do all his interviewees talk like Englishmen? Perhaps—and no doubt I should regard it as an intended compliment.

Well, what the phukk, gotta get back to work now. Am typing up a piece on "Life in a Lookout Tower" for *Audubon* while postponing as long as possible the dread moment in which I must somehow resume work on the novel which, for seven years now (and they have been very kind and forbearing), I have owed to your colleagues McGraw and Hill.

Good luck with our book.

Yrs, Edward Abbey—Moab

Don Congdon, New York City (28 OCTOBER 1975)

Dear Don:

Thanks for your letter of Oct 21st.

Naturally I think Lippincott should make an effort to sell *Monkey Wrench Gang*, with or without reviews from them swine at *Time*, *Newsweek*, etc. I cannot believe we will not get a review in the *Sunday* [NY] *Times* at least.

Furthermore, *MWG* has been reviewed so far in some fifty to sixty newspapers and magazines nationwide, including good ones in *National Observer*, *Wash Post*, *Denver Post*, *Saturday Review*, *PW*, *Kirkus*, *Barkham* (whatever that is), *Audubon*, *Smithsonian*, *Playboy*, *Harper's Bookletter*, etc etc etc, even UPI and many other papers from Rhode Island to California. The worst review so far was in a miserable rag which calls itself *The Phoenix Gazette*, in which the reviewer's chief complaint is that there is no such place as "Wolfe City, Arizona" (sic). Lippincott certainly knows about these reviews because that's where I got them from.

As for the movie deal or non-deal, I do think you should contact [Robert] Redford's agent before granting an option-renewal to Katzka and United Artists. Naturally, I did not press Redford for any kind of commitment but he did say to me that he would like to make a film of the *MWG* book and that his agent had already contacted you or your office about it, learned about the option, and is now waiting for Katzka and UA to make up their minds. My impression was that Redford and Co. do not wish to get involved with Mr. Katzka in any sort of auction for the movie rights.

I'll tell you all about the "Outlaw Trail Ride" sometime; much fun and many good stories. Redford himself struck me as a good man—a little shy but very intelligent, much concerned, serious about his art, overflowing with energy. But can't sing worth a shit.

I am disgusted with *Newsweek*. How dare they refuse to print my Kaiparowits [Plateau, Arizona] bulletin! And refusing to review my book! Conspiracy of silence, enough to make a man paranoid. (Anyone not paranoid in this world must be crazy.) Walter Clemons, as you'll recall, was the editor of *Desert Solitaire*; isn't he still reviewing books for *Newsweek*? Goddamn their eyes. . . .

Speaking of paranoia, it's true that I do not know exactly who my enemies are. But that of course is exactly why I'm paranoid. Or consider this proposition, copied from the men's room wall in a bar in Flagstaff: "Will trade three blind crabs for two without teeth." Appears to be no connection at all with the first part of this paragraph, right? Very suspicious.

Well Don, as you see, I'm still coasting along on the manic wave of my psychosis. The depressive phase begins when I confront that blank sheet of paper that necessarily prefigures my next book. Tell Fred Hills that I am writing a novel for him this winter and if the family novel still proves impossible I have two other good ones percolating in my brains. How's this for a title?: *Good News*—a novel about work, marriage, redneck pickup trucks (my brother Howard works as a truck driver back in Pennsylvania), death and other forms of divorce, love in Hoboken and other tales of the supernatural, etc., survival, Sunday mornings, Friday nights, baseball, troopships, hospitals and the smell of trauma, Mexico, Scotland, food stamps, the sorrows of August in Kellysburg, Pennsylvania, lost in the woods, rain on the roof, ghosts on the stairway, fire in the attic.... No more fantasies, no more topical Westerns, no more self-indulgent wishful thinking, but a dense, intense, suspenseful book about—survival, yes, that's the subject, recorded in simple declarative sentences quite unlike this sentence. To seize the thing which has no name.

If only I could write the book as easily as I can imagine it.

Ah well, back to the mundane and the profane. The trouble is, living here in bright dazzling desert Utah, with snow-covered mountains rising above redrock cliffs and the cliffs above green fields of alfalfa and the cottonwoods shimmering with gold foil and the meadowlarks preparing to depart, it is so goddamned hard to take anything seriously. One must struggle against the desire to just sit here, munching on lotus, chewing our peyote buttons, dreaming the dream that only dreams are real.

You see the trouble. Down to Phoenix next month to have a few words with the editor of the *Phoenix Gazette* and to join with old Bill Eastlake in some kind of autographing party for "Arizona Authors." I'll be there, of course, to represent Wolf Hole.

Someone or something is mutilating our cows, excising assholes, depupilating eyeballs, amputating tongues, with surgical precision. No kidding. Maybe you've heard about it. Cowboys packing guns again. UFOs (Unidentified Fucking Objects) reported in the skies at twilight. *Molto misterioso.*

Enough, enough of all this gibberish.

Ed A.

Joshua Abbey   (24 NOVEMBER 1975)

Dear Josh—

Enclosed are three letters which I hope will help you out. Rather than wait for you to send me the addresses I am sending them to you to mail yourself. Quicker and simpler. Be sure to type up the envelopes in a tidy professional style and put my name and address on the return address corner. Am also enclosing your resumes. The carbon copies are for your own records. Sorry I didn't think of this myself; it really never occurred to me that that old Cowboy movie might be a means of helping you out. But as I said in Las Vegas, I did plan to try to get you a job when and if *Monkey Wrench* is sold to the movies.

Be sure to check out the addresses. I merely used Universal to make the letters look business-like; you can put different addresses on the envelopes if necessary or desirable.

I will also write to Robert Redford as soon as the *Monkey Wrench* matter is settled—either way. The book is now under option to something called Palladium Productions but their option expires at the end of this month and I don't know what, if anything, will happen next. I do hear rumors that Redford is seriously interested in the book—in fact he told me so himself—but you know better than I how utterly unreliable is any promise connected with Hollywood. We'll see. And if *Monkey* becomes a film I will certainly do all that I can to get you a part in it. In the meantime be cautious with your hopes and go on with your work. Sooner or later you will get the break you deserve.

I also enclose a letter from Suzi, and my annual check from Universal, which arrived, by strange and hopeful chance, just today. I really do not know if I am considered a member of SAG [Screen Actors Guild]. I don't think I ever got a card. Maybe you can find out. If I am a member, maybe I could help you get into the union. In fact I'll write SAG today. Never paid any dues.

Well. So much for business.

I probably failed to convey to you how wonderful it was to see you again, after so long. But it was a wonderful experience for me. I came home in a glow of pride and happiness and exhilaration which has not worn off yet and I hope never will. You are truly a beautiful and impressive and sensitive and wise and solid young man—I wish I could claim some credit for it. You seem already to be more grown-up than I ever was. . . .

Anyway: could you come for a visit on Christmas? Aaron too, of course. (Check enclosed for plane fare. And see if you can find the letter I sent you last July c/o Lee Strasburg School.) We'll be in Phoenix then, with Renee's parents, who are eager to meet you. Maybe you could fly to Phoenix on Christmas Eve, after you finish your Santa Claws bit, if you make reservations early. I'll call you about it later at your friend Jeff's place. Be sure to send me your own phone number as soon as you get one.

Of course we'll pick you up at airport or train station (nice train ride by the way) if you can come. If you cannot come, I want you to spend the check on champagne and flowers for your sweet and delightful girl Jane. Tell her I'll autograph a book for her anytime.

Write to us. From now on I want to hear about everything you do and every development in your career as an actor, playwright, director, lover, philosopher and traveler.

See you again soon. Much love from your old man,

Ed—Oracle, Arizona

Laurence Gonzales & David Standish & Karol Pozniak,
Playboy **Magazine, Chicago**   (21 NOVEMBER 1975)

Dear Larry & Dave & Karol:

Thanks very much for the hospitality at Playboy Towers Inc. I like your little two-bit town, despite the windy corners and the incredibly banal clip joints. Seriously. . . .

If you were serious about having me write again for *Playboy*—and certainly I want to—here are a few essays, of various length and depth, which I have in mind:

1. Women's Liberation: Some Second Thoughts—a semi-humorous reexamination of the basic issues; a winnowing of the reasonable from the unreasonable; the man-hating theme; a review of the biological basis of male-female relations; the anthropological basis of male domination; the essential meaning of the sexual act itself; etc.

2. The Right to Arms—a defense of the right to own and bear arms (including handguns) from my own libertarian, agrarian-anarchist, left-wing liberal point of view; too important an issue to be left to the National

Rifle Association, the John Birchers and other right-wing crackpots; i.e., if guns are registered (then confiscated, then outlawed), cops—and the military—and the secret police—and a few outlaws—will have guns; consider: the democratic rifle as opposed to the authoritarian tank, the totalitarian B-52; widespread citizen ownership of firearms as the final popular defense against the tyranny of the State; etc.; tyranny always based on a monopoly of the means of violence; all authoritarian societies based on a disarmed population, a class-controlled restriction on ownership of weapons, etc., etc.

3. Drunk in the Afternoon—some small-town Western bars I know and love, and what goes on there on August afternoons (not much) and Saturday nights (too much). . . .

4. Mountain Men and Mountain Music—Why I love Beethoven, Bruckner and Bach, and why I regard Bob "Dylan" and others of his aging-adolescent unisex-bearded ilk as so many Pop-Kulchur schmucks; (I can guarantee this essay as the most-hated you would ever publish). . . .

5. Death Valley Acid—what it's like to drop 350 micrograms of LSD at twilight on the sand dunes out in the middle of Nowhere between the Panamint Mts and the Funeral Range. . . .

6. Down the Green River with Major Powell—a trip on a little boat thru Gates of Lodore, Split Mt., Desolation, Stillwater, Labyrinth and Cataract Canyons, in the watery footsteps of J. Wesley Powell. . . .

7. Shithead Literature and Fuckhead Crap: Studies in Contemporary American Psycho-Babble and Other Varieties of Teenybopper Intellectualism—That is, a critique of such current pop lit as Casteneda, Herman Hesse, Seth Speaks, Be Here Now, Hugh Prather, Naked Massage, etc etc ad infinitum ad nauseum. . . .

8. A Journey By Foot, Horse, Camel & Rover Through the Empty Interior of the Australian Desert—This is something I've always wanted to do and if I can get Playboy, Audubon, National Geographic and Sierra Club to help pay the expenses, I'll do it . . . .

9. Warfare in the Desert: A Walk Around the Sinai—with special attention to the battle at Mitla Pass, and some consideration of the effects of modern tank and aerial warfare on a desert environment in the old Mosaic Wilderness.

Well you see, I've got plenty of ideas, and more where those came from. Let me know if any of them interest you.

Has the *Playboy* Book Club taken a look at *The Monkey Wrench Gang?* Seems to me that *MWG* might be a book to interest your readers.

So much for now. It was good to meet you people and I wish you all the best of luck in your work and play.

Regards, Edward Abbey—Moab

Frederick W. Hills, Editor in Chief, McGraw-Hill Book Co., New York City (20 JANUARY 1976)

Dear Fred:

Much tanks for your recent letter. I find it consoling to learn that you, too, believe that *Monkey Wrench* got a bad deal from the NYC press. The *Times* has always reviewed my books before; why they should persist in boycotting this new one creates an exasperating mystery where no mystery should be necessary. Let them dislike, scorn or hate the book if they so wish; but it seems to me only fair that opinions should be openly stated, reasons given. The silent treatment is unjust.

Have made only slow and painful progress on "our" novel, *The Good Life,* or, as I am now thinking of calling it, *Good News.* (Various ironies intended.) I find it difficult to write a story based on the actual lives of people I love, who are close to me, and all still very much alive. Would find it easier to write about even myself. Which suggests this proposition:

If I were to defer completing *Good News* for yet another year or two, would you be interested in considering a different book in its place, in lieu of fulfilling the contract for the other? Here are two projects I have had in mind for years:

1) autobiographical: an account of my life—so far—as a writer. Twenty years in the pursuit of fame, fortune and understanding, with mixed results. Or what it's like to be a half-successful "famous unknown author." Making a living but not making it. What it does to loves and marriages and friends. Jobs and places, schools and abandoned careers, lost opportunities, discovered compensations. Like *A Fan's Notes,* mostly true. A few modest lies, perhaps. Other writers I have known. The joys, sorrows and complicated ambiguities of this most wide, free, exasperating art. What it does to one's children—the writer as father. What it does to the nervous system.

Alcoholism, melancholy, lechery and an early death. (Too long deferred in this case; now too old for a romantic passing on, I see that I must stick it out to the untidy and no doubt lugubrious end.) Etc. etc. Many, many laughs. I have a nice title for it, to wit: *Abbey's Road—Take the Other: The Secrets of a Literary Bum. Confessions of a Barbarian.*

2) *Sundown Legend.* One more attempt to improve on Cervantes. An old man, crazed by reading too much Zane Grey and Louis L'Amour, takes to the open road with rusty six-gun and hollow horse (you can see the moon through its ribcage), bent out of shape on righting wrong. "Write right, write good, right wrong." Contemporary setting, more or less. Equipped and properly costumed, the old man works his way with supreme confidence toward the inevitable surprise. One final attempt (on my part at least) to abstract, pin down, grasp, extract, idealize once and for all the essence of the myth of the Old West. A short novel in a style as clear, cool and simple as I can make it. Windmills. Country taverns. The Arizona desert. Ghost towns. A bar maid with sweaty armpits. A bad man with good intentions. Flashy sunsets and well water in a tin cup.

And a third I want to do sometime soon: *Salty Dogs*—a novel about working men, today. Bartenders (I was a bartender for a time), truck drivers (my brother is a truck driver), rednecks, lovers, husbands and philanderers. About meeting the mortgage on the new "mobile home." About Saturday nights in Woody's Bar. About deer season on opening day. About the little woman's bowling team and that sonofabitch who sold her the insurance policy on my life. About cowhands and melon farmers. About the war, about death and boredom, about the gritty grimy sweaty underside of American life. About hard work, the vanishing paycheck, the drunk tank in the city jail. About the black hole in the middle of the sky. About a salty dog who sticks with his wife and bullies his kids through school. About hope, and nerve, and endurance.

Ah yes, the head is full of books. The hard part is to force them down through the bloodstream and out through the fingers.

Regards, Ed Abbey—Moab

New York Review of Books, New York City   (FEBRUARY 1976)

Dear Sirs:

The review of Gary Snyder's *Turtle Island* [*NYRB* 1/22/76] by Mr. Irvin Erhenpries is stupid.

That takes care of the matter to my satisfaction, but perhaps I should add an explanatory remark or two. Or three.

Mr. Erhenpries is baffled by the problem of evil institutions rising from the benevolent dispositions of human beings. But the answer to that, as human history demonstrates, is fairly clear: corporate institutions, such as the State, create a morality of their own, inferior not superior to the morality of ordinary men and women in their homes, clans, villages and towns. Through the diffusion of responsibility, the remoteness of control and the impersonality of its large-scale operations, the social institution is capable of crimes which mere people, in their face to face dealings with one another, could not even imagine. Thus a little wretch like Harry Truman could boast that he "never lost a night's sleep" over the incineration of Nagasaki and Hiroshima. Adolf Eichmann merely obeyed orders. Hannah Arendt called it the banality of evil. In other words, there is something in the character of large-scale organization itself which is qualitatively different from and is not derived from anything in the character of its individual components—i.e., people, ordinary people, the majority of us, who wish only to be let and left alone to pursue our rather simple interests among family, friends and community.

Mr. Erhenpries suggests that before the advent of technology, urbanization, and mass production, the condition of life for most people was "threadbare, uncomfortable and nightmarishly dependent upon the caprice of men in power." That could be true; there are good reasons for believing otherwise. In any case his words appear to me as a precise description not of the past but of contemporary life, the very conditions under which most men struggle for survival today. It is because contemporary life imposes on most of us a threadbare, uncomfortable and nightmarishly dependent existence that so many are seeking a way out from under the grotesque social machine developed by industrialism, urbanism and the national state.

Nor is "the life of harmony with natural rhythms" designed for only a "saving remnant." It is—or was—the life lived by most of mankind for most of human history. Were that not so we would not be here today. Life lived in disharmony with nature leads rapidly to extinction. Precisely the nature of the threat we face now, in this dying and most unpopular of centuries.

Yours sincerely, Edward Abbey—Moab

Don Congdon, New York City   (2 FEBRUARY 1976)

Dear Don:

Enclosed is a fragment "left over" from the *Playboy* rape article. Maybe you could sell it to *Harpers? Esquire? New Yorker?* (The latter two have never bought any words from me, the swine.)

Now that the Kaiparowits [Plateau, Arizona] affair has received more publicity, perhaps it would be worthwhile trying again to interest *Newsweek* in the "Great Kaiparowits Rip-Off" article—what do you think?

I wish *Atlantic* would print that "Telluride Blues" story soon, before the ski season is all over again.

Received the movie option renewal check, thanks.

In a few days I'll be sending you some three hundred pages of collected magazine pieces which I'm thinking of calling *Desert Music: Essays and Assays 1969–1976*. My plan, if we can get a contract for the book, is to give it a little more coherence and unity by arranging the material in a certain order, either chronological or by subject matter, and by adding explanatory and/or autobiographical pages between each chapter or article: i.e., background information, how or why the piece came to be written, what changes have occurred since in the place, situation, person, etc. As you know from your copy of Jack Macrae's letter of Jan 22nd, he has practically promised to publish the book, but I'll believe it better when I see a contract. If you decide it is worthwhile making copies of the ms. please send a copy to Jon Beckmann, Editor-in-Chief, Sierra Club Books, Mills Tower, San Francisco; I have promised him a look at it. And if you think Hills and Burlingame might also be interested in a crack at it, that's fine with me.

Despite the alleged failure of *Monkey Wrench Gang*, I have already received more letters, reviews, speaking invitations, proposals and propositions decent and indecent (one lady M.D. in California has offered me "female companionship and free medical care for the rest of my natural life—if I live that long"), hate letters and veiled threats as a result of that "obscene," "sexist," "outrageous and scandalous" book than in the previous nineteen years of my alleged literary career. Keeps Renee busy answering the correspondence from strange wimmin. The "Wolf Hole" dodge is not working. Thank you for passing Joshua's resume on to Katzka and Douglas.

Best, Ed—Moab

Edward Hoagland   (16 APRIL 1976)

Dear Ted,

Thanks for your letter. I presume you've just returned from Africa and that we'll read all about it in the next new book. I hope so. Me, I'm on my way to Australia in two weeks: will spend a month or so there exploring the desert interior (for [National] Geographic), then on to Calcutta, Bombay, Tehran, Athens etc etc before a rather hasty return to the States. Got to be back in Utah in time for the fall watermelon festival, rodeos, roundups and alfalfa harvest. Will stop off in NYC in August and look for you.

I am grateful for your attempts to find out what happened to my Monkey Wrench book in New York. Actually, I'd gotten over my bitterness about it and pretty well forgotten the whole mysterious business—until your letter. Now all my exasperations have revived and I am outraged all over again.

The Monkey Wrench book, nation-wide, did very well compared to anything else I've ever had published. It's sold more copies in six months than the Desert Solitaire book (my only other "popular" production) has sold in eight years, got five times more reviews (mostly favorable) and resulted in more letters decent and indecent, friendly and hateful, than I care to try to answer anymore.

But in New York itself (the big puddle?), there were no reviews at all, unless you count Newsweek as a NYC publication. I don't. Even the Sunday Times failed or declined to have it reviewed and that I find absolutely inexplicable, unjust and unfair. And am still mighty pissed about it, now that you've reminded me. I don't care if they don't like the book, they should have the guts to say so and say why they don't like it, rather than try to bury it alive.

Oh well, what the hell. There's still the inner satisfaction. Of all the books I've composed so far, two give me that sensation Nabokov calls "aesthetic bliss," the feeling that I've finally done something right, and one of

those two is *The Monkey Wrench Gang* and the other is *Black Sun*. The rest
is juvenilia and journalism (though not without art, I hope). So to hell with
the New York book reviewing crowd. I can survive without them. Except
for your generous plug in the *Sunday Times* several years ago, none of them
never were any help to me anyhow.

As for frogs and puddles, who can say? That is a matter of perspective.
Except for the publishing industry, New York City appears from here as a
small and waning force in American culture. I feel that the real battle to
determine the character of America's future (if any) will take place west of
the Mississippi. I certainly do not feel isolated from your "red-hot center"—
quite the contrary. The West is now the scene of what may be seen decades
from now as epic struggles, of which the Kaiparowits affair is merely one
minor skirmish. (Our greatest negative victory so far though—we had an
epic celebration in Salt Lake City a couple of nights ago.)

If I really wanted peace and quiet in my life I'd go home to Pennsylvania—or back to Hoboken or Brooklyn. I always felt, living in those places,
that things were pretty well shaken down and settled; that in fact there
was really nothing very interesting going on, that the dominant emotional
atmosphere is one of humorous resignation, cynical hopelessness. The
European phase in the maturing and decay of America. No doubt it will
eventually creep over the West as well.

But not while I'm around. (I'll be gone.)

To belabor this subject a bit further, I wonder if there even really is such
a thing as a "red-hot center" in American literary life? When I try to think
of the contemporary American writers, poets, novelists I most admire, they
seem to be scattered all over the landscape: McGuane in Montana, Harrison
in Michigan, Eastlake and Harrington in Arizona, Creeley in California,
Pynchon in California (or so I hear), Berry in Kentucky, McMurtry in DC,
Kesey in Oregon (although he has apparently quit), Kinnell in Spain, old
Henry in California, Algren somewhere in New Jersey now, Hoagland in
Vermont and all over, Gary Snyder in California, Mumford in—well I don't
know—he is my candidate for the Nobel Prize, by the way; Hunter Thompson in Colorado, John Graves in Texas, Exley in Florida and so on. Well,
there must be others but I can't think of them offhand.

And I think this is right and wholesome. I think that writers and artists
should be scattered, spread out, living among working people (as most of
us do), rather than clustered together in herds, interlocking elbows with
agents and editors.

There's a topic for your next essay: "The Desolation and Barrenness of the New York Literary Scene."

Enough of all this gibberish. Good luck. Write again.

(I've enclosed some photos of life in the West, for your amusement.)

Ed A.—Moab

High Country News, Lander, Wyoming (1 MAY 1976)

Dear Friends:

Please don't print that dumb interview from the *New Mexico Independent*. I must've been drunk or hung over. That's not me talking, that's me trying to impersonate a responsible conservationist. I am not a responsible conservationist, I am a wild preservative. If I knew how to blow up Glen Canyon Dam, I'd be out there working on it tonight.

Yrs truly, Ed Abbey—Wolfe Hole

P.S.: Contribution enclosed.

**Miss Michaels, High School Teacher,
Bicentennial Affair** (3 JULY 1976)

Dear Miss Michaels:

You asked for a few words about Utah. Okay, here are a few words about Utah:

Utah is my home. It is also the home of rattlesnakes, scorpions, coyotes, eagles, mountain lions, bighorn sheep, mule deer, kit foxes, bobcats, wild horses, pronghorn antelopes, vultures, Indians and some people. (Not too many.) Utah is one of the wildest, least-inhabited, freest, most beautiful places in North America and we like it that way. Help us keep the strip-mining industry, the power-plant industry, the river-damnation industry, the shale-oil industry, the ORV industry, the logging industry and the freeway-building industry out of Utah and when you come to visit we who live here will help you to see and enjoy the national parks, the national forests and the national public lands which are the property of all Americans.

You're welcome, Edward Abbey—Moab

Gilbert Neiman, English Department, Clarion State College, Clarion, Pennsylvania (17 JULY 1976)

Dear Gilberto—

Thanks for your letter of May 29th. Sorry to be so late in replying but I just got back from Australia. (Investigating how the lower half live for a couple of Stateside journals.)

I'd be happy to do the visiting writer bit at Clarion most anytime this fall between say Sept. 15th and Christmas. You set the date. In setting it, however, I would appreciate it if you would contact the English Dept at I.U.P.—Indiana University of Pennsylvania (near my old hometown, where my parents and brother still live)—and see if they would also be interested in a guest appearance by Abbey. They said they were last year, if I gave them sufficient advance notice. Then if they say yes, try to work out two dates within a week or ten days of each other. That way I might make enough money to pay travel expenses and have some left over for a wild binge in New York. (Come along.)

My new wife Renee (half French, half Mormon!) will probably be accompanying me. She's nuts about New York.

By "usual writer bit" I mean informal get-togethers with teachers & students, plus a formal public reading or lecture, plus of course the usual excessive indulgence in alcoholic intoxicants, cigar-smoking and ghastly restaurant food. I am ashamed to admit that I have learned to enjoy these things—in moderation, i.e., two or three times a year.

My official U.S. Superstate IBM # is 198-20-1947.

Would really be great to see you again. Want to hear about your brothel novel, among other things. We have much to talk about.

Best, Ed—Moab

Paul W. Allen (24 JULY 1976)

Dear Mr. Allen:

In reply to your letter of July 20th:

Yes, the smoke from a copper smelter looks white as it leaves the stacks. But as those gases level out and form a plume they react with sunlight and take on a yellowish-brown color. Anyone who lives in southern Arizona knows this. I have seen it for years from Tucson, from the Catalina Mts, from the air, from Table Mt above the San Pedro Valley, where I worked for three years on the Whittell Ranch, and from Organ Pipe, where I worked several winters as a park ranger. I have a friend working now as a fire lookout in the Tonto Forest; he sends me regular reports on the extent and distribution of smelter smog. The Group Against Smelter Pollution (G.A.S.P.) in Tucson has been trying for years to get the goddamned EPA to enforce the Clean Air Act in southern Arizona. Everyone knows the problem exists, except the state politicians and their employers, the officials of the copper industry.

Your response is so typical. Instead of doing something constructive about smelter pollution, you attempt to deny that it exists. Instead of attacking the problem, you attack your critics. Instead of installing the B.A.T., you build higher stacks, dispersing the filth over a wider area rather than keeping it out of the public air entirely.

It is this concern for profit above the public good that makes me question the practice of absentee or out-of-state ownership of the Arizona copper industry. Perhaps if you and other copper industry officials and the major stockholders made your homes in southern Arizona you would show a little more concern for human health, not so much for your profit margins. We can live with less copper, or with no copper at all, but we cannot long survive without clean air.

Yours sincerely, Edward Abbey—Moab

Martin Litton, Grand Canyon Dories,
Stanford, California (17 AUGUST 1976)

Dear Martin:

Thank you very much for the free ride down through the Grand [Canyon]. My wife and I had a Grand time and loved every minute of it. You are a generous man and I wish you the best of luck with your riverine enterprises. And everything else you're up to.

I was much impressed by the dories. They are not only beautiful to look at but beautiful to ride and row, much superior to baloney boats in every respect. (A fact which I shall not hesitate to stress in writing the words for Blaustein's book.)

Finally, I must say something about your boatpeople—oarsmen and cooks. They are really a wonderful bunch of men and women. I was sick with envy at their skill and competence, filled with admiration by their never-failing cheerfulness, tact and gentleness in dealing with problem passengers (like myself, for example), and amazed at the many other talents they revealed—tin-can compaction, for instance, and music, and psychiatry, and high diving, and wit and humor and general knowledge on many, many matters. It will be a long time—if ever—before I forget people like Jane and Kenly, Wally and Rich, Dane and Mike and Sharky, Miltie and that other one—what's his name?—the one with the cameras and the contacts and mustache who's always shuffling his foot in the sand and falling in love with twelve-year-olds. Anyway, they make a great crew, and I want to be on their side. Always.

All the best, Ed Abbey—Moab

Esquire Magazine, New York City (11 SEPTEMBER 1976)

Dear Sirs:

I read with interest your two stories in the September issue promoting "Traction"—ORVs or "escape machines," as your writers call them.

Let me tell you what a lot of us who live out here in the American West think about your goddamned Off-Road Vehicles. We think they are a goddamned plague. Like the snowmobile in New England, the dune buggy on the seashore, the ORV out here in the desert and mesa country is a public nuisance, a destroyer of plant life and wildlife, a gross polluter of fresh air, stillness, peace and solitude.

The fat pink soft slobs who go roaring over the landscape in these oversized over-priced over-advertised mechanical mastodons are people too lazy to walk, too ignorant to saddle a horse, too cheap and clumsy to paddle a canoe. Like cattle or sheep, they travel in herds, scared to death of going anywhere alone, and they leave their sign and spoor all over the back country: Coors beer cans, Styrofoam cups, plastic spoons, balls of Kleenex, wads of toilet paper, spent cartridge shells, crushed gopher snakes, smashed sagebrush, broken trees, dead chipmunks, wounded deer, eroded trails, bullet-riddled petroglyphs, spray-painted signatures, vandalized Indian ruins, fouled-up waterholes, polluted springs and smoldering campfires piled with incombustible tinfoil, filter tips, broken bottles. Etc.

It is not the bureaucrats back in Washington who are trying to stop this motorized invasion of what little wild country still remains in America; on the contrary, the bureaucrats are doing far too little. What feeble resistance has so far appeared comes from concerned citizens here and there who are trying to prod and encourage the bureaucrats to do their duty: namely, to save the public lands for their primary purpose, which is wildlife, habitat, livestock forage, watershed protection and non-motorized human recreation.

Thank God for the coming and inevitable day of gasoline rationing, which will retire all these goddamned ORVs and "escape machines" to the junkyards where they belong.

Ed Abbey—Moab

Mike Di Leo (14 SEPTEMBER 1976)

Dear Mike:

Sounds pretty lively around your place, with naked hysterical lesbians and flaming forest fires. All we've got here at present are money-mad Mormons and Christ-crazy Christians. Sort of quiet and peaceful.

Your questions are tough but I'll try to answer some of them.

Question 1. Don't know. I doubt that politics, harangues or books will do much good. The power of example will do more and has already done much to persuade people there may be a better way to live. But most of us—myself for example—are not going to give up our VWs and our pickup trucks and our electrified kitchens until we are forced to by economic pressures. Those pressures will come. Meanwhile, though we know better, we drift along on the currents of sloth, inertia and general insouciant indifference.

Q2. Culture vs civilization. Perhaps my use of those two words in that old *Desert* book was careless; many have objected. I was using "culture" in its anthropological sense, meaning the social thought and reason, the institutions by which any given society is dominated. America, Europe, Japan are urban-industrial cultures. "Civilization," on the other hand, is something which has never existed. Civilization is the realm of ideas and ideals, the invisible republic of visions. Civilization suggests a city, true; but that city is the City of Humanity—incorporeal, everywhere and nowhere, found only in courage and brotherhood, in poetry and visions and the highest music. Culture refers to cultivation and farming, among other things, but as my friend Seldom Seen Smith mentioned in *The Monkey Wrench Gang*, the invention of agriculture may have been a great step backward for the human race. It was a farmer, Cain, who murdered his brother Abel, the rancher. See *Tiger and Fox, The Imperial Animal*, for a fuller development of this notion. It seems quite possible that the hunting, gathering and pastoral societies might have been the freest and most adventurous ever known. Anyhow, the meaning of "culture" and "civilization," used as symbolic contraries in *Desert Solitaire*, is spelled out there at great length with clear and simple examples. Those who object to the terminology are free to substitute more fitting labels, if they wish and if they can find them.

Q3. George W. Hayduke, violence, and beer cans on the highway. Yes, we may need Hayduke someday. When? When other means fail. When the violence of the ever-expanding industrial culture threatens our homes, our ways of life, those places on earth that we love and need, then some of us may choose to resist by whatever effective means are available. Violence, of course, is traditional in our country, as American as pizza pie. But I speak for myself only. I mean for myself and George. What the rest of you are up to, I don't want to know. Officially I am absolutely opposed to all forms of illegality—except at night. I don't mince words.

Q4. I doubt that my sense of personal freedom is any stronger than anybody else's. I'm happy to respect authority when it's genuine authority, based on moral or intellectual or even technical superiority. I'm eager to follow a hero if we can find one. But I tend to resist or evade any kind of authority based merely on the power to coerce. Government, for example. The Army tried to train us to salute the uniform, not the man. Failed. I will salute the man, maybe, if I think he's worthy of it, but I don't salute uniforms anymore.

Q5. Fiction and the Fat Masterpiece. The art of storytelling must be as ancient as language itself. A good story dramatizes our deepest hopes, fears, loves and other passions. The story is primordial as rhythm. "Be primordial or decay," says Dahlberg, quite correctly. My own particular preferred mode of sharing these passions is through the novel. Having failed last week for the fourth time in a row to climb Mt Wilson—14,250 feet of rotten rock and dirty frozen rotten snow (near Telluride, Colorado)—I am more determined than ever to complete my Fat Masterpiece. Though it may take years. And when I do I shall retire from this writing business and retreat to my hut in the desert and spend the rest of eternity contemplating—my novel.

Q6. My next book? I'm glad you asked that question. It's a collection of essays to be called *Malice Aforethought: Essays in Defense of the American West*, and will be published by Dutton sometime early in 1977, in case anyone is still around then. Writing habits? None. But I work best under duress. In fact, I work only under duress.

Q7. Yes, I'm in favor of back-to-the-land movements, homesteading and the family farm. But I was born and raised on a family farm, escaped, am having a fat and easy life now, and am in no hurry to return. But I will, eventually, when I overcome my sloth and melancholy. Eventually we shall all return to the land. Naturally.

Q8. "There is a way of being wrong which is also necessarily right." I don't know what the hell I meant by that statement, but I know it's right.

Q9. The joy of the spadefoot toad. Yes, I think I share that joy. Like the toad, I spend most of my life under the mud, aestivating in sloth and melancholy, but on those rare and wonderful occasions when it rains, out here in the desert, then I too crawl forth and sing along with the rest of the crowd. I am hopeful, though not full of hope, and the only reason I don't believe in happy endings is because I don't believe in endings.

Thanks, Mike Di Leo. I've had fun trying to answer your questions, as you can see, and I know you can also see around all the facetious corners. One request: please don't mention that I live in Moab or Green River; as you will understand, I sometimes get some pretty funny people looking for me. The official address is "near Wolf Hole, Arizona."

Best regards and come visit again sometime.

Florence Krall, Professor, University of Utah,
Salt Lake City (26 SEPTEMBER 1976)

Dear Flo—

I threw away those notes from the final evening of the workshop but will try to recall what I said then:

It was a pleasure meeting you people. Sorry we didn't have time to get to know each other better. Anyhow, I did enjoy talking with you and showing you a little of this country I love so much. I hope that you love it too.

Loving it, we are obliged to defend it as best we can. An anarchist myself, I have always been reluctant to join any organization. But if we are going to defend the American West against industrial exploitation, we will have to cooperate with one another in some kind of political, social and legal action. (I am opposed to all forms of illegality—except at night.) I think we can best do this by supporting candidates for public office who will put the public interest before corporate-business interests. The two are seldom the same. At present, in Utah, we have no such candidates—none at all. We'll have to find some, or invent some.

We are obliged to join or work for, or at least contribute money to, the citizen conservation organizations which are trying to defend the environment. Since I give little time or effort to such societies myself, I appease my guilty conscience by giving a tithe of my income—like a good Mormon should—to several of them: the Sierra Club, the Wilderness Society, Friends of the Earth and ad hoc organizations such as the Escalante Wilderness Committee, the Kaiparowits Awareness Group, etc. Other organizations which I believe deserve our support are Defenders of Wildlife, the Environmental Defense Fund (Robt Redford's creation), the Izaak Walton League, the Environmentalists for Full Employment (Washington DC), the Audubon Society, etc. And publications like *High Country News*. (Addresses of these are available at your nearest Sierra Club office.)

Devoted though we must be to the conservation cause, I do not believe that any of us should give it all of our time or effort or heart. Give what you can, but do not burn yourselves out—or break your hearts. Let us save at least half of our lives for the enjoyment of this wonderful world which still exists. Leave your dens, abandon your cars and walk out into the great mountains, the deserts, the forests, the seashores. Those treasures still belong to all of us. Enjoy them to the full, stretch your legs, expand your lungs, enliven your hearts—and we will outlive the greedy swine who want to destroy it all in the name of what they call GROWTH.

God bless America—let's save some of it.

Long live the weeds and the wilderness yet!

Ed Abbey

Jimmy Carter (Next President, U.S. of A.),
Plains, Georgia (THANKSGIVING DAY, 1976)

Dear Jimmy,

A few helpful suggestions for your first Hundred Days:

1. Unconditional amnesty (not a pardon, not amnesia) for all the young men in exile, in prison or in trouble because of their opposition to the Vietnam war;

2. A pardon for all living American war criminals, that is, for example, Lt. Calley, Gen. Abrams, Gen. Westmoreland, Dean Rusk, Henry Kissinger and that other one, what's his name, now writing his memoirs in San Clemente;

3. Reparations in full to the survivors—in Vietnam, Laos and Cambodia—of our Presidential Wars, in exchange for final settlement of the question of Americans missing in action;

4. Appointment of Joan Baez or Bella Abzug as Secretary of State;

5. Remodeling of the Pentagon by Allen Ginsberg and Gary Snyder;

6. A merger of the Departments of Agriculture and Interior into one Department of Natural Resources, with Luna Leopold, Stewart Udall, Elvis Stahr, Barry Commoner or Schumacher as Secretary;

7. Guaranteed employment for all seeking work;

8. A vigorous policy of energy conservation, with David Brower as administrator;

9. A vigorous policy of population stabilization and eventually population reduction by means of economic and tax incentives, Paul Ehrlich, administrator.

10. Lots of luck from yours truly,

Edward Abbey—Pariah, Utah

1977–1978

ABBEY TURNS FIFTY . . . reads his pornographic poetry to standing-room audience for two consecutive nights at the University of Arizona . . . paints Las Vegas with his three children, Josh, Aaron, and Susie . . . resides in Moab, at Aztec Peak fire lookout (Arizona), back to Moab, and finally in Tucson. The two books published during these two years were *The Hidden Canyon* (with photographer John Blaustein) and *The Journey Home* (collected essays). A time of introspection and "endless magazine interviews."

Natural History Magazine, New York City   (14 JANUARY 1977)

Dear Editors:

An orchid is not a parasite. An orchid is not a parasite. An orchid is an epiphyte, as the author of a book review ("Ah Wilderness!" *NH*, November 1976) has now been reminded by about twenty different readers from all parts of America. To them all, he offers his apology for insulting—merely from ignorance, not malice—their beloved air-eating vegetable. Now don't tell me the orchid is not a vegetable either.

I also wrote, in the same review, that critics and reviewers are parasites. So far not a single member or cultivator of those species has risen to deny the slur. Does that mean it's true?

I must apologize as well to Mr. Mike Tomkies, author of *A World of My Own*, for accusing him of probably living in Los Angeles. Not True. Mr. Tomkies informs me, *par avion*, that he is now a resident of an isle in Scotland called Wilderness. Ah, Wilderness!

Yours truly, Edward Abbey—Pariah, Utah

Bookletter, New York City   (22 JANUARY 1977)

Dear Editors:

I was shocked by Seymour Krim's review of *Mauve Gloves [and Mad Men]*. Tom Wolfe a "major American writer"!? That's an insult to the living memory of the real Tom Wolfe—Thomas Wolfe the novelist. This current Tom Wolfe is merely a journalist, and one of the most sycophantic of the generally spineless species. He has all the instincts of the intellectual courtier, defending the rich, the sleek, the powerful from their critics by attacking safe and easy targets like professors, *schierkunst* painters, New York intellectuals (of which he is one) and penthouse liberals.

Where was Wolfe when the Pentagon was waging its cowardly war against the rice farmers of Vietnam? Why, he was dancing on the sidelines, cheerleading for the Grim and Roaring Majority, idolizing the bomber-colonels eating steak in air-conditioned wardrooms while the victims were trying to remove steel flechettes from the bodies of children, women and teenage soldiers. Tom Wolfe is the leading pom-pom girl of American journalism. If he worked in Prague he'd be doing the same thing he does here, denouncing dissidents. As for his much-admired style, it looks to me like laboriously contrived, imitation-teenybopper, hippie-type hype, a barely controlled hysteria verging continually on the edge of a screaming breakdown. On the other hand—let's be fair—he is sometimes very funny. I wouldn't miss a word.

Ed Abbey, Novelist—Oracle

Kenneth Atchity and Marsha Kinder,
The Dream Journal (17 JUNE 1977)

Dear Sir and Madam:

Thank you for your invitation to contribute a dream to your *Journal*. I am honored and flattered by your interest, and went to bed last night resolving to dream a good dream for you. However, nothing much occurred; if I dreamt anything at all, it evaporated with the dawn.

I believe I've had the usual assortment of weird, satirical, comical, paranoid and nonsensical dreams that everyone else apparently has. I've never found any of my own dreams very interesting or, so far as I could tell, of much significance. The nearest thing to a significant dream that I remember is one which I retold in a novel called *Black Sun*—the dream of the incompleted house on a seashore. If you want to, you're welcome to reprint that passage. The book was published by Simon and Schuster in 1971, reprinted in paperback by Pocketbooks in 1972. Haven't got a copy on hand.

I find other people's dreams even less interesting than my own; nothing is more boring, really, than free fantasy unattached to the real—especially in literature. Most dreams, I think, are simply the horseplay of the brain; an unwinding and running down after the tensions and efforts of the day. No dream I've ever read or heard of gives me one-tenth of the pleasure I get from awakening in the morning, watching the sun come up over the mountains, hearing the curved-bill thrasher whistle as I stroll down the path to the old shithouse and sit there for a while, smoking a cigar and thinking about—nothing much at all.

Yours sincerely, Edward Abbey—Oracle

The William Eastlakes   (29 AUGUST 1977)

Dear Bill and Marilyn,

Much thanks for the hospitality. We much enjoyed your company, the fine dinner, the most excellent pinot black from Espana. In the wicker basket.

Too bad we wasted so much time talking about real estate again, that dreary subject. I wanted to talk about the sad case of Jim Jones—what happened to him anyway? Why did he go to France? (Such a conventional thing to do!) I suppose he thought, in the trite tradition of e.e. cummings, Hemingway, Fitzgerald et al. that it was obligatory, the sort of thing an American writer has to do to be recognized as an American writer. The dumb bastard. He could have seen the American West while it was still the West. He could have gone to Mexico, Crete, North Africa, Chile, Sweden (Stockholm is a much more beautiful city than Paris—and full of much more interesting people), Africa. . . .

Instead, he went to Paris, like a good dutiful litterateur, or whatever you call 'em, and never after wrote anything worth a damn. And then to let himself be trapped into a horrible hospital death, wasting away amidst bottles and tubes and technicians taking notes—the most depressing fate of all. I cannot understand it, why he did what he did, after so wonderful a beginning with that first book. He should have stayed in Indiana and wrote about truck drivers and bartenders and disabled veterans; he'd have done much better, both as a person and as a novelist. If he'd been true to his origins he could have been another B. Traven (America's greatest writer).

Anyway, those are some of the things I wanted to say and somehow never got around to saying. What do you say?

Dear Bill, why do you want to move to Aspen for godsake? That hip-boutique Kulchur infested with rich hippies and the worthless rich. For a glimpse of John Denver? You're not a mountaineer or a skier—what the hell would you do there? True, there are an awful lot of pretty girls in Aspen (for me, the town's sole attraction), but you're not a satyrmaniac either. So what's the point?

If you want to move again, come to Moab: live as I do among real people—truck drivers, bartenders, miners, prospectors, ranchers, stockcar racers, real estate developers—it keeps your soul alive. I've made more good friends in that little town (and Green River) than I did in ten years in the cities; the loneliest years of my life were those I spent in Hoboken–New

York. Oh well, no doubt I'm crazy; in truth I don't fit in very well anywhere. The Mormons of Moab tolerate me chiefly because they're unaware of my existence—and vice versa. What the hell.

Actually, after every venture into the cities of the plains, down to the lowlands, I find it a great relief and delight to return to my lookout tower on Aztec Peak, where I don't have to accommodate to anybody—except my wife and my dog and the patient turkey vultures. Still waiting.

Best, Ed, Fire Lookout—Roosevelt, Arizona

P.S. This will interest you. Bruce Babbitt was up here Sunday—he's a fan of mine. (He says—a real politician!) Visiting with his friend Haldiman down below on the chicken ranch. Anyway, when I asked Bruce what he's doing these days he said "fighting crime" (with a grin) and "thinking of running for Governor." I urged him to go for it; and even gave him a $20 check for the campaign. He said he'd think about it even harder and that he would, in any event, keep the check.

George Sessions, Sierra College,
California (30 SEPTEMBER 1977)

Dear Mr. Sessions,

I have read your paper with care and find it illuminating. It is encouraging to learn that professional philosophers such as yourself are getting involved in the eco-environmental concerns of our day. The last time I had any contact with academic philosophy, back in the fat and futile fifties, American philosophy was bogged down in such dreary dead ends as symbolic logic (which I flunked at Yale) and linguistic analysis (which I almost flunked). It's good to know that at least some philosophers are again looking beyond narrow specialties out onto the bigger world of which we humans are the creatures, not the creators.

Whether it's safe to base a comprehensive man & nature philosophy on Spinoza's *Ethics* I am not competent to judge, but you make a good case for it. Of course, I tried several times to get through Spinoza but never could make it: the language, the style, the method, put me off. I admire the man's stand for freedom of expression and political democracy, as he understood it, but his pantheistic "God" struck me as a euphemism—no doubt necessary at the time, if he was to avoid Bruno's fate—and his "intellectual love" for Nature-God does not interest me at all. I suspect that Spinoza was not in love with his God-Nature but rather with his own system of ideas, which, whether true, false or somewhere between (as in all systems), seem to be the product of the mind and the library, not of living engagement with persons, places, things, events, all the infinite variety and particularity of the world we actually know.

Actually know? Know? Of course you can't make any such statement without at once entangling yourself in a whole web of further questions—is it not that which makes philosophy so fascinating and exasperating? Anyhow—epistemologically speaking, I consider myself a naive realist, and to hell with it. When I hear the word "phenomenology," I reach for my revolver.

Anyhow—I meant to say, about Spinoza and his notion of what constitutes happiness, the theory of the cosmos, the intellectual love of "God," are all very well for the professional metaphysician, who seeks somehow to comprehend all, the Whole (whatever that is), and when he can't find them—since neither is evident in ordinary experience, or even in extraordinary intensified hallucinatory experience—he creates them. In the head. So that Spinoza ends up as subjectivistic as Kant or Hegel and all of their descendants.

The trouble with creating a coherent, internally logical system is that in order to do so, you have to leave too much out. Spinoza's philosophy, Spinoza's ethics, Spinoza's notion of love and happiness, were well suited to Spinoza—but they no more suit me (comfortably) than would his pants, shoes and hat. (As Santayana—to me a more appealing thinker—might have said.)

· Holy Christ, am I getting my foot in the typewriter now! I knew I should never have started this letter.

What I'm trying to say, what I think I meant to say, is that, for me, Dostoyevsky's Underground Man makes more sense than Spinoza's logic-drunken mystic. When Dostoyevsky asserts that (I quote from memory) "the axiom that two plus two equals four and always must equal four is a piece of insolence," I understand him at once. Spinoza claims [that] if we understood well enough what constitutes our own self-interest we would necessarily—necessarily!—act in a predetermined manner. However, if we wish to insist on some kind of freedom, freedom of the will, the spirit, the emotions, we may perversely choose to act in a manner that defies logic, common sense, our own good, the public good, any good. So too, Spinoza's axioms, theorems, corrolaries etc form a hierarchical structure of flamboyant insolence, if you ask me. And you did. What is "intellectual love" but simply the love of intellect?

I love the intellect too—but I love my friends, my wife, my children, the trees and rocks and animals, clouds and lizards and rattlesnakes, far more. Desire leads to pain: so be it. Passion leads to bondage: how true. How human. How tragic. And how right. "Reason is and ought to be the slave of the passions," said Hume. I agree; no matter how misleading Hume's ideas may be in other ways, he had a moment of insight there. One of the reasons I admire Bertrand Russell so much is that he was not afraid, he never played it safe, he took risks, even risked making a fool of himself (as he sometimes did), by always, throughout his life, taking a huge bite out of life, hurling himself into human affairs with all his heart and mind and soul.

Maybe I'm being unjust to Spinoza. I can recall little of what I learned about his personal life. But his philosophy, his system, his morality, seem to me—not cowardly—but too cautious. Like those Oriental philosophies now so much the vogue in California and Greenwich Village, he would have us seek a calm, contemplative security of mind by cultivating non-attachment, disinterest, directing our attention and love toward that imaginary Whole or One or Energy Flow or whatever capitalized abstraction may be the mental God of the Week. (And the weak.)

All is One? I doubt it. One what, anyway? There may not be any Sum of Things at all. And if there is, how can we ever see it, feel it, know it? Who cares, in any case?—even if God exists I'm not seriously interested. Let Him go His way, I'll go mine.

Anyone who says he loves the Universe, or God, or Life, is probably neglecting his wife. If he has one. I doubt Spinoza ever married—or even fell in love—with a woman. When the mother came to Buddha, grieving for her lost child, he advised her to avoid further suffering in the future by training herself to relinquish, suppress, refrain from desire. Refrain from desire! And he called himself a wise man! I find the woman, in her grief, far more noble, alive and wise than that holy fakir, squatting under a banyan tree, sunk in the stupor of self-absorbed narcissism that is called meditation. And what did Buddhism, Hinduism, Taoism and Zen have to do with respect for the natural world? The most devastated lands on earth are those of India, China, and Japan. (Though the rest of the world is catching up rapidly.) If the earth is illusion, why care for it?

Well, I'm rambling on, committing one non sequitur after another, losing the thread of some idea I thought I had in the maze of my own confusion. How did I sink from Spinoza to Al Watts? Christ, I don't know. That's why I gave up systematic philosophy for—things. Not people, but a few persons I happen to know; not the Universe, but the earth, and not much of that either; not the Forest, but these lightning-blasted yellow-pines sitting up here on this mountain with me (wishing I would leave); not Dogginess, but my dog, and so on.

"No ideas but in things," said good sound Doctor Williams. Hear, hear!

"Keep your eye upon the doughnut and not upon the Whole," says my old man. And he's no pragmatist either.

Dear me, this is beginning to look like a word-intoxicated attack upon the entire intellectual enterprise. Not so, not so; I regard philosophy, serious thinking, as completely respectable activities, on a par with carpentry, flute-playing, novel-writing, child-raising, plumbing, school-teaching, cattle-growing, space exploring, science, hang-gliding and so on. To be more precise, I regard philosophy as being exactly one of the fine arts, as high an art and high a calling as any other. The power of Spinoza's work lies in its perfect self-coherence, complete self-consistency, terminological exactitude, mathematical self-sufficiency—not in its pretense at telling us the truth. In its beauty, not its wisdom.

There is no truth. I can prove it. Only multitudes of partial truths. We can know the world in much of its details, but not all of them, and in much of its pattern of organization, principles of process, but not in its entirety. Essentially, inside and out, wherever you begin, the truth is Mystery. That is the only truth we know and all we need to know. And Mystery—my only concession to the mania of abstraction—is not a thing.

How's that for insolence? (Frankly, I don't know what the hell I'm talking about and I think I'll cease making it so plain.)

I liked your article very much and am honored at being named in so majestic a list. (You'll probably delete my name now.) But send me a copy when it's printed.

Best regards, Ed

Ms. Heist, University of New Mexico Press (22 NOVEMBER 1977)

Dear Ms. Heist:

An addendum to my letter of a couple of days ago:

In looking again at Mr. Haslam's proposed introduction to *Fire on the Mountain* I am a bit shocked at his very first line. It is quite false to say that I am a writer whose primary and exclusive concern is "wilderness preservation." I cannot for the life of me understand where he got that idea. If my books have a common theme, it would be something like human freedom in an industrial society; wilderness is merely one among [many] means toward that end.

And if Mr. Haslam would take a look at my other books he would see at once that they cover a wide range of subjects, viz: The first novel, *Jonathan Troy*, is concerned with adolescence in an Appalachian mining town and the relationship between a father and his son; the second, *The Brave Cowboy*, is a political fantasy—liberty versus technology; which is also, of course, the obvious matter of *The Monkey Wrench Gang*; the novel *Black Sun* is about sex, romantic love and death; only in my nonfiction books *Desert Solitaire* and *The Journey Home* is "wilderness preservation" a major theme, and even in those two books it is only one among several dominant subjects. As for *Fire on the Mountain* itself, there is almost nothing in that book about "wilderness preservation"; the subject, quite plainly, is again, as in my other books, personal liberty versus the modern industrial, military State.

Please forward a copy of this letter to Mr. Haslam with my request that he rephrase that first line in a way to make it conform better with the facts. Most of my books have already been so misrepresented and over-simplified by reviewers and critics I would hate to see the idea get started now that I am a writer about wilderness—and nothing else!

Aside from this objection, I found Mr. Haslam's introduction quite interesting.

Yours sincerely, Edward Abbey—Moab

Mr. Williams, *Utah Holiday* **Magazine**   (26 NOVEMBER 1977)

Dear Mr. Williams:

I agree that a written interview lacks spark as well as spontaneity. However, I'm going to answer some of your questions anyway, just to make sure that we get certain matters on the record. Then we can continue the interview next time I get to Salt Lake; or if you wish, you can watch me perform at the University of Idaho next Thursday eve, December 1st (Moscow), and again at Livingston the following night, where I'm giving a reading for the Montana Wilderness Association. You might find it interesting to see the kind of people I seem to attract (a weird and wonderful bunch) and how they react. Now, your questions:

1. Southern Utah is hardly in a wild and natural state anymore, except for a few isolated small areas here and there. What I do advocate is [to] keep it, so far as possible, a farming and ranching and small town sort of society, tourism being the least destructive form of economic development. It's a question, as the politicians like to say, of balance. And I agree. Since most of America has been heavily industrialized it might be a good idea to keep the intermountain and Rocky Mountain West a basically agrarian region, free of the smog, crime, overcrowding and hopelessly complicated social problems that bedevil most of the nation.

It's true that a majority of businessmen in southern Utah are in favor of industrial development, for the obvious reason that they hope to profit from it. That does not mean that heavy industry, such as mining and power generation, would be of much benefit to most of the present inhabitants. (And there are only a few thousand of us anyway.)

Actually, we who live in southern Utah are perhaps the luckiest people in the nation. Housing is relatively cheap, fuel is free (in the form of firewood), meat is cheap (beef and venison), the air is still clear and clean, the environment favorable to good health, unregulated recreation and wide-open physical adventure. Anyone who would trade the advantages of Moab or Kanab for the filth and disease and social lunacy of a Salt Lake City must be crazy—or should move there.

Yes, a lot of people down here complain that their children, when they grow up (so to speak), have to go elsewhere to find jobs. Quite so—when you have eight to twelve children. One must speak plainly on this question: any couple who have more than two children are not only placing an unfair burden on their neighbors and on society in general, they are also placing these numerous offspring in a disadvantageous position in the scramble for survival. If we must have more industry in southern Utah, I would suggest that what we need most is some form of light manufacturing: let's say, a nice clean well-lighted condom factory. A desert region cannot support a dense human population.

Industrialism might provide jobs for the three hundred or so officially unemployed persons in Garfield and Kane Counties. (Right: three hundred!) It would undoubtedly enrich a few landowners and businessmen. But for the rest of us, it would create far more problems than it would solve.

In any case, there's a larger question involved here than the preferences of the fifteen thousand or so people who presently live in south-central and southeastern Utah. And that question is, who owns the land? No one disputes the legal privilege of private property owners to exploit to the limit those lands to which they hold title. But what right have southern Utahns to determine the fate of our national parks, national forests, national monuments and recreation areas and BLM-administered public lands? Most of southern Utah is the rightful property, not of local Chambers of Commerce, but of all Americans. All Americans—from California to Maine, from Alaska to Florida. Therefore, any decision as to the further industrial exploitation of these public treasures is one that should be made by the American people as a whole.

Now, if most Americans eventually decide that they want to make Utah the boiler-room of the West ("Best of the West") and surround our national parks with an industrial slum of strip mines, power plants, trailerhouse cities, mine roads, damned-up rivers, clear-cut forests, disposal dumps, power lines, etc etc, there's not much that people like me can do about it except complain and maybe move on—if there's any place left to move to.

If Americans decide, on the other hand, that they would rather reserve the West—their West—primarily for the purpose of human pleasure, delight, wonder, recreation and contemplation, then heavy industry can have no place here and those southern Utahns who would really rather live in an industrialized area (and they are very few—if any), they are the ones who will have to seek . . . grayer pastures. God speed them.

2. I've never suggested shutting down any mines or power plants now in operation. We should insist, however, that all polluters be retrofitted with the best possible pollution control equipment. The Navajo power plant at

Page [Arizona], for example, is a disgrace. And why you Salt Lakers submit, year after year, to the greed and insults of Kennecott Copper is beyond my comprehension. Make them clean up; and if they try to blackmail you again with threats of closing down, then have Utah County take over the plants, let the unions manage them. Could hardly be any worse than what you've got now.

As many economists have pointed out, cleaning up the environment will not put people out of work; it will create more jobs. Anyhow, I've already answered this question, in detail, in that book *Journey Home*. Sooner or later, we Americans are going to have to grow beyond the Greed & Gluttony Lifestyle into something a little simpler, saner, quieter, more human and humane. The only question is, Shall we do it voluntarily, rationally, in a way that is fair for all, or shall we continue to drift toward ecological disaster, violence and civil strife, and either nuclear war or technological tyranny as the ultimate solution?

3. The Russians and Japanese are facing the same problems we are. All industrial societies have reached the point of diminishing returns. What is needed is not the abolition of industrialism but the moderation of it, a sensible and wholesome balance between industrialism and agrarianism, the decentralization of all forms of power, including economic power, cutting the awful nation-state down to human size—and most important, putting limits on human population. We are clearly breeding ourselves into a planetary prison-house. There is, I believe, a direct correlation between human numbers and the value we place on individual human life. Population increase inevitably diminishes the importance (as well as the dignity, freedom and economic well-being) of the individual.

One of the pleasant things about small town life is that everyone, whether rich or poor, liked or disliked, has some kind of a role and place in the community. I never felt that living in a city—as I once did for a couple of years.

4. In the short run, literature and philosophy and the other arts change nothing. They merely entertain. But in the long run, they change everything. We live today under the domination of ideas first formulated hundreds of years ago.

In the long run? In the long run, said Keynes, we will all be dead. Keynes was wrong. We as individuals will be dead, but—unless we commit some irrevocable mistakes in the near future—our children and our children's children will still be here. Our descendants continue the human adventure. Those who have no sense of posterity or any concern for future generations are the ones who are really dead. I mean, they are dead right now. Walking zombies. You can see them in the U. S. Senate and in any boardroom meeting of Kennecott, Peabody Coal, Exxon Oil, General Motors, U.S. Steel and all the other giant national and multi-national corporations that presently make the basic decisions about the way we will be permitted to conduct our lives.

5. One of the wisest things Wright ever said was this (when someone asked him if he was a socialist): "No public ownership of private needs. No private ownership of public needs." As for the great cities, I hope they survive. Our civilization would become a dreary place without them. I'm speaking of real cities, of course—not Salt Lake City. The point is to prevent the whole country from being urbanized, to preserve diversity, to give people a choice.

6. None. Not one. Except William O. Douglas. But he is out of it. The rest are dismal mediocrities; especially such chameleons as Jimmy Carter and Jerry Brown.

7. Heroes? I've known a few. People who do good, useful work, who succeed in raising a couple of decent children, who can stay in one place and become citizens of a working human community. My own parents, for example.

Words, words, words!

Ed A.—Moab

Edward Hoagland (13 DECEMBER 1977)

Dear Ted,

I was startled by the anger in your last letter. I had no idea that [John] McPhee was so important to you or that you might construe my criticism of him as criticism of you. Since I don't have so many friends that I can afford to lose even one, I guess I'd better attempt to restore myself to your good graces.

It should have occurred to me that McPhee is probably an old friend of yours, but it didn't. (I would never review a friend's book myself; suppose the book were no good?) And now I recall that in one of your books you mention that you and McPhee were classmates somewhere.

So it's easy to understand, in that light, your violent reaction to my admittedly rather harsh remarks. But as I said, I haven't read McPhee's new book: all that I know about it is what I read in your review and John Leonard's. But in both, I found sufficient hints that I would probably not only dislike the book but would find parts of it downright insulting and insufferable.

E.g., it's bad enough that he should call the conservation movement "the Sierra Club syndrome" and conservationists "eco-centrics and sneaker-faces." Or that he fails to understand why the Arctic tundra is considered fragile by ecologists. Or that he can apparently find nothing more significant to say about the Alaskan pipeline than that moose lean against it in winter and that from high in the air it resembles a thread stretched across Staten Island. (What an absolutely dumb observation. How utterly inane. The first railroad into the West would have looked like a "thread" across the landscape, I suppose; but to the Sioux and the Cheyenne and the buffalo it meant the end of their world.) Or that he finds lovable that grotesque character in the plastic cowboy hat, disemboweling a mountain valley for the sake of a few ounces of gold dust. Talk about fear in a handful of dust.

Trauma! And that valley belongs to me. To all of us. Not to that greed-crazed looney—"reaping where he never planted," as Thoreau would say—acting out the 1872 Mining Act and serving as advance man for international corporations like AMAX and Tenneco and Rio Algom and Kennecott and Exxon and so on.

I quite agree with you that McPhee is a first rate investigative reporter. He has a keen eye for the quaint and the picturesque. But in the two reviews you sent me, I find no hint at all of what is the point of this Alaska book. Or the point of view. He traveled a lot, he saw a lot, that much you make clear—but what did he learn? How does he feel about what's happening to Alaska? Is he really concerned at all? Judging from your review and Leonard's, he is not concerned. And that sort of thing, of course, is what makes me so angry.

I imagine [McPhee] coming to the West and showing the same indifference to our efforts to save a little of the land, to preserve the agrarian way of life before the tidal wave of industrialism. I think of my friend Slim Randles, who lives at Mile 249 on the Alaskan Railway, trying to fight off the mining corporations . . .

[The remainder of this letter is missing. Although Ed and Ted had been compatible correspondents for years, their dispute over the social worth of McPhee and other popular contemporary writers would persist, gradually eroding their correspondence if not their friendship. As Abbey notes with comic sadness in a November 26, 1977, journal entry *(Confessions of a Barbarian)*: "Making a fresh new enemy. Hoagland is very angry with me now because I called his friend McPhee a temporizer and fence-straddler—no balls. He accuses me of envy and jealousy because McPhee's books get better reviews than mine do. But how can that be? My books don't get reviewed at all."]

Mr. Lewis H. Lapham, Editor, *Harper's* Magazine, New York City (22 FEBRUARY 1978)

Dear Mr. Lapham:

For your own amusement and for the information of those among your recent contributors who have been advancing the (really absurd) proposition that the conservation movement is by and for the wealthy, I enclose a typical document from a typical conservation outfit—the Sierra Club of Arizona. Where are these rich backers we read about in *Harper's*? We could sure use some of their money in the West.

I have been loosely in touch with various conservation groups and causes for much of the last ten years. Almost all the people involved are lower-middleclass types: college students, a few professors, a very few medics and lawyers, and—where their lives are being directly affected, as in Wyoming and Montana—a considerable number of farmers and ranchers. I have yet to meet a single corporation executive in the ranks or leadership of any conservation organization. (There may be some, but I have yet to hear of them.)

The opposition to conservation, environmentalism, the "earth conscience," whatever you want to call it, comes from the rich and powerful (at least here in the West): from the mining industry, the highway and dam-building industry, the international oil corporations (most of the uranium mining and coal strip-mining is being done by subsidiaries of Exxon, Mobil, Texaco, etc), the timber industry, a few powerful unions like the Teamsters and the Operating Engineers (bulldozer drivers), the Mormon Church (managing a virtual theocracy here in Utah) and of course the majority of Western politicians—most of them the bonded servants of the above-named industries. Plus the Federal government as represented by the Forest Service, the Bureau of Land Management, the Department of Energy, the Geological Survey (largely a tool of the oil and mining interests) and even, alas, the Park Service, which all too often compromises its mandate to wilderness protection by yielding to the insistent demands of the "recreational vehicle" industry and the motorized tourism industry. For example.

These are facts, easily documented, brought to our attention most vigorously every day, or whenever some attempt is made, however timid, to save a little of the rural, agrarian or still-primitive public lands from the apparently insatiable appetites of the modern industrial State. Though I am not personally familiar with the effects of this contest in other regions of the United States, I have no doubt that the conflict is equally bitter and equally one-sided almost everywhere.

I sympathize with your efforts to subject environmentalism to criticism; the movement—if that's what it is—has perhaps enjoyed too good a press for too long. But *Harper's* appears to have gone completely the other way; I don't think I've seen a single issue in the last two years which has not contained at least one attack on environmentalists or other critics of Technology Unlimited. Surely a better balance would be in order. Surely you can find a few competent journalists willing and able to present the dissenting view. (And I am not suggesting myself; I am weary of writing on the subject.) Writers like George Sibley, for example, or Wendell Berry, or Roderick Nash (I enclose also one of his recent pieces), or McPhee or Hoagland or Dave Brower (why not give the arch-druid himself a chance to reply to some of your contributors' Chamber-of-Commerce-like polemics?), or Gary Snyder or Amory Lovins. I could probably think of many others if I set my mind to it.

Harper's is a great magazine (for a magazine), maybe the most consistently interesting still available in America. I can't think of any that's better. I am honored to have seen some of my own stuff published in your pages. But I do think that the most important function of *Harper's* is to continue to serve as an open forum of ideas, presenting the best thought from various and different and—unavoidably—antagonistic points of view. Don't you agree?

This letter, obviously, is not meant for publication. Just trying to help you do your job.

Best regards, Edward Abbey—Moab

1979–1981

WITH HIS CELEBRITY by now in full swing, Abbey is told by a team of doctors that he has pancreatic cancer and only, perhaps, six months to live. His reaction: "Well, at least I won't have to floss anymore." The doctors are wrong—not pancreatic cancer, but acute and chronic pancreatitis, painful but not likely lethal. Having met his ultimate wife, Clarke Cartwright Abbey, Ed settles down to work and family life in Tucson. The capping event of these years is Abbey's marathon "Walk in the Desert Hills," a solitary journey of some 110 miles through the Sonoran wilderness in six days and nights. Meanwhile, three more books are published: *Abbey's Road* (an essay collection), *Desert Images* (with photographer David Muench), and *Good News* (a comically prescient novel).

Clarence D. Stephenson, Indiana County History,
Marion Center, Pennsylvania (18 APRIL 1979)

Dear Mr. Stephenson:

My mother has forwarded to me your form letter requesting biographical information for a history of distinguished Indiana County citizens. I am honored, of course, that you should request such information of me for inclusion in your "Who's Who."

However, I think the request is misplaced. If you are really compiling a book of worthy Indiana County residents, I believe it should begin by including an account of the lives of my parents Mildred Abbey and Paul R. Abbey. Both were born in Indiana County, both have lived all of their already long lives in Indiana County and both have distinguished themselves as citizens, parents and leaders in many and varied ways. In fact, their sum contributions (so far) to the economic, social, cultural, intellectual and educational life of Indiana County far exceed my ability, or anyone's ability, to measure such things. Their contributions certainly exceed mine; I think, therefore, that I would prefer not to be included in your book unless you also include them.

Yours sincerely, Edward Abbey—Oracle

Fred Hills, McGraw-Hill, New York City (20 JULY 1979)

Dear Fred,

Thanks for your letter of June 20th. I'm sure you're right about *Black Sun*. I'll see if I can get some "small press" to reprint it.

Your notion of a novel about people lost in the woods, facing a survival situation, interests me; I've been entertaining a similar idea for a couple of years. In fact I suggested such a story to Peter Mayer of Pocketbooks a long time ago (at his request), but he seems to have disappeared. At any rate, he never followed it up. Perhaps you could find my letter in the files at Pocketbooks Inc.

My idea was this: Two men and a woman stranded on a desert island in the Sea of Cortez. Read the chapter called "A Desert Isle" in *Abbey's Road* and you'll see the setting I have in mind. The story begins with two Americans, a man and a woman (of course), being flown by a Mexican pilot from,

say, Guaymas to La Paz. A storm or engine trouble forces a crash landing
on this small, waterless, uninhabited island in the sea. Radio disabled, of
course; and the pilot, of course, had not bothered to file a flight plan.

So there they are, stranded, with little water and no food. Robinson
Crusoe all over again, but this time with some company, and ethnic and
sexual conflicts, naturally, playing a big part.

All three are pretty ignorant of desert survival techniques; they have to
learn from scratch. They'll learn to find mussels under the rocks, catch fish
from the sea, roast a few lizards and rattlesnakes now and then for fresh
meat. They find water (as I did) in a natural storage basin far up a palm
canyon, far from shore. Perhaps the two men fight to the death over the
woman; perhaps they agree to share her; perhaps she tells them both to
go fuck off—we'll see. (I never know myself what's going to happen when
I begin a story.)

Eventually, I suppose, some form of rescue appears. Perhaps a cabin
cruiser in perfect condition, but without a soul on board, appears offshore,
waiting for them. Maybe the boat is a phantom, a delusion, but the image
of it appeals to me—I don't know what it means. Maybe the couple, or
threesome, have a child, decide to remain on the island indefinitely. Or
maybe something quite different, perhaps terrible, arrives to solve all questions for them.

I see the story as basically one of adventure and survival, but with meta-
physical, perhaps even supernatural, overtones. Undertones? A simple tale,
but intense—with the island itself being the principal . . . presence.

Edward Abbey—Oracle

Harvey Shapiro, Editor, *New York Times Book Review*,
New York City (14 AUGUST 1979)

Dear Mr. Shapiro:

After twenty-five years in the book writing business, I am naturally accustomed to simple-minded reviews. (In fact, I have yet to see a review of any
of my books, anywhere, that I couldn't have written much better myself.)
But the review (Aug. 5) of my book *Abbey's Road* goes beyond simple-
mindedness into the higher realm of malicious falsehood. Your reviewer,
Lucinda Franks, deliberately misrepresents the tone, manner and content

of this book: e.g., her version of my views on the Indians of Mexico and the Aborigines of Australia is exactly the opposite of what I actually stated, as any fair-minded reader can easily discover for himself. (Or herself.)

I know nothing about Lucinda Franks and can't imagine why she has it in for me. But I can guess. Based on internal evidence, I suspect that she objects to the book because the author is a man (by choice) and writes like a man—not like a Garp, a Cowgirl with the Blues, or some other species of androgyne. In short, I accuse Mizz Franks of raw sexism!

Ed Abbey—Wolf Hole

**George Sessions, Philosophy Professor,
Sierra College, California** (30 AUGUST 1979)

Dear George,

Sorry your friend [Bill] Devall and you couldn't come. Since you didn't, I shall pass on a few remarks via typewriter.

As I said, I think the new *Eco-Philosophy* contains many interesting, important and daring ideas. But I have three quibbles:

1. I dislike the pejorative term "shallow environmentalism," and the pretentious term "deep ecology." It is vital that we avoid any hint of moral superiority in our dealings with one another in the environmental movement; if it developed into factionalism it would destroy us, as factionalism has destroyed so many other progressive movements in America. E.g., I was quite disappointed by Stewart Brand's silly attack on the Sierra Club (promptly publicized by *Esquire* Magazine and other Shithead publications) because some Sierra Clubber in San Francisco obstructed his plans for a *Co-Evolution* fund-raising picnic on public parklands.

If we must have labels, why not something like "eco-activists" and "eco-philosophers." Each implies the other anyway, and most of us are, or try to be, something of both. While I grant the intellectual value of providing environmentalism with a sound philosophical basis, the people that I actually most admire are those who put their bodies where their minds are—i.e., Mark Dubois, and patient tireless organizers like David Brower, and the field reps of the various conservation organizations, the people who confront and deal directly with politicians, industrialists, the media.

I think it far more important to save one square mile of wilderness, anywhere, by any means, than to produce another book on the subject.

I am weary of the old and tiresome and banal question "Why save the wilderness?" The important and difficult question is "How? How save the wilderness?" I am not much concerned with the state of the world a thousand years from now, for in that long-range view I am an optimist: I think that the greed and stupidity of industrial culture will save us from ourselves by self-destruction. What I am concerned about is the world my children will have to live in, and maybe, if my children ever get around to it, the world of my grandchildren.

2. One of these days the Orientalizers will have to face the question of why the homelands of Hinduism, Taoism, Buddhism and Zen—namely, India, China, Japan—are also the most abused, ravaged, insulted, overpopulated and desperate lands on planet earth.

Why? I have my theories about it, of course, implied by things I've written elsewhere; but how do you and Devall and Gary Snyder explain it? If you're going to make your theories cohere with fact, you've got to do some thinking about the real role of any large-scale, institutional religion in human life and the life of the planet.

In my view, the Oriental religions are no better than Christianity (itself of Oriental origin, of course) or Islam; all of them tend to divorce men and women from the earth, from other forms of life, by their mystical emphasis upon the general, the abstract, the invisible, and by their psychological tendency, in prayer and meditation, to turn the mind inward, toward self-love, self-importance, self-obsession. Salvation. Satori. Union with God, union with the All-Source, union with The One. (Which one? my daughter Suzi, age eleven, says—bless her native common sense.) Of course, the devotees of these mystical rites claim the opposite—that they are engaged in self-transcendence. I think they delude themselves; rather than escaping the self, they are wallowing, luxuriating, in a most enormous vanity. The same is true of all the many lesser cults now flourishing, like fungi in a bog, among us bored and idle Americans—EST, for example, and Esalen, and TM, and psychoanalysis, and anal-analysis, and good God! all the many other sickly little superstitions that pollute the psychic atmosphere.

(However, I tell myself . . . it's all part of the carnival. All part of the human comedy. These things have always been with us and always will. Each to his fate, predetermined (perhaps) by his character. I must confess that I often tire of my own role as the sneering buzzard on the dead tree. There are times when I envy those with the freedom to hurl themselves into the mob, to lose themselves in the flood of life. Ideally, I suppose, we should be able to enjoy every form of experience. Including suffering? even torture? even slavery?)

Paralyzing philosophy. But always entertaining.

Action, there's the thing. Action! When I grow sick with the buzzing of the brain, I like to go climb a rock. Cut down a billboard. Disable a bulldozer. (*Eine kleine Nachtwerke*) Climb a mountain. Run a rapid. Pursue a woman. Etc.

Enough of these trivial asides. On to Quibble #3:

3. Animal egalitarianism. If all animals are equal, then we humans, obviously, are no better than any other animals. Being no better, we cannot be expected to behave any better. Therefore, it is perfectly logical, as well as natural, that we do as others do—expand to the limits of our range, exterminate competitors, multiply our numbers well beyond the carrying capacity of our territory, submit to mass die-offs periodically, and so on. On the other hand, if we demand of ourselves that we behave rationally, display tolerance and even love for all other forms of life, then it would seem to follow that we are asking of humans a moral sensitivity unknown to lesser—excuse me!—other animals.

Having raised the question, I think I see the answer. In demanding that humans behave with justice, tolerance, reason, love toward other forms of life, we are doing no more than demanding that humans be human—that is, be true to the best aspects of human nature.

Humans being human, therefore, cannot consider themselves morally superior to, say, bears being bear-like, eagles being eagle-like, etc. No doubt Spinoza had much to say about this. Despite his disdain for nonhuman forms of life.

Let beings be, says Heidegger. Very good. Be true to the earth, says Nietzsche. I like that. Death is the most exciting form of life! said General George Patton. Well no, that doesn't fit here. Give your heart to the hawks, said my favorite American poet—after Whitman. How about a similar nifty slogan from Spinoza? Can you offer us one, George?

I liked Devall's review of *Person/Planet*. Very much to the point. But [I] think, in his letter to NMA, that he must have missed a few chapters in my own book. In "Science w/a Human Face" and "Conscience of the

Conqueror," he will find that I attempt to deal directly with some of the questions that he is most concerned with.

And yes, I do distrust mysticism. I regard it as too easy a way out. Whenever I find myself sliding into mysticism in my writing—I never do it in my feeling and seeing—I know that my mind is relaxing, taking the easy way around a hard pitch of thought. Just as those who casually throw in the word "God" think that they are answering questions which may very well have no answer. Not all questions can be answered. I think that Carl Sagan is a bit naive in his scientific optimism, just as those who call themselves mystics are naive in identifying their personal inner visions with universal reality.

Random thoughts. No more for the time being. Please continue to send me the *Eco-Philosophy* newsletter. And you are welcome, if you wish, to print parts of my letters, or parts of my books, in that newsletter. I would be honored, and most interested in reading the reaction of others to the words of an anti-metaphysical metaphysician. Among metaphysicians, I would prefer to be a G.P.—a general practitioner.

Best regards—Oracle

The New Republic, Washington, D.C.   (9 SEPTEMBER 1979)

Hey, after twenty-five years of benign neglect, the *NR* finally gets around to reviewing one of my books. Thanks a lot, fellas.

Of course, I'm sorry that my feeble attempts at irony, humor, self-mockery were lost on your reviewer, the extremely literal-minded Ms. (Miss? Mrs.?) "S. C." But she's right in charging me with "visionary liberalism"; it's true, I'm guilty, I've been a visionary liberal ever since 1937, when, as a little boy in the hills of Pa., I was rooting for John L. Lewis, the Pittsburgh Pirates and the Sp[anish] Loyalists. I gather from the review that that sort of thing is no longer in style. Disappointing, but not surprising; try as I might, I just never have been able to keep up with all the twists and turns of literary fashion.

Yrs, E.A.

Edward Hoagland   (15 SEPTEMBER 1979)

Dear Ted,

I'm sorry my letters exasperate you so. I wasn't trying to make you angry but merely to engage you, so to speak, in a little exchange of ideas now and then. Since it is so difficult for us to see each other, I thought it would be nice to carry on a genuine co-respondence. Are you so busy that you haven't time to write a real letter occasionally? Maybe the problem is that I enjoy writing letters to my friends and you apparently don't.

Anyhow, I'll try once more. In one of your recent postcard communiqué's you accused me of "writing off the future." Please explain, because I am bewildered by the accusation. Where, when or how have I written off the future? Really, now, my friend, I have three children—two boys in college and my eleven-year-old Susie, the solace and delight of my middle-age, who has no parent but me; her mother died nine years ago, of leukemia (the poor girl had lived too much of her life in New Jersey, before I rescued her). Thus, you see, I cannot write off the future, even if I wished to; I am already very much a part of the future. Please explain what you meant.

I'd say that I'm more of an optimist than you. I believe that the military-industrial state will eventually collapse, possibly even in our lifetime, and that a majority of us (if prepared) will muddle through to a freer, more open, less crowded, green and spacious agrarian society. (Maybe; of course it may be only a repeat of the middle ages.) In any case, as you say, life in some form will surely continue, even after a nuclear war. To point out, however, that the 20th century will be succeeded by the 21st, while that's good arithmetic, is not an optimistic basis, in itself, for optimism.

Ah well, enough of the heavy stuff. Back to the fun and personalities: I meant no "slight" of your ex-friend Marge Percy, of whom I know little and care less. The point of the anecdote was, and is, the incorrigible, incurable female-ness of most young females, at least out here in the country. They know in their hearts and bowels, if not in their heads, what both tension and joy are all about. Doris Lessing said it, not I: "In the world we live in, feminism is a trivial cause."

As for the book reviews, well, that's old stuff too, to which I am (impatiently) accustomed. Every two years I run into a few feminist buzz-saws, as you know. It was thoughtful of you to mention the two most hostile, which otherwise I would probably have missed. You need not apologize for your friend Franks; she is welcome to dislike me and my book, but it was unfair of her to deliberately misrepresent it. Why can't I be reviewed by my peers sometime? By you, or Matthiessen, or even (ugh) McPhee? Did I go to the wrong school? Live in the wrong town? (Hoboken won't do?)

Speaking of hostile book reviews, you should've seen the one in the *Berkeley Bard*. Or was it the *L.A. Free Press*? Anyway, that lady reviewer concluded her denunciation by urging that I be "neutered and locked away for life." Ouch. Now that really hurts.

From rave to rage. So it goes.

Hope I'm not irking you too much again. But hell, I do like to write letters. Much easier than writing books. What are you working on these days? I'm about halfway through the final version of another novel, this one to be called *Good News: An Action-Packed Adventure Thriller*. Do you like it? Does it make you itch to rush out and buy it?

Too many ideas, not enough industry. Too many mountains, not enough time, or ambition. I want to write a novel about my redneck brothers—*Country Blues*. About two men and a woman (beautiful of course) stranded on a desert isle—*Shadow Island*? About my own life—is not every author entitled to one autobiographical novel?—which I'll call . . . but the title's too good, you might steal it.

Two more weeks on this tin tower. Too many visitors this summer—so many I snuck away for two weeks for a river trip in Alaska. My second visit to Alaska. Floated down a river called the Tatshenshini, whatever that means. Nobody there seemed to know. You can read all about it in some future issue of *Mariah/Outside*.

Saw another bear yesterday. And a peregrine falcon. The raspberries are gone. The autumn flowers are in bloom—sunflowers, asters, penstemon, black-eyed susans, goldenrod, skyrocket gilia, others—and there's a chill of winter in the air after sundown. And so on. Mustn't start sounding like Annie Dillard. (Your hero, I know.)

Enough shop talk. Enough, enough. If you've read this far, please respond. Not an equal length, but with some indication of interest and good will. I'll be in New York in early November; hope to see you then. Perhaps a few beers shared in your local pub will ease our somewhat testy relation. Might even fluidify the path toward actual friendship.

Yrs, Ed—Oracle

Tucson Newsreel (17 SEPTEMBER 1979)

Dear Editor:

That "Interview from the Wilderness" with Edward Abbey was fairly entertaining, but your interviewee was misquoted or misunderstood on at least one topic.

I did not say, or certainly did not mean to say, that we should let the Russians occupy our country rather than continue the nuclear arms race. If the Russians, or any other foreign power, were ever silly enough to invade our shores in a military manner, then of course we would have to resist them by military means. Along with most Americans, I'd take the old deer rifle down from the wall and go tottering off with all the other drunks and maniacs to kill or be killed. Better to die fighting than live in slavery? Of course; although this is not a choice I would think of imposing on others.

What I thought I said, or meant to say, was this: Rather than continue the arms race, as we are doing (with or without SALT II), which means an ever-increasing risk of a catastrophic war, we should be doing all in our power to induce the Russians, the Chinese, the French, the English, to begin a step-by-step reduction in nuclear weapons. And to encourage such a process, I think that we—the American government—should be willing to take the first step. To take a small risk now, rather than risk total disaster later. I am sure that the Russians would follow our example and also begin reducing, rather than forever increasing, the mega-death stockpile. And if they did not, we would retain the option of returning to the arms race.

(And as for invasion by a foreign power—the Mexicans have been dumping their surplus human population on our welfare rolls for several years now; why don't we do something about that?)

Don't let anybody tell you these are matters for experts. War and peace are matters too important to be entrusted to our "experts." I would rather turn over the administration of our foreign policy to the first fifty names from the Tucson phone book than entrust it any longer to those Ivy League, Wall Street "experts" who have led us from one disaster to another for the last thirty years.

Sincerely, Edward Abbey—Oracle

Thomas McGuane, Livingston, Montana   (25 SEPTEMBER 1979)

Dear Tom,

Read your piece on Montana in the current *Mariah/Outside*. Cryptic and clever, wise and wry, as always. (Now the "but.")

But I am puzzled by your attitude toward environmentalists, conservationists, eco-freaks, whatever you want to call them. They are not, as you seem to think, a bunch of doomsayers and despair-mongers, nor are their publications, like *High Country News* or *Friends of the Earth*, filled with nothing but jeremiads of outrage. What they are mainly concerned with is letting people know what's going on and then organizing intelligent opposition to the greedy and stupid; intelligent support for the good and generous. That's all, and that's enough.

I don't consider myself a crusader. I give a tithe of my income, in good years and bad, to the eco-freaks, spreading it around among many, and mostly local, groups. I write letters to Congressmen, since it apparently does help. I give a free speech now and then, mainly for the laughs and the girls. And of course I write about it all in about ten percent of what I write. (Plus the joys of *Eine kleine Nachtwerk*.)

I don't know if we can prevent the eventual industrialization of the West. But we can slow it down, if we make a fight, and in delay may lie our best hope. Passive non-resistance, on the other hand, merely hastens the destruction. If we love our country, how can we refuse to defend it?

When I first came to the West to live, back in the '40s, I spent a lot of time playing cowboy in the corral. I roomed with a "native," a New Mexican named Buddy Mack Adams, who owned a little bronco ranchette in the hills east of Albuquerque. In the mornings we raced to school in his black Lincoln convertible—thirty miles in twenty minutes. In the evenings and weekends we played with those goddamned horses, trying to make dude ranch hacks out of rodeo renegades. I spent more time climbing back on than I did riding. And the day before deer season we went deer hunting—with revolvers. Fun. But after a couple of years I discovered things more interesting: women, books, music, ideas, the call of the canyons and the freedom of the hills. I have never given a damn since whether those who were born out here accept me as an equal or not; to hell with them; and besides, I have now lived in the West longer than most of those (like my children) who were born here. Thirty-three years.

As for "light-hearted developers" and "lively speculators," here ·in Arizona they are mostly Mafioso types, and in Utah they are Mormons: a deadly serious lot. Not funny at all. (Ridiculous, but not funny.)

Okay, enough lecturing. Write us another novel. (*Panama* is great.) See you in Livingston one of these days.

Best regards—Oracle

The Nation, New York City (26 SEPTEMBER 1979)

Dear Sir:

The review of Vonnegut's *Jailbird* by Saul Maloff is spiteful, mean, petty. Unjust. Vonnegut is one of America's basic artists, a true and worthy heir to the grand tradition of Thoreau, Whitman, Twain, Dreiser, Traven, Tom Wolfe (the real Tom Wolfe, I mean) and Steinbeck.

In other words, he writes out of a concern for justice, love, honesty, and hope. This makes him unfashionable among the Manhattan critics. If he could only shape up he'd be writing very serious novels about the ethnic introspection project (Roth, Bellow), the miseries of suburban hanky-panky (Updike, Cheever, Irving), race (all those embittered ex-females beating off on their typewriters), and of course novels about novel-writing (*Garp* & Co. etc.).

Sincerely, Edward Abbey—Oracle

Thomas McGuane, Livingston, Montana (6 DECEMBER 1979)

Dear McGuane,

Read your "reply" to my letter in *Mariah/Outside* (December '79). I generously assume that you were stoned or drunk when you wrote that. Otherwise my seconds would be around to see you in the morning: bullshit at ten paces—your favorite weapon.

Drop down to Tucson sometime.

Regards, etc., Ed Abbey—Tucson

Barry Lopez, Finn Rock, Oregon   (6 DECEMBER 1979)

Dear Barry,

Got back from the East [Coast] a couple of weeks ago, plagued by the urban ague. Which gave me the chance to finally read *Of Wolves and Men*. A marvelous book. An impressive work of scholarship, observation, feeling and writing. And you're only about—what—thirty or so! "I salute you at the beginning of a great career!"

Write to me whenever you feel like it. I like to get letters from good people and I always answer them—sometimes at great length.

Yours fraternally, Ed Abbey—Tucson

Audubon Magazine, New York City   (23 DECEMBER 1979)

Editor:

John Mitchell (an excellent fellow & an admirable writer) could clarify the hunting controversy if he were willing to make the simple, obvious & necessary distinction between hunters and sportsmen.

A hunter pursues wild game in order to provide meat for himself, kin and kith. This is a craft as old as life, and perfectly honorable. A sportsman kills for the sake of fun or pleasure, or what he calls "sport." This is not honorable.

In our pathologically over-crowded society the hunter is a rare, endangered species. The sportsman, on the other hand, is much too abundant. Hunting for sport always appears in over-developed, socially-stratified, over-refined cultures. It is a reliable indicator of privilege, hierarchy and moral decay. From ancient Assyria thru feudal Europe to contemporary jet-age Montana this pattern has held true.

There is of course an intermediate and overlapping phase in this historic, cyclic process, as the sportsman gradually displaces the hunter, which gives the issue an appearance of ethical complexity. But the basic distinction remains clear: the hunter hunts out of need; the sportsman kills for pleasure.

For my part, I admire the hunter & despise the sportsman. And if the return & triumph of the former seems to require the dismantling of our industrial machine, and the gradual reduction (thru normal attrition) of human numbers, then so be it. In fact, I'm all for it.

(*Note to Editor: This parenthetical superfluity may be deleted.)

Barry Lopez, Finn Rock, Oregon (22 DECEMBER 1980)

Dear Barry,

My thanks to you and your wife for the hospitality. And for returning that shirt—cleaned and pressed even! You shoulda kept it. Hope to see you next spring in Arizona.

Regards, Ed A.

Bill Plummer (16 AUGUST 1981)

(re your book about Neal Cassady & Friends):

. . . an interesting, honest, highly readable account of that recent episode in our nat'l history, pathetic but amusing, which we might call the Children's Crusade—a misdirected but earnest effort at human liberation and worthy of the serious attention which you give to it. If this sounds condescending, I can't help it; altho I too was much excited by *On the Road* & *Howl* when they first appeared, I've never been able to take Kerouac & Ginsberg seriously as writers or guides to thought. As for the drug culture in general, it was born, passed me by and then croaked while I was still plodding along on my own road. There was anyway something faggotty & soft, rotten, childish & selfish about all of it, as the fate of the cult leaders (Cassady, Kesey, Leary, Kerouac, Ginsberg—Naropa!) makes clear.

Harper's Magazine, New York City (18 SEPTEMBER 1981)

Dear Sir:

Congratulations to Walter Karp for his article "Coolidge Redux." His analysis makes it clear enough that the so-called new conservatives operating through Reagan & Co are not conservatives at all but rather the most extreme of authoritarian revolutionaries. Like their rivals in the Kremlin, with whom they have so much in common, the Reaganites are out to impose on their own nation (and if possible on the earth as a whole) a kind of monolithic military-industrial state in which social diversity, traditional human values such as equality and democracy, and the surviving remnants of the natural world are all sacrificed to the demands of industrialism, centralized power and technology. (The three mesh nicely together, cog-in-cog.) In this respect the differences between the USA and the USSR are those of evangelical dinosaurs competing for domination on one small planet: the first deifies Jesus Christ, the other Karl Marx. Neither has much practical interest in what those two sincere and hard-working fellows actually preached.

Sincerely, Edward Abbey—Oracle

John Macrae, New York City (5 NOVEMBER 1981)

Dear Jack,

Brochure enclosed; "Sundancer" is only a half-mile from my house, across a stretch of undeveloped desert. Only the Rex Ranch, near Amado, thirty mi S of here, combines dude wrangling with actual cattle ranching. I haven't seen the place, but they'll send you information. Nogales, Mexico, is another thirty miles beyond Amado. You're welcome to use my car; we've got two.

Let me know if you'd like to meet any of the following writers/poets, and I'll arrange it: Leslie Silko (*Ceremony*), Robt Houston (*Bisbee '17*), Wm Eastlake (maybe once was enough with him), Alan Harrington (*The White Rainbow, Immortalist*, etc), Jonathan Penner (*Going Blind*), Peter Wild and Richard Shelton (poets), Mary Carter (*La Maestra*); can't think of any others living in this area. Some of these people might have new work to show you; I don't know. If Mo Udall is in town, I might be able to get him to come to a party. Or Bruce Babbitt, if you're interested in meeting any politicos.

Best, Ed

Arizona Highways, Phoenix   (11 NOVEMBER 1981)

Dear Editor:

I much enjoyed your recent issue on Arizona wilderness areas. I was especially pleased to read our Governor Babbitt announcing himself as a wilderness lover. This is good news indeed.

We can now depend on his help, I presume, in such matters as saving the Grand Canyon from aircraft intrusion and other forms of commercial exploitation; in saving the Baboquivari Mountains from the DPS, the mining industry and the over-grazers; in saving Aztec Peak and the Sierra Anchas from the uranium industry; in defending the Kofa and Cabeza Prieta Wildlife Preserves from the beef industry; in defending the Gila, Salt and Verde Rivers from the dam builders; in pushing the BLM and Forest Service into protecting our remaining roadless areas; in keeping the developers out of the Tucson Mountains; in promoting a moratorium on the killing of mountain lions and bighorn sheep in Arizona; in enforcing the air pollution laws; and, in general, doing all that he can to prevent further industrial development (more power plants, for example) and urbanization (Phoenix and Tucson are really big enough) in our still beautiful state.

Wonderful news!

Sincerely, Edward Abbey—Oracle

Rocky Mountain Magazine, Denver, Colorado   (12 NOVEMBER 1981)

Dear Sir:

Re the "bitter journey" of the Big Mountain Navajos: This reader of your handsome periodical was much impressed by John Running's always distinguished photography, and by the dignity, beauty, nobility of the people he has shown us. But—there is much more to be said: Though the commentary mentions that the Navajo population has now reached a figure of 150,000, the writer fails to point out that the Navajo population in 1890, when the huge Navajo reservation was established, was then estimated at fifteen thousand. In other words, the Navajo have grown ten-fold in ninety years—three generations—and continue to grow exponentially at a rate of some 3.5 percent per year.

The blunt truth must be stated by somebody: The Navajos have out-bred their range; their abused and ravaged land cannot support so great a number. That is why the tribe expanded onto Hopi territory and why the Navajos, from tribal chairman up to sheepherder, remain largely dependent on various forms of Federal welfare for survival. There is a lesson for us all in the Navajo's difficulties: We must begin to limit our numbers; we must begin to learn some respect for the earth which sustains us.

Edward Abbey—Oracle

Tucson Daily Citizen (12 NOVEMBER 1981)

Dear Editors:

Allow me to offer a modest proposal for a solution of Tucson's disgusting, exasperating, nerve-wracking traffic problem—I mean bicycles! And bicycle streets! There are many thousands of us in this mad fungoid city who'd be happy to ride bicycles to work each day if only we didn't have to fear being knocked into surgery, intensive care and wheelchairs by some marginal humanoid with a penis problem driving his double-barreled eight-cylinder tractor-wheeled 4x4 high-rider up and down the city streets. Reserve at least a few streets for human-powered traffic only, and at no expense whatever to us taxpayers; with vast reduction in private expenses, at great benefit to the public air and the public health and the public treasury and the public equanimity, we could make Tucson once more what it once was—a decent, clean and pleasant town for full-grown human beings. With its balmy, arid climate and gently rolling terrain, our city offers the perfect outdoor laboratory for such a simple and worthy experiment.

Sincerely, Edward Abbey—Oracle

(Note to editors: I'd be happy to write a feature article on this subject if you're interested.)

**Secretary, Department of Energy,
Washington, D.C.** (28 NOVEMBER 1981)

Dear Sir:

We the undersigned are opposed to the further exploration of southeast Utah as a possible repository for nuclear wastes. The mining and milling of uranium have already caused great environmental and social damage to the land and people of Utah; we cannot tolerate further exploitation of this region for the sake of the nuclear power industry and the nuclear weapons industry. We are especially shocked by the idea of storing poisonous nuclear wastes in the Gibson Dome area next door to the great Canyonlands National Park. This is the most irresponsible and narrow-minded proposal yet to appear. That the Government would even consider invading this beautiful, still primitive and relatively clean area with its roads, railroads, drill rigs, power plants and other industrial installations is an outrage.

We respectfully suggest that you take your nuclear wastes, pack them into the space shuttle and launch them off to the moon. Yes, and take the nuclear engineers, the nuclear administrators (including yourself), the nuclear speculators, the nuclear industrialists and all the other varieties of nuclear developers with you. And don't come back.

Sincerely, Edward Abbey—Monticello, Utah

Morton Kamins (14 DECEMBER 1981)

Dear Morton:

Herewith an answer to your queries:

Q 1: I've done long solo hikes before, mainly in Utah, northern Arizona, Death Valley, Grand Canyon, but never thru the Sonoran Desert of southern Arizona. So, I did it because I enjoy that sort of thing, and because I wanted to see some new country, intimately, as can only be done on foot, through direct personal engagement with sand, stone, sun, space, moon, stars, craggy hills and those wonderful beautiful isolated waterholes that always turned out to have water (thank God!) when I got there.

Walking is the only form of transportation in which a man proceeds erect—like a man—on his own legs, under his own power. There is immense satisfaction in that. All other modes of transport require sitting down, which I find tiresome. Traveling by horse is the next best thing, and I've done plenty of that too: for two years, as a ranger on the Whittell Wildlife Preserve near Aravaipa Canyon, AZ, I was in charge of and responsible for a string of twelve saddle horses, and did most of my patrolling on horseback, but unlike some people we've heard of, I never feel in love with a horse. (Either end.)

Q 2. Wolf Hole is an actual place, a ghost town on the Arizona Strip north of Grand Canyon. I own a small place near there, under the Vermilion Cliffs, and next summer my wife Clarke and I are going to build a house there, a house of stone and logs, with ramada and corral and a hay shed; will keep us busy and out of trouble for the next few years, I imagine. There's a spring on the place, and enough water and forage for two grownups, several children and a couple of horses.

And oh yes, I am not and never will be a cowboy. A cowboy spends most of his life studying the hind end of a cow; that does not interest me much.

Q 3. I've been married five times and have three children. My sons are in college in California and New York; my daughter Susie, thirteen, lives with me, most of the time now, though she was mostly raised by her grandmother (my former mother-in-law) after the death of Susie's mother eleven yrs ago. Leukemia killed her at age twenty-eight. Grandmother and I are good friends; she lives in Tucson.

Q 4: We have a small two-bedroom adobe-brick house in the open desert a few miles out of Tucson. Quite modest: no swimming pool, no horses, no tennis court, no TV, no home computer, no microwave oven, no close neighbors. We came here three years ago (from Moab, Utah) so that my wife could finish college; we'll be leaving in a year or so. We heat with wood, cool with a swamp cooler and generally spend the summers on a Forest Service fire lookout up in the mts.

Q 5, 6, 7, 8, 9: I am pro-marriage, pro-family, pro-life, and pro-love, esp romantic love, yes. I also believe absolutely in Negative Population Growth and don't intend to have any more kids, except maybe one or two with my new and final wife.

Q 10: When I'm writing a book I pack a lunchbox every morning, retire to my shack down by the wash and hide for four or five hours. Between books I take vacations that tend to linger on for months. Indolence-and-melancholy then becomes my major vice, until I get back to work. A writer must be hard to live with: when not working he is miserable, and when he is working he is obsessed. Or so it is with me. Thus my writing life consists of spells of languor alternating with fits and spasms of mad typing. At all times, though, I keep a journal, a record book, and most everything begins in the form of notes scribbled down on the pages of that journal. Am now halfway thru volume XVII.

Q 11: No. . . .

Q 12: Yes, my female characters are based upon, or drawn from, women I have known, although I have never attempted a portrait of anybody, female or male. And yes, I am most strongly attracted to women who combine beauty with intelligence, sweetness with strength—in a word, character. Most women I have known, and loved, have seemed to me superior to men in the essential way: morally. They are simply nicer, better, gentler humans than men. I hope they stay that way. I think they are a different race, and sometimes wonder that we men can even interbreed with them. I am against androgynes and androgyny. Men and women really are deeply different, and it is that difference which creates the tension and delight. Without it humankind would be no more interesting than beef cattle, or factory chickens, or ants and bees.

Thus I must also oppose the Beehive Society now being imposed on us by the new technological military industrial planetary superstate. Down with the State! Up with community! Long live anarchy!

(Which reminds me of something you said Norman Mailer said, that he now believes in "order" (undefined). I hope that I never become rich and fat, if the chief result is to make one talk as fat rich men have always talked.)

Q 13: Technique: I imagine that I've been influenced by the classic writers of England and America; but I also admire, very much, Rabelais and Villon, Lao-Tse and Job and Ecclesiastes, Tolstoy, Chekhov and Andreyev.

Q 14: "If I came into a lot of money . . . ?" I have a lot more money than I need right now. By the standards of my old farmer-logger father, I am a rich man (at the moment). I can make a decent living as a fire lookout, $5000-6000 a year. So I write mainly for the fun of it, the hell of it, the duty of it. I enjoy writing and will probly be a scribbler on my dying day, sprawled on some stony trail halfway between two dry waterholes.

Q 15: How become a writer? Naturally.

Q 16: Should a writer have a social purpose? Any honest writer is bound to become a critic of the society he lives in, and sometimes, like Mark

Twain or Kurt Vonnegut or Leo Tolstoy or Francois Rabelais, a very harsh critic indeed. The others are sycophants, courtiers, servitors, entertainers. Shakespeare was a sycophant; however, he was and is also a very good poet, and so we continue to read him.

Q 17: Like most writers, I feel that my latest work (*Good News*, and the forthcoming *Down the River*) is my best. I also feel that my best work still lies ahead—the FAT MASTERPIECE. Otherwise, why keep on with this lunatic art? Would rather be a good banjo player than a great but played-out novelist.

Q 18: When I'm writing I sweat a lot. But not blood. It's really a form of play, this writing of books, and if the reviewers, esp those literal-minded androgynes in New York, ever took a close look at my books they would find that they consist mostly of play. Play! for Christ's sake!

Well, enough of this frivolity, I could drivel on at the typewriter for days doing this, it's so easy and so much fun. Must now get to work. You should be getting an advance copy of *Down the River* in about a week; I hope you can read it before you complete your article. And please send me an advance copy of it—I will not attempt to censor you in any way but would like an opportunity to suggest changes if I think you've got something seriously wrong.

Best regards, Ed

New York Review of Books, New York City (17 DECEMBER 1981)

To the Editors:

John M. Crewdson's review of Miller's *On the Border* and Hansen's *The Border Economy*, though lengthy, provides little essential information on the illegal immigration problem, and misinterprets what information it does provide. Those of us who actually live in the U.S.-Mexican border region owe it to other readers of the *NYR* to correct Mr Crewdson's misunderstandings and fill in his lacunae.

It is absurd, for example, for Mr Crewdson to repeat Tom Miller's facetious "calculation" that it would take two and a half million men, standing shoulder to shoulder, to close the Mexican border to illegal aliens. In fact most of the border runs through flat, wide open, sparsely vegetated desert country. Except for the far-scattered towns and cities, most of the border could be easily patrolled and easily "sealed"; a force of twenty thousand, or ten men per mile, properly armed and equipped, would have no difficulty—short of a military attack—in keeping out unwelcome intruders. In and near the few towns and cities a physical barrier is obviously needed, of the type routinely used everywhere else to restrict and control access. People do not cut holes through fences when the fences are watched and guarded.

Furthermore, there is widespread popular support for closing our southern border to the Latino invasion. A recent NPR [National Public Radio] broadcast (the *All Things Considered* program) cited various national polls indicating that 80 to 90 percent of Americans now object strongly to these mass immigrations from Mexico and other Hispanic countries. A poll by Arizona's Senator DeConcini revealed that 79 percent of his constituents (and this in a state with a large and rapidly growing Hispanic population) want the illegal aliens deported and the immigration laws strictly enforced.

No doubt there is an element of ethnic chauvinism in this hostility to Mexicans et al.—and that element will grow violent and much larger if the influx continues—but the sentiment is based on the clear awareness that these aliens do indeed take jobs away from American citizens and that the estimated ten billion dollars remitted annually from Mexican aliens to their relatives still in Mexico is money that should be going into the pockets of American workers.

To say, as Mr Crewdson does, that the presence of these foreign millions "creates" employment for American workers is [in line with] the magical economics of Reagan & Co., that wondrous world wherein food is produced in supermarkets and rabbits are born in hats. If, as Mr Crewdson seems to believe, the proliferation of human bodies somehow "creates" new wealth for all, then Mexico would be a rich nation without need to push its surplus population northward, and India and China would be the richest nations on earth.

The actual reason why our immigration laws are not enforced is simple, obvious and well-known (though seldom mentioned in polite print): there are small but powerful groups on both sides of the border who benefit from this expanding northerly migration.

Cui bono? is now as always the appropriate question, and the answer is, first, American employers in all fields, from industrialized agriculture to factory manufacturing, who thrive on this unlimited supply of cheap, docile, non-union labor. One simple way to halt the alien incursion would be to penalize employers, with jail sentences if necessary, who hire illegal aliens. Simple but politically unlikely to be enforced; no doubt it will be easier to militarize the international border.

The second group of beneficiaries are the merchants on the American side of the border towns, who do a brisk trade in selling American goods to Mexicans. A third group are the Mexican-American politicians in the Southwestern states, eager to expand their power base. The fourth group are the wealthy and dominant classes in Mexico itself, who require the safety valve of emigration in order to postpone for as long as possible the next, and inevitable, revolution in their desperately overpopulated nation.

American "interests" (the term "ruling class" is now taboo, right?), anxious to secure access to Mexico's oil, must therefore appease Mexican "interests" by overlooking illegal immigration while at the same time offering at least a token response to the popular demand for a halt to it; thus we have the cosmetic but ineffectual proposals of the Carter and Reagan administrations.

These are harsh, even cruel propositions, but in fact the American boat is full, if not already overloaded; we cannot allow further mass immigration. The American public is fully aware of this truth even if our "leaders" prefer to attempt to ignore it. We know what they will not acknowledge, that the tendency of large-scale immigration is to degrade and cheapen American life. Anyone who has made a recent visit to Mexico, to East L. A., or even to Miami, Florida, knows what I mean.

When the call for compassion is raised (a word now hopelessly corrupted by its use in the mouths of such as Nixon, Carter and Reagan), we must answer that the most compassionate thing we can do for nations such as Mexico is to encourage them, somehow, to commence the policies of radical internal reform and vigorous population control that are clearly necessary.

Edward Abbey—Tucson

Edward Abbey as a military policeman in 1946

In New Mexico circa 1950

At White Sands, New Mexico, 1952

At Arches National Park, Utah, 1957

At Half Moon Bay, California, 1958

With Rita, Joshua, and Aaron in Taos, New Mexico, 1960

With parents, Paul and Mildred Abbey, circa 1970

Writing at his home office in Moab, Utah, circa 1975

Camping with Susie along the Colorado River, 1978

In 1978

With Becky in San Francisco, 1986

The only watercolor Abbey painted in his journals

August 10, 1969

To the Editor
<u>Arizona Daily Star</u>
Tucson

Dear Sir:

A friend recently sent me a clipping from ~~your newspaper~~ *yr aliz??*. It's an editorial aptly
entitled "Baloney" from your June 29th
issue, ▆▆ in which you seem to accuse
both Wallace Stegner and myself of writing
about the West without adequate knowledge
of the region. But on this point Wallace
Stegner requires no defense, as anyone even
slightly acquainted with his career should
know; and for myself, though I have lived
only twenty-two years in the Southwest (so
far) I am willing to bet my ▆▆ bottom
dollar that I have seen at least as much
of it as the writer of your editorial.

When I wrote in my review of Stegner's book
that "there is no West anymore" I meant
the West as a distinct <u>cultural</u> region.
Of course our unique landscape still remains
(or those portions of it which have not
yet been flooded by ▆▆▆▆▆▆ dams,
disemboweled by ▆▆ copper mines, buried
under asphalt and obscured by fungus-bearing
smog) but the general way of life, as typified
by our overgrown cities, is ▆▆▆▆▆▆
patterned after that of Los Angeles. Can
you deny it?

You claim the Old West ▆▆▆▆▆▆▆▆▆
still exists in much of its "primitiveness
and squalor" (your words). Here I agree with
you; it still exists, all right, in the
primitive minds and squalid greed of those
promoters and expansionists whose highest
ambition appears to be the debasement of Arizona,
New Mexico and Utah to the level of southern
California's ant-hill existence.

Edward Abbey
Edward Abbey
North Rim
Arizona 86022

Original letter to the *Arizona Daily Star,* which appears on page 14

11-6-73

Mr. John Davis
Mr. William J. Briggle
Glacier National Parks, Montana

Dear Sirs

People down here _have_ heard about the wilderness and development proposals for Glacier N.P. and like most of your own local citizens who are seriously interested in Glacier, and the national park system in general, we too believe that the park should be preserved in its natural, wild state to the maximum extent possible. That, after all, is what the parks are for. This means that all of the park not already "built-up" with permanent developments should be given official wilderness status.

As for transportation into & within the park, it must be plain to all by now that the private automobile (and other motorized forms of access) is both destructive to park values and wasteful of what is supposed to be a dwindling resource — oil. Cars, motorbikes, powerboats should be banned completely from all national parks. For those too old, infirm or obese to walk, the Park Service should provide shuttle-bus service to principal points of interest. That way the park would remain open to all, with special privileges for none. Please include this letter in the hearing records. Yrs truly, Edw. Abbett,
(copy to Director, N.P.S.)   Box 702, Oracle, Arizona 85623

Original letter to John Davis, which appears on page 29

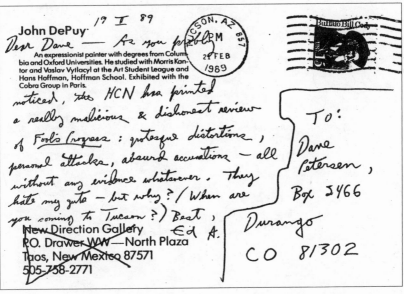

John DePuy

An expressionist painter with degrees from Columbia and Oxford Universities. He studied with Morris Kantor and Vaslav Vytlacyl at the Art Student League and Hans Hoffman, Hoffman School. Exhibited with the Cobra Group in Paris.

19 I 89

Dear Dave — As you probably noticed, the HCN has printed a really malicious & dishonest review of *Fool's Progress* : grotesque distortions, personal attacks, absurd accusations — all without any evidence whatsoever. They hate my guts — but why? / When are you coming to Tucson?) Best ,

Ed A.

~~New Direction Gallery~~
~~P.O. Drawer WW—North Plaza~~
~~Taos, New Mexico 87571~~
~~505-758-2771~~

To:

Dave
Petersen ,
Box 3466

Durango
CO 81302

A postcard to David Petersen, which appears on page 266

A sketch from Abbey's journals

Edward Abbey and David Petersen

Abbey's gravestone, location undisclosed at the resident's request

1982-1983

THE FIFTH TIME'S A CHARM. . . . Ed enjoys a marriage meant to last, at last. . . . Increasingly annoyed by acute and chronic pancreatitis, nagging pain, and "patch patch patch." "I do not want to become a grouchy, growling, grumpy old man." River-tripping in Alaska. Baby Rebecca is born (October 10, 1983): "I finally did something right!" *Down the River*, widely considered Abbey's flagship essay collection, is published.

Arizona Daily Star, Tucson   (7 JANUARY 1982)

Dear Editors:

In response to your editorial "A Nice Fellow" in your issue of December 30th, let me attempt to defend myself as follows: In my letter to the *New York Review of Books,* I was not talking about "cultural influences" but about the social and economic effects of unchecked mass immigration from the impoverished nations to our south, particularly Mexico. Certainly Mexico has contributed much to the Southwestern heritage; I like tacos, tequila and ranchero music about as much as anybody else does. But mass immigration is another matter.

It is not "smugly elitest," but simply common sense to point out that we in America have not so far been able to solve our own problems of poverty and unemployment, crime and racial conflict—and that taking in the surplus populations of Latin America will increase our economic-social troubles without really doing much to help Mexico and others. American employers benefit in having a cheap, docile and growing labor pool in our midst; but working people, and especially teenagers, women, blacks, Indians and Hispanic-Americans will suffer in a more intense competition for scarce jobs and a diminishing federal welfare program.

What alternative? The reality of contemporary Mexican life is dramatically, shockingly apparent the moment you walk across the border: poverty, filth, squalor, overcrowding, injustice, the background menace of police and military oppression. What Mexico needs is radical internal reform and a serious policy of population control—negative population growth. In short, a social and moral revolution. Otherwise, we can foresee the future of Mexico in the present state of affairs in Guatemala, El Salvador, Honduras and many other Latin countries, where class conflict has developed, inevitably, into open warfare between the rich and the poor.

Myself, I support the cause of the poor; justice is on their side, and I see nothing to be gained in postponing the necessary revolution. It is for that reason, therefore, as a defender of humanity, that I think we should halt every *campesino* at the border, give him a revolver, a good rifle and a case of ammunition—and send him home. He will know what to do with our gifts; the Mexican people know who their enemies are.

Sincerely, Edward Abbey—Oracle

Russell Martin, Dolores, Colorado (11 JANUARY 1982)

Dear Mr. Martin:

Your recent article in the NY *Times Mag*, called "Writers of the Purple Sage," is fairly interesting, so far as it goes, but raises some questions and reveals some curious omissions.

First, on what grounds do you classify McGuane as a "Western" writer? He is a new arrival on the scene and so far has published nothing that deals with the American West—the land, or its people, or its troubles—nor has he taken any part in the region's environmental battles.

Second, if current residency is the only requirement, then how could you fail to say anything about another very good American writer, Alan Harrington, who has lived in Arizona for more than ten years? Strange.

Why no mention of Robert Houston, whose novel *Bisbee '17* is the best piece of fiction about the West, by a Westerner, to appear in many years? Mighty strange.

Why no mention of that old New Mexican master Paul Horgan?

Strangest of all, how could you fail to devote major attention to William Eastlake, who has been living in and writing about the West for at least thirty years? Haven't you read *Go In Beauty*, or *The Bronc People*, or *Portrait of the Artist with 26 Horses*, or *Dancers in the Scalphouse*, or *Castle Keep*, or *The Bamboo Bed*? Eastlake is surely the best of all living Western novelists, better even than Stegner, or Wright Morris, another whom you somehow overlooked. Mighty peculiar.

Mighty queer goings-on in the old NYC literary corral again, seems like.

As for your unkind remarks about me and my books, I'll overlook it this time. But you should read a few of them before passing such severe judgments. You'll find that the style varies widely, for example, from book to book; except for the essay collections like *Desert Solitaire* and *Abbey's Road*, no two are much alike. You might even like my next, *Down the River*, written in a fairly restrained manner (Dutton, March 1982).

You called *Good News* "tedious" and "depressing," but the book is really play, a parody of traditional genres; and it has a happy ending. (I really do believe that the techno-industrial empire will soon collapse, or destroy itself, so I am hardly a "smirking pessimist" at all; quite the opposite.) Reviewers may dislike the book; but so far it's sold over twenty-four thousand copies in the original trade edition and has now gone into a fourth printing. What does that prove? I don't know. Who cares? None of my books ever received much support from reviewers and critics, but every single one except the very first (*J. Troy*, an awful novel) is still in print. Whatever I've achieved as a writer I've done on my own; no institutional help at all. I'm proud of that.

Edward Abbey—Oracle

Thomas McGuane, Livingston, Montana   (19 JANUARY 1982)

Dear Tom,

I see by the papers that you have definitely decided that Montana will be your new home. I'm glad to hear that. Welcome to the West. Maybe now you'll help us try to save what's left of it. And I don't mean just write about it, that's already been done, many times over, but actually get down off the fence and join in the fight. We need help.

Don't worry so much about getting depressed. Once you get involved in a real fight, something serious and important and therefore interesting, your existential angsts will drop away like old wives and girlfriends. You won't need your hobbies anymore. The only depressing thing I see are those people with time and money and talent who tell us how much they love the West but won't lend a hand to help defend it.

What's more, if you join us, you'll meet the best people. Like me. Like Doug Peacock and Bruce Hamilton and Ed Dobson and Howie Wolke and Dave Foreman, and many others; once you get to know them, real outdoorsmen, you'll realize how dreary and mean and trivial those Hollywood coke-sniffers and rodeo cowboys are—them Marlboro types. (Their main passion is really real estate.)

You know I admire your novels very much. All four of them. I think you are one of the half dozen or so best fiction writers now working in these U.S. I like your style and wit. But your heroes are too short. I mean, self-obsessed. What they need, it finally occurs to me, is something to do. They are dying of too much money, education, leisure and boredom. They need some work—man's work.

Indolence leads to melancholy, as Sam Johnson pointed out. And Burton and Shakespeare and Ecclesiastes et al.

Of course, your main job is writing novels. I sympathize with that. But in your spare time, you know, between typewriters, you might—lend a hand. Grab a-hold. We need all the help we can get. I know you'll enjoy this kindly advice from your older brother,

Ed Abbey—Oracle

KUAT Radio, Tucson (5 MARCH 1982)

Dear Manager:

Although I am contributing, once again, another $100 to KUAT, I would like to say that I and many of my friends are increasingly disappointed with the quality of KUAT-FM programming.

All that recorded classical music is fine, of course, and we expect that it should always fill the bulk of your radio time. And *All Things Considered* is certainly the best of all radio news programs.

But—Dick Estelle is a bore. Those hack best-sellers he insists on reading are a bore. With all the dramatic talent available here in Tucson, and even on the UofA campus, why can't you get a good reader with flair and verve and have him read real books?—I mean books of top literary quality, unusual interest, and lively and controversial subject matter? That Estelle has the tastes of a St. David school board censor.

Furthermore: your local newscasts are dull and flat, no better than newspaper stories. With all of the interesting and exciting things going on in Arizona, why no representation of wider and diverse points of view? Why no debates, serious, full-time prime-time debates on such issues as smelter pollution (did you people even bother to interview the Greenpeace activists?), urban expansion into the desert, ground water pollution, misdirected police activity (e.g. coke busts instead of murder investigations), the gasoline tax hike, our Chamber of Commerce growth-for-the-sake-of-growth religion, creationism vs. evolution (there was a good debate on that subject only two weeks ago at UofA; did you bother to record and broadcast it? No), and many many other serious and important issues.

Last week we had Tim O'Brien on campus reading from his next novel—a delightful and bawdy comedy. Why didn't you tape and broadcast that? Does anybody at KUAT even know who Tim O'Brien is? Why no live dramatic shows? Why no book, film, drama, or even concert reviews?

Why is KUAT so dull, unimaginative, and timid? One gets the impression that the station is run by a bunch of fuddy-duddy old D.A.R. teacup-holding spinsters. Awake!

Edward Abbey—Oracle

Thomas McGuane, Livingston, Montana   (5 MARCH 1982)

Dear Tom,

Can't blame you for getting mad: nobody likes to be smoked out of his hole in the middle of February. But when did I ever accuse you of "loving" the West? I was merely suggesting, in my discreet and subtle way, that if you're gonna make a home out here, you might be interested in helping to protect your own home (for chrissake!) from all those eastern and mid-western relatives of yours who want to flood you out or strip mine you or radiate you or smother you w/smog etc.

Passive non-resistance will get you nothing. "Westerners" like that are no better, in my eyes, than common tourists. Or worse: like ticks on a dog, ornamental but dysfunctional. Or as my neighbor Joe McKearny says (he's a mining engineer), "useless as tits on a motor."

Oh well. Nobody's perfect. Look at me: though born and raised on a submarginal Appalachian farm, and though I've spent most of my life in the rural West, I have never yet—not once!—fallen in love with a horse.

Either end.

And if you really don't "care about the country" (I don't believe you), then where to next? Oahu? Take up surfing? O'Neil space capsule? Zero-gravity masturbation? Etc?

Yours fraternally, Eddy—Oracle

John Gardner   (5 APRIL 1982)

Dear Mr. Gardner:

Finally took the time to read your little book On Moral Fiction. A brilliant performance—and more important, and more gratifying, I share your basic theses: that it is the writer's duty to write fiction which promotes virtue, the good, the beautiful, and above all, the true. (Who could disagree?)

But (here comes the but) I find your application of our common belief a little disappointing. First, the writers you single out for praise (however faint), namely such as Bellow, Cheever, Updike, Irving and Salinger (that juvenile neurotic!), are the dullest and blandest of contemporary American writers, the type who always play it safe, who serve in effect as sycophants to the rich and powerful, supporting and never attacking the modern military-industrial state, with all its monstrous crimes and horrors. They are the kind, and I can hardly think of a more damning test, who receive and even accept invitations to the White House. Or, as the case may be, with their opposite numbers abroad, to the Kremlin. They write not moral fiction but moralistic fiction, finding intricate ways to accept, without revulsion, the ancient doctrine of the powerful, that whatever is, is right.

My own notion of moral fiction I'd phrase like this: It is the writer's duty to hate injustice, to defy the powerful, and to speak for the voiceless. To be, as Isaiah was, and St Francis, and Diogenes, and Rabelais, and Villon, and Thoreau and Mark Twain and Tolstoy, to name but a handful, the severest critics of our own societies.

Any fool and coward can rail away at foreign enemies; moral courage implies the willingness to risk attacking those who call themselves our friends, protectors, lords etc. Moral fiction, and moral art in general, must take a part in the apparently endless struggle not merely to keep old ideals alive and functioning, but to prevent evil from triumphing through our tendency to passive acquiescence. We must measure the worth of America, e.g., not by comparing it to Russia or Argentina (those regimes of torture, terror, extermination, which our "authorities" always end up supporting), but by comparing it to what it could be.

Vast generalities, of course. But a proper reply to your book would require another book. (I'm working on it.) (In novel form, of course.)

Regards, Edward Abbey—Oracle

The Nation, New York City   (7 MAY 1982)

Dear Sir:

In his/her review of a book called *Down the River*, your reviewer Dennis/Denise (?) Drabelle gives us a good forthright description of the book's author. As the undersigned can testify from personal acquaintance, Edward Abbey is indeed an "arrogant," "xenophobic," "puerile," "smug" and "dopey" sort of fellow. So far, fair enough. But what about the book? Mr./ Ms. Drabelle never does get around to telling us what the book is about. Rivers, maybe? It would appear that, in his/her determination to review the author, Mr./Ms..Drabelle forgot to review the book.

Sincerely, Edward Abbey—Oracle

Aaron Abbey   (9 MAY 1982)

Dear Aaron,

Thanks for the letter.

Sorry we didn't get together in L.A. I was only there for one night but spent two nights down in San Diego, where I gave something called the "4th Annual Belkin Lecture" at UCSD. A great and lively crowd. You shoulda been there—didn't you hear about it? I thought you'd call and when you didn't, I decided you must've been in LV [Las Vegas] or Aspen. Josh tells me you go to Aspen a lot.

Oh well. At least now I've got yr address in LA. Do you have a phone there too? Send me the number.

Susie says "High." Yes, you have a sister, and a pretty damn good one too. Now 13½ yrs old, she's a first-rate pianist, a good ballet dancer, writer of stories, artist, hiker, camper and boatwoman. (Last year she rowed a skiff down the San Juan River in Utah—ran all the rapids without a flip.)

I'm glad to hear you're still playing the guitar. How about the piano? Composing a guitar piece for a film sounds like an interesting project—lots of luck with it.

As for writing, that's a cruel hard business. Unless you're very lucky it'll break your heart. Even the very talented, as I'm sure you know, have about one chance in a thousand of ever making a living at it. You should prepare a fall-back position for yourself, as I often wish I had done. As I tell Josh, it would be best to learn a good honest trade on the side: shoe repair, horse shoeing, welding, carpentry, cattle stealing, plumbing, para-medicine or some such. Hard times are a-coming, and people without useful, practical skills are going to suffer. Or suffer most.

The one Abbey I most admire, after my father, is my brother Howard, who makes his living as a truck driver, construction worker (high steel man), tree surgeon, gardener, deer hunter. He'll survive when all us fine sensitive artistic types are scrabbling for lunch in garbage cans down on Skid Row, USA.

But maybe I'm wrong. I sure hope so. Maybe we'll muddle through into a world where there will still be jobs for writers, teachers, musicians, dancers and so on. Would be a grim world without us, eh?

Write again, more often. Come visit sometime. You would like Susie very much, and she would like you. Call collect whenever you feel like it.

The New York Times, New York City (15 AUGUST 1982)

Dear Editor-in-Chief:

Early last May one of your sub-editors—perhaps it was Gideon Gil but I'm not certain—contacted me (by telephone) to write a fourteen-hundred-word essay for your Op-Ed page. I said I'd be happy to do it, but having had experience with editors before, suggested that we agree first on a topic for the essay. Which we did: illegal immigration. In the most flattering and ingratiating terms, this man insisted that the Times would be happy to publish whatever I produced on the subject.

Thus encouraged, I promptly produced the requested fourteen-hundred-word essay on the agreed-upon subject. Your editor asked that I mail in the piece "as soon as possible" so that it could be published before your NYC readers began deserting your city for the summer. Within a week I did my part; then followed a lengthy delay of a month or so, at which time I was informed that my essay was too long and too "personal," whatever that means, and would I please condense it to about seven or eight hundred words. Once again I obliged and promptly returned a shortened and "depersonalized" version of the same essay.

Another long delay, of about two months; then I received the attached letter from Mr Gideon Gil, stating that the Op-Ed Page lacks sufficient "room" for my article.

This is ridiculous. I hereby return the article for re-consideration by yourself or whoever is in charge there, if anyone. If you are still unwilling to print it, then I request that you do me the simple basic courtesy of explaining why, i.e., my essay is stupid, or badly written, or illogical, or scandalous or outrageous, or racist, or genocidal or whatever. As the author of a solicited piece of work, I am entitled to at least that much rudimentary fair play.

And oh yes: if printed, I expect to be paid whatever is customary for Op-Ed pieces. If again rejected, then I expect the customary kill-fee. $500 would be about right.

Sincerely, Edward Abbey—Tucson

John Nichols, Taos, New Mexico   (17 AUGUST 1982)

Dear John,

Finally got around to reading *Nirvana Blues*, and I want to tell you I think it's a delightful book—witty, precisely honest, rich & true in characterization and situation. I think it's your best novel to date, better than *Milagro* [*Beanfield War*], esp. because you pull no punches. You have a great gift for satire.

The trouble w/ *Milagro*, tho' it too is a delightful book, is/was that in your contempt for our Anglo culture, you tended to sentimentalize the Mexican. Let's face it—the Mexicans, Chicanos, whatever you want to call them—as a group, as a class, are no better than the rest of us. Contemporary Chicano culture is based on TV, welfare, the R.C. church, drugs, crime, politics. Nothing more. As you well know, most of them have nothing but fear, contempt, even hatred for nature—the natural world. Have you been to Mexico lately? A desperate squalid mess.

Anyhow, what the hell, you are a great writer. Now I must eat my words in *Down the River*; there is at least one good writer in New Mexico now and his name is Nichols. Continue to tell the truth, avoid ideology, and you will go on to even better books. I look forward to your next. Best of luck and my best regards,

Ed Abbey—Oracle

Tom Pew, Editor, *American West*, Tucson (22 AUGUST 1982)

Dear Mr. Pew:

I am troubled by your editorial remarks in the current issue of *American West*. Do you really believe that all is well in the contemporary West, simply because it is still possible to go for a picnic in the hills and the cowboys are still doing what they've always done? There's something fake about your pretended naiveté. You know better, and you know that we know it.

Yes, the cowboys are still out there, a few of them, working mostly for absentee ownership, still wearing their comical hats, still overgrazing the hell out of our public lands and still shooting down the last of our eagles, mountain lions, bears, etc. That much remains the same. But the American West as a whole is under a massive attack by industrial greed—the mining, lumbering, land development industries—and you know it. James Watt is the perfect personification of all that is most corrupt and rotten in American life—and Watt and his buddies are now in power!

Right here in Arizona, the copper industry continues to have its own way, dumping its poisonous filth into the public air while their political flunkies like Bruce "Shithead" Babbitt and those moral dwarfs in the state legislature continue to grovel at the industry's feet. It's high time for the copper industry in Arizona to clean up or shut down—and you know it. Don't give me any crocodile tears about unemployed copper miners either. Good God, there's over ten million people out of work in this country, many more millions who've given up looking for work and some twenty or thirty million living below the poverty line. We don't need a copper industry—but we do need a revolution!

American West was once a fairly feisty magazine, when T. H. Watkins was editor, displaying some concern about preserving the quality of life in our West. But if this current issue is typical (I'll admit I haven't looked at the magazine for years), then you are sinking to the intellectual level of Bruce Babbitt and his *Arizona Highways*. And lower than that you cannot sink. That slick slimy publication reminds me of what astronomers call "black holes"—objects so contracted, small and dense that they can neither emit nor reflect light. Assholes of the universe.

Have you read or reviewed James Byrkit's *Forging the Copper Collar*? A very good book about the copper companies strangle hold on Arizona life and politics. I recommend it. (Univ. of Arizona Press, 1982).

Regards, Edward Abbey—Oracle

George Sessions (22 AUGUST 1982)

Dear George:

Thank you for keeping me up to date with the *Eco-Philosophy* newsletter. Too bad you couldn't make it to the July 4th Earth First! rally in Wyoming—we had a good deep ecological get-together there—good talk and good music in a splendid setting. Only J. Paul Getty & Co failed to show, thus robbing us of the anticipated confrontation.

I published a book last Spring which should be of interest to you and your readers—*Down the River*. In that book I deal with most of the questions about man and nature that are currently coming to the fore. Not in a systematic way, of course, but—in my own way. In fact, most of my books since 1968 have dealt with these matters that you call "deep ecology." It annoys me that some people apparently have the idea that I never got beyond the superficial notions of *Desert Solitaire*.

Another thing: I am still waiting for an answer to the questions I raised in my first letter to you several years ago, particularly the question about the relation of Oriental religions, such as Buddhism, to the actual character of life in the Orient. E.g., it seems apparent that the most miserable, most abused, most man-centered cultures on earth are those of India, China, Japan. Nowhere has the land been so devastated by human numbers and human greed, though in each case in a greatly different manner. Japan is a horror of technological busyness, China a totalitarian purgatory and India simply the sickest nation on earth. Now, how do you cultists of the "Eastern Way" reconcile the actual facts of Eastern life with your idealized (if not sentimalized) version of Eastern religions?

Also, it has been my observation that most of these American Zen Buddhist types are completely self-absorbed. They are obsessed with attaining what they call "enlightenment," which seems to mean, in practice, nothing but a state of selfish, irresponsible self-indulgence. Most of them couldn't care less what happens to the natural world or to human society, since in their view these things are nothing but "illusion" anyway.

Now, Gary Snyder may be an exception to this rule—he has certainly written some sound, sensible things about man-in-nature—but even he advocates passive non-resistance to the advance of industrialism, even suggesting that bulldozers have "souls" and should be treated with veneration. (See his letter to Dave Foreman of Earth First!) What good is that sort of thing? You people have got to get out of your California grooves! There's a bigger world out yonder.

Ah well, enough of this carping. Carry on. I do enjoy reading your eco-philosophical reports and hope the movement continues to grow. (Three cheers for Bookchin—now there's a masculine mind, unpolluted by Orientalism.)

Best regards—Oracle

Earth First! Journal, Tucson (6 OCTOBER 1982)

Dear Editors:

A reading list for Nature Lovers, resistance fighters, "deep ecologists" and regular working environmentalists—why not? The literature is immense and old as civilization; I have read but a small part of it myself. One could range across the world, from ancient China—the writings of Lao-Tse and his disciple Chuang-Tse—to surviving fragments of certain pre-Socratic philosophers—Democritus, Heraclitus, Diogenes—to the sermons of Saint Francis, and such modern Europeans as the novelists Knut Hamsun and Jean Giono, the historian Toynbee, the philosophers Spinoza (for his pantheism), Heidegger, Naess and others. But for the sake of brevity, I shall confine myself to American writers, some obvious, some little known:

Thoreau (of course); John Muir (dull but important); William Bartram; John C. Van Dyke; John Burroughs; Raymond Dasmann; Garrett Hardin; Barry Lopez; Murray Bookchin (see especially his *Ecology of Freedom*, 1982, and *Our Synthetic Environment*, which anticipated Rachel Carson by several years); Bernard DeVoto; William O. Douglas; René Dubos (but only in part, with major reservations—not recommended); Loren Eiseley; Paul Ehrlich; William Faulkner (in such as "The Bear," "Big Woods," "Go Down, Moses" and other stories); Colin Fletcher; the poets Walt Whitman, Robinson Jeffers, Robert Frost, Gary Snyder, Robert Bly, Wallace Stevens, Theodore Roethke, Jim Harrison, Peter Wild—to name but a few; Sigurd Olson; Wallace Stegner; Wendell Berry; Renny Russell; Joseph Wood Krutch (one of the best); Aldo Leopold (basic); Jack London (for his *Call of the Wild*); Annie Dillard; Ann Zwinger; Mary Austin; Rachel Carson; Paul Shepard; Paul Ehrenfeld *(The Arrogance of Humanism)*; several others I'll think of too late; and Lewis Mumford, who has provided us, in such books as *The Pentagon of Power* and *The City in History*, with the best critique yet of our modern military-industrial culture—Mumford, in my opinion, is the one living American author who fully deserves the Nobel Prize for literature.

Ah well, many books. Of the making of books there is no end. I would like to close by reminding myself and others that writing, reading, thinking are of value only when combined with effective action. Those I most admire are those who *do* something, such men as David Brower, Mark Dubois and the legendary Bulgarian brigand Georges Heiduk. Philosophy without action is the ruin of the soul. One brave deed is worth a hundred books, a thousand theories, a million words. Now as always we need heroes. And heroines! Down with the passive and the limp. Avoid the Swami Moonbeams, the Yogi Yahoos, the Roshi Bubbleheads and all other "gurus" whether native American or imported, that swarm of fakes and fakirs who pander to and fleece the foolish, the gullible, the sick, the desperate. Be your own guru. Your own gurette. Little is gained by gaping at a blank wall in a stupor of meditation.

If it's knowledge and wisdom you want, then seek out the company of those who do real work for an honest purpose—e.g., cattlemen and sheep-herders; woodcutters, rangers and wildlife biologists; midwives, nurses and school teachers; farriers, boot makers, gunsmiths, stone masons, veterinarians, carpenters, gardeners; astronomers and geologists; old soldiers and veteran seamen; and others I could name if I set me mind to it.

Fraternally, Edward Abbey—Oracle

Arizona Republic (22 OCTOBER 1982)

Dear Editors:

Once again we citizens of Arizona confront the farce of another make-believe election. Dunn versus DeConcini; Babbitt versus Corbet versus Steiger. Tweedledum, tweedledee and tweedledoo—the bad, the worse, the ridiculous. Once again we are supposed to try to figure out which is the lesser evil. In truth there is no choice; all of the major candidates are financed by corporate money, all of them support and promote the industrial expansion and commercial greed which is gradually destroying

Arizona. Politics has become a game for millionaires or the cronies of millionaires; no wonder that our quisling officials work for the interests of the rich and powerful. As Will Rogers once said, "We have the best politicians that money can buy."

To vote in such a rigged scheme amounts to tacit consent. If it were not for the presence on the ballot of some propositions deserving our support (placed there by the citizens, of course, not by our cowardly politicians), one would be tempted to ignore the whole sick comedy. But there is one more rule worth considering: when in doubt, when there is little choice, always vote against the incumbent. Keep the rascals rotating. The one thing worse than a hack politician is a hack politician entrenched in power. Power corrupts, and the longer in power, the more corrupt they become.

Sincerely, Edward Abbey—Oracle

Edward Hoagland   (31 OCTOBER 1982)

Dear Ted,

Yr loyalty to yr friend Updike is touching and admirable. But it's no use: Updike cannot rise or be raised above the mediocrity of his origins, training, ambition & nature. His work lacks vision—he cannot see beyond the suburbs. He lacks passion—has nothing of interest to tell us of anything important. A smug, fatal complacency has stunted his growth; his books are essentially trivial. Like so many writers of that little pre-school Ivy League coterie, a streak of servility flaws his outlook; he has the soul of a sycophant. Faulkner summed up the type: "They write good . . . but they don't seem to have anything to say."

OK? (Now comes the amateur Village psychologizing.)—Updike in Rose Garden kissing Nancy Reagan's foot.

Fraternally, Ed A

**Eugene C. Hargrove, Editor, *Environmental Ethics*,
University of Georgia**   (3 NOVEMBER 1982)

Dear Mr. Hargrove:

Thank you for inviting me to respond to your editorial re Earth First! and *The Monkey Wrench Gang:*

So far as I know, Earth First! as an organization—though it's more a spontaneous grouping than an organization, having neither officers nor by-laws—is not "pledged to ecological sabotage." If *Newsweek* said that, *Newsweek* is hallucinating (again). We are considering acts of civil disobedience, in the usual sense of that term, when and where they might be useful. For example, when and if the Getty Oil Co attempts to invade the Gros Ventre wilderness (Wyoming) with bulldozers, we intend to peaceably assemble and block the invasion with guitars, American flags, live human bodies and maybe an opposing D-9 tractor. If arrested, we shall go to jail, pay the fines and try again. We invite your readers to join us. A good time will be had by all.

As for that book, please note that *The Monkey Wrench Gang* is a novel, a work of fiction and—I like to think—a work of art. It would be naive to read it as a tract, a program for action or a manifesto. The book is a comedy, with a happy ending. It was written to entertain, to inspire tears and laughter, to amuse my friends and to aggravate our enemies. (Aggravate their ulcers.) So far, about a half million readers seem to have found that approach appealing.

The book does not condone terrorism in any form. Let's have some precision in language here: terrorism means deadly violence—for a political and/or economic purpose—carried out against people and other living things, and is usually conducted by governments against their own citizens (as at Kent State, or in Vietnam, or in Poland, or in most of Latin America right now), or by corporate entities such as J. Paul Getty, Exxon, Mobil Oil, etc etc., against the land and all creatures that depend upon the land for life and livelihood. A bulldozer ripping up a hillside to strip mine for coal is committing terrorism; the damnation of a flowing river followed by the drowning of Cherokee graves, of forest and farmland, is an act of terrorism.

Sabotage, on the other hand, means the use of force against inanimate property, such as machinery, which is being used (e.g.) to deprive human beings of their rightful work (as in the case of Ned Ludd and his mates); sabotage (*le sabot* dropped in a spinning jenny)—for whatever purpose— has never meant and has never implied the use of violence against living creatures. The characters in *Monkey Wrench* engage in industrial sabotage in order to defend a land they love against industrial terrorism.

They do this only when it appears that in certain cases and places all other means of defense of land and life have failed and that force—the final resort—becomes morally justified. Not only justified but a moral obliga- tion, as in the defense of one's own life, one's own family, one's own home, one's own nature, against a violent assault.

Such is the basis of my characters' rationale in *The Monkey Wrench Gang*. How the reader chooses to interpret all this is the reader's business. And if the reader is impelled to act out in real life the exploits of Doc, Bonnie, Slim & Hayduke, that too is a matter for decision by the individual con- science. But first and last, it should be remembered that the book is fiction, make-believe, a story and no more than a story.

As for my own views on environmental ethics, I have tried to state them explicitly in the essay form: see *The Journey Home* (1977), *Abbey's Road* (1979), and *Down the River* (1982).

Sincerely, Edward Abbey—Oracle

George Sessions (20 NOVEMBER 1982)

Dear George:

I've read with interest and almost total approval your latest paper, "The Development of Natural Resources etc"; I hope *Environmental Ethics* prints it; I'm sure they will. I agree with you about everything you write and am pleased to find you fellows coming around to my point of view after all these years of mutual ignorance. I think you'll find that I've been saying exactly the same things, tho in different terminology and by a greatly dif- ferent approach, in most of my books since 1970. (See, for example, the chapter "Dust" in *Journey Home*; "Down There in the Rocks" in *Abbey's Road*; "Down the River w/Thoreau" or "Reply to Dubos" or "Floating" in *Down the River*, etc etc—the same basic view and emotion is present in nearly everything I've written, even in those trashy picture books I made with Porter, Hyde, Muench and others.)

However: The difficult question, which you do not attempt to deal with in this paper of yours, is the old question, How do we get there from here? Always the tough question. Since you and I and Gary Snyder and many others are directly bucking the tide of modern history, swimming upstream against a powerful river, I am not very hopeful. In fact, I suspect that our only hope is disaster. Cruel tho' it is to say it, there has got to be a vast die-off in the human population—likely including us and our families—before the survivors find themselves in a world where a new and humble and "religious" adaptation with nature is possible.

Disaster is not necessary; the better world could be achieved through reason and common sense and a sense of fellowship—but most of the present human world is dead set against us. Thus I was forced to the disagreeable resolutions (not solutions) which I attempted to sketch out in the novel *Good News*. The title is of course deliberately ambiguous.

So much for that. I enclose a letter from Gary Snyder which I invite you to print as a reply to my letter in your *Eco-Philosophy* newsletter. I merely wished to raise the general question of the value of Oriental religions and attitudes for modern deep ecologizers; I have no wish and haven't the time or intellectual competence to engage in individual debates with each of your readers; would much rather hear what others have to say on the matter in the pages of your journal.

My postcard reply to Gary goes as follows: "... I'm sorry that I haven't the heart right now to give your letter the response it deserves and requires. . . . Will say only this for now: I do not find your defense of Indian, Chinese and Japanese cultures adequate. However, it seems to me that a defense of them is not necessary unless you insist on an identification with them. Why can't we simply borrow what is useful to us from Buddhism, Hinduism, Taoism, especially Zen, as we borrow from Christianity, science, American Indian traditions and world literature in general, including philosophy, and let the rest go hang? Borrow what we need but rely principally upon our own senses, common sense and daily living experience. . . ." Print that if you wish.

Thanks for the invitation to Yosemite. If you're ever in the Tucson area, give me a call.

Best regards and carry on,

Ed A.

John Nichols, Taos, New Mexico (1 DECEMBER 1982)

Dear John,

Thank you for the books. You'll not be displeased to learn that I already owned both. Will give them away for Xmas then and keep the signed copies, *mil gracias*. Would love to debate most everything you say in your letter but my urge to write letters flares & fades like most other hard-ons. Come to Tucson sometime, give me a call and we'll discuss it over a few beers.

Will say only this for now: Most every charge you level at American capitalism applies with equal force to communism, with this nice difference, that the Reds make no pretense at such frivolities as civil liberties or environmentalism. The differences in degree are so great that they result in a radical difference in kind. As for "culture," I usually use that word in its anthropological sense. When I hear it, I load my shotgun.

Cheers, Ed—Oracle

Barry Lopez, Finn Rock, Oregon (3 JANUARY 1983)

Dear Barry,

Thanks for the card. Yes, I had a dose of pancreatitis last August but am back to normal now. Except must "moderate" the booze intake. Old age advancing on me, I guess.

I *was* invited to Notre Dame but haven't yet seen the color of their money. Green?

Am going down the Owyhee River May 5th with some river guide named Bob Dopplett. Join us if you can.

Best regards, Ed A.

***National Review*, New York City** (29 JANUARY 1983)

Dear Editor:

Thank you for publishing A. Solzhenitsyn's splendid indictment of the Soviet empire. His denunciation rings true, despite some contrary reports (on the economy there) by the CIA. The most disturbing aspect of S's attack on the USSR, however, is the fact that almost everything he says applies w/ equal force, at least in principle, to most of the rest of the world as well: the concentration of power in a hierarchy of the few, the destruction of our God-created (tossed in that meaningless term to appease NR's Catholicism) environment; the insane lust to dominate manipulate control almost every part of both nature & human nature; the deliberate suppression, by military force, of every effort at popular liberation; the demoralization of the general population; the mad pursuit of military power at all costs.

The gross evil of our time defies all labels.

Yrs, E.A.

Arizona Daily Star (12 MAY 1983)

Dear Editors:

Since the editors of the *Daily Star* are so devoted to promoting mass immigration from Mexico, it seems to me you might well change the name of your paper to the *Daily Estrellita*. Better yet, set up your editorial offices in South Nogales, where you can enjoy today the poverty, misery, squalor and gross injustice which will be the fate of America tomorrow, if we allow the Latino invasion of our country to continue.

Sincerely, Edward Abbey—Oracle

Arizona Daily Star (5 JUNE 1983)

To the Editor:

I regret that Stephan Gomez (June 5) should accuse me of racism and zenophobia. He ought to know better. But anyone who takes a public stand on touchy topics (such as illegal immigration) must expect to be called names. I've also been labeled an "elitest," a "genocidist," a "Commie preservationist" and once (my favorite) a "creeping Fascist hyena."

I don't mind. We have it so easy in this country. If I lived in Russia I'd be in a psychiatric prison. If I lived in Poland I'd be in hiding. If I lived in almost any Latin American nation I'd long ago have been "disappeared" (now a transitive verb), tortured, murdered, buried in a secret mass grave. Maybe that's why all the population seems to be moving one way—from south to north. Even Gabriel Garcia-Marquez lives in exile. I don't know of any American citizens who wish to emigrate to Mexico, Guatemala, Columbia or other points S & SE.

These crude facts tell us what we need to know about the character of life for the majority of people in Latin America. We also know that our own U. S. Government is largely responsible for the forcible maintenance of this state of misery, ugliness, injustice and hate. ("Social stability.") My conclusion from these facts is this: Uncle Sam should keep his big beak at home and allow our Latino neighbors to carry out and complete the revolutions which most of them desperately require. *Viva la causa? Por supuesto.*

Edward Abbey—Oracle

Arizona Republic (7 JUNE 1983)

Dear Editors:

It's true that I am opposed to illegal immigration, as are the great majority of other Americans, including the U. S. Senate. But your catchy headline "Author wants illegal aliens returned to garbage dumps" (May 31) is unfair and the story which follows gives a badly garbled version of what I have said and written on this delicate issue.

As I carefully explained to your reporter, I share the general opinion that illegal aliens who have resided in this country continuously for a period of, say, five years or more, and who can prove that they have established families, homes and livelihoods here, should be granted legal status of some kind. It would be cruel to do otherwise. But we are under no obligation, moral or political, to provide permanent homes for the five to ten million others.

I apologize to my Mexican-American friends and neighbors for the tactless term "garbage dumps"; perhaps it will console them if I reveal my belief that most American towns and cities, including Tucson and Phoenix, are also rapidly becoming huge, unmanageable, unlivable commercial-industrial slums. The differences are mainly of degree.

Finally, I am much too busy writing books and trying to stay out of trouble to have time for "crusading," whether the crusade be for virtue, conservation, wild rivers, peace, well-regulated borders or anything else.

Edward Abbey

Arizona Daily Star   (15 JUNE 1983)

Dear Editors:

So Jacqui Tully, in her review of *Octopussy*, thinks that "we" should "stop condoning" the use of beautiful women in James Bond movies? (And in all other movies, no doubt.) But who do you mean by "we," white woman? Everybody? And what do you mean by "stop condoning"? Censorship? A return of Puritanism?

Men enjoy looking at beautiful women—always have enjoyed it and always will. What of it? Most women enjoy being admired by men. The girls in the Bond movies appear to enjoy their work. I presume they are well paid. They don't seem to be doing it at gun point. Who's exploiting who, anyhow? Or whom, if you prefer.

This form of sexism is as normal, natural and wholesome as sex itself. If this is sexism, let's have more of it. Women in America still have some legitimate grievances. (Although, as Doris Lessing has written, "In the world we live in, feminism is a trivial cause.") But the attempt by a tiny minority of feminist evangelists to repeal a million years of basic primate biology makes them and their movement look silly and ridiculous. And if this be sexism—so what?

Edward Abbey—Oracle

(Aside to the editors: I know these crank letters are a bore. But half the fun of reading *The Daily Estrellita* lies in responding to the daily absurdities.)

Joe Kanon, Dutton Books, New York City   (20 JULY 1983)

Dear Mr. Kanon:

Thank you for your letter of June 20th. I would have replied sooner but returned only two days ago from a month in Alaska.

I am sending a letter to Don Congdon today asking him to make an agreement with you for publication of an "Abbey Reader." I too think this should be a simple matter and never had any wish to involve you or [Jack] Macrae in any competitive bidding for rights to such a prefabricated book.

The book need not be entirely prefabricated. I would like to write an introductory essay for it, dealing with such matters as nature writing and the art of fiction; a lengthy essay, perhaps, straightforward and serious, avoiding the tongue-in-cheek and foot-in-mouth style which I now think rather mars the introductions which I wrote for *The Journey Home* and *Abbey's Road*. No more Don Rickles stuff. I have offended so many people over the years, especially those stuffy NYC reviewers, and made so many enemies, that—I am satisfied.

The essay would also be my farewell to environmental journalism. Let younger voices carry on. I have nothing new to say. From now on I intend to write nothing but fiction, and maybe a few travel books: on Mexico, on Australia and India, for example.

A title? *Slumgullion Stew: An Abbey Reader.*

Sincerely, Edward Abbey—Tucson

Century Magazine, Brooklyn, New York (3 AUGUST 1983)

Dear Editor:

Carol Anderson works hard to find a scientific basis for a truce between developers and preservers. The result, however, is only one more illustration of the narrow limitations of scientific methodology—"the irrationality of rationality," as Heidegger said. Nobody needs an understanding of physics to understand why, for example, most people object to having a four-lane freeway blasted through the neighborhood in which they live. Nor was the motive force of economic greed and the desire to dominate nature and human nature invented by Isaac Newton or Adam Smith; these evils have been plaguing mankind for at least ten thousand years, or ever since the invention of the hoe, the plow and slavery. The conflict is ancient; only the technology has been improved.

Nothing could be more dangerous than to attempt to base human values, life values, upon the murky ground of modern physics. The fact (if it is a fact) that the high priests of quantum mechanics don't know which way a proton will jump next tells us nothing whatsoever of any much usefulness about the world that we actually live in. To think that it does is to commit the fallacy of reducing living experience to the abstractions of mathematics.

The one great contribution that the nuclear physicists have made to contemporary civilization is the nuclear bomb. (How can we ever thank them?) The fact (if it is a fact) that matter is reducible to indeterminate patterns of energy—"wavicles"—does not mean that rocks, trees, clouds, dogs, chickens, people etc are nothing but such patterns. Anyone who can't see the difference between his wife and a cluster of equations on a blackboard needs help; I mean medical help. Or else should be sequestered in a cell on the Lama Foundation bullshit plantation.

I see that I have strayed a bit from the initial topic. Therefore I shall continue. The idolatry of science and the worship of technology are part of a unique modern problem. What we need is a civilian review board to oversee the activities of those thousands of little men in the white smocks. They are creating a world that is becoming increasingly unpleasant to live in. No, I am not advocating thought control; I am advocating popular control, through direct democratic means, of the misapplications of scientific discovery.

Modern science has given us many gifts—not only the nuclear bomb but also the MX [missile], nerve gas, neutron bomb, napalm, television, the computerized university, sphincter transplants, fetal surgery, Hostess Twinkies, dioxin, PCBs, Three Mile Island, etc. One could go on for pages. Outside of the scientific-industrial world, none of us ever asked for or even wanted or even needed any of these marvels. Therefore it seems only fair that we, the simple untrained majority, should demand a vote with veto power in all further life-shaping decisions. The motto of the World Science Exposition in Chicago in 1933 was "Science discovers; Industry applies; Man conforms." We have been living under that authoritarian ideology for half a century. Time for a nice wholesome rebellion, I'd say.

Now back to the initial topic. The conflict between the greed of developers and the freedom of the rest of us is as old as civilization. But now the developers come at us armed with the weapons of industrial technology. We're not going to stop the bulldozers with lectures in theoretical physics. We can only stop them with active resistance, steadfast unyielding opposition both personal and organized. Throw out of office the flunky politicians who serve [the developers]. Drown in laughter the bald-headed transistorized near-sighted factory-made economists (with their floppy-disc brains) who prepare their position papers. (Such as Milton Friedman and Julian Simon, for example.) And if the computer gives you any back talk, pour some well-sugared office coffee into its evil little silicon brain. As Edna St. Vincent Millay once said, "Humankind will never be free until the last corporation executive is strangled with the entrails of the last systems engineer analyst."

"But what about jobs?" they'll cry, opening up their business suits to reveal their fake bleeding hearts with the genuine simulated polystyrene tears, "the people need jobs." To which I reply: I need a job. My brother-in-law needs a job. All God's children need jobs. Get off our backs, get out of our land, go back to the moon where you came from, and we'll find plenty of work to do. Good work. And we'll share it.

Edward Abbey—Oracle

Arizona Daily Star   (5 AUGUST 1983)

Dear Editors:

Why should we, as Tucson citizens, make any effort to conserve water or support the C.A.P. when the only purpose of such an effort is to make possible more and more industrial and population growth in southern Arizona? Do we really want Tucson to become another vast sprawling commercial slum like Phoenix? When the developers, boomers, promoters and land speculators tell us that there is no Constitutional way to prevent more people from coming here, they are being dishonest and evasive.

In fact, the tumor-like growth of Tucson is the result of deliberate policy on the part of the little crowd which runs this town. By encouraging industry to relocate here, by deviously promoting more "parkways," by pushing for the great C.A.P. boondoggle, by pro-development zoning, by anti-labor politics (Right-to-Scab law) and by a host of other measures, they have created the runaway growth which plagues us now. A few profit, the rest of us lose. By reversing the above policies, we could slow the expansion of Tucson to a manageable and self-limiting pace.

Years ago, the writer Joseph Wood Krutch urged us to "Keep Tucson Small." We ignored him. Now we must adopt a new slogan: Tucson is big enough.

(You can say that again, Abbey!)

Okay, I will: TUCSON IS BIG ENOUGH.

Edward Abbey—Oracle

The Atlantic Monthly, **Boston**   (30 SEPTEMBER 1983)

Dear Editor:

The little essay on Hemingway by James Atlas was good; but his estimate of Thomas Wolfe as "no longer readable" strikes this reader as false,
unjust and all too conventional. False because thousands of people, here
and abroad, still read Wolfe, every year, year after year, forty-five years after
his death. His books stay in print. This happens despite the fact that Wolfe
receives no support from the academics; unlike Fitzgerald, for example,
who still "holds up" because he is held up by institutional inertia.

[Atlas's] judgment is unjust because it implies that Wolfe is no longer
worth reading. In fact, no other modern American writer has given us so
deep, rich, detailed, human and humane a sense of the texture and quality of American life in the first thirty-five years of this century. He was, as
Faulkner once said somewhere, "the best of us all." (And only thirty-eight
when he croaked.)

Finally, the rejection of Wolfe is so damned cautiously conventional, so
commonplace among our official critics that it makes you wonder if it is
based on anything more than custom. Why is it, anyway, that our literary
critics always face in the same direction, like a herd of sheep? Always swim
in unison, like a school of fish? Thomas Wolfe belongs among our great
American novelists and one of these years some daring young new literary
explorer is going to "rediscover" him and "revive" his work. Then of course
we'll see the whole class of critical crickets dance off in a new direction,
dropping poor Scott what's-his-name like a husk of chitin.

Sincerely, Edward Abbey—Oracle

Annie Dillard   (15 NOVEMBER 1983)

Dear Miss Dillard:

I've just finished reading *Living By Fiction,* and wish to say that I am
impressed once again, as always in your work, by the elegance, simplicity
and clarity with which you present your thesis.

But one thing bugs me. On pp 153–154 you refer to the novel notion
that humankind are destroying their own habitat (and equally important,

the habitat of most other creatures) as a "miserable cliché." How come? In what sense can such a general idea, almost certainly valid and thereby of fundamental importance, be a cliché? And why a miserable cliché? Are some clichés more miserable than others?

In any case, it seems an odd remark, out of place in your book (no other miserable clichés are singled out) and totally out of character in a writer such as yourself who is well known as a nature writer, nature lover in fact, and environmentalist. Why the left hook at some unspecified opponent?

Furthermore, is the idea truly a cliché? As general ideas go, it is of recent origin, hardly a generation old, and an idea still unknown to the majority, ignored by the ignorant, bitterly resisted by the powerful and scorned by our misnamed "conservatives," such as, for example, Saul Bellow and James Watt. (Two of a kind, those fellas, in many ways, alike in their malignant politics, their hatred of environmentalists and their creepy eschatologies.)

Anyhow, cliché or not, the growing awareness of the interdependence of life forms is an awareness that has so far escaped writers of fiction. Although people like Lewis Mumford (my nominee for the Nobel Prize), Jacques Ellul, Ivan Illich and others have dealt with the question, I don't know of any novelist who has taken it up. Jean Giono? Thomas Pynchon? In fact, it would require a novelist combining the powers of Thomas Pynchon, Thomas Wolfe and Thomas Mann to embrace so vast and intricate a subject within the limits of a novel—would it not? No wonder that most of us feel constrained to limit our efforts to the familiar ground of human relationships, whether comical, tragical or comical-tragical.

The writer, says Henry James, must be granted his premises. Which seems to mean that a great work of literary art can be based on any platitude, however stupid. "God is Love," for example, or "The Earth is our Mother," for another, or "Life is a tale told by an idiot" for a third. But I don't think that you, anymore than a "Marxist or fundamentalist" (your page 153), can really go along with that doctrine. And neither do I. We both believe that good art is based on truth, whatever in Heaven or Hell that may be. I'd be interested in your response.

Fraternally, Edward Abbey—Oracle

John Macrae, New York City   (23 NOVEMBER 1983)

Dear Jack,

In response to your request for better blurbs for *Beyond the Wall*, I have searched thru my files and old scrapbooks and found only the enclosed, a copy of the ad that you (or someone) wrote for *Abbey's Road* four years ago. All the other reviews etc I must have thrown away or sent home to my mother. Anyhow, even though John Leonard was writing about a previous book of mine, I think it would be fair to use the first part of his remarks on the jacket copy of *Beyond the Wall*—but not in another *NY Times* ad.

I cannot find the card from James Dickey in which he praised *Down the River* in general but generous terms. I'm sure I mailed it to you or Jeanne Bornstein when you were both still at Dutton. Perhaps Joe Kanon could find it. Dickey's statement, as I recall, was of the same general nature as Leonard's and therefore could fairly be applied to *Beyond the Wall*.

Edward Hoagland also had some kind words about my work in general in a review of *Down the River*, which he wrote for a magazine called *Backpacker*. I think that mag has its office in NYC; you might give them a call. That review, like Dickey's card, I sent to you at Dutton over a year and a half ago.

Please do not use McGuane's "fly in the ointment" bit anymore; I think we've already used it too often. Also, please do not solicit any blurbs from my old friends Alan Harrington and Wm Eastlake, or Wendell Berry— too much mutual back-scratching there, you know. I don't know if Peter Matthiessen and Hunter Thompson ever write blurbs for anybody, but you might give them a try. I would like to think that they both like my books.

Who else? Well, the sad truth is that I don't have many friends in the higher echelons of the literary world, especially back East. And it is the East which I would like to crack, naturally. Someday. That's why I think Leonard's and Hoagland's words would help.

As for book signing at bookstores, I'm willing to give it one more go-around if you really think it's worth Holt's expense and my embarrassment. Remember that, altho' we drew a good crowd at Denver's Tattered Cover bookstore, that was only two years ago. Boulder was not very good, for some reason, maybe because it's only twenty miles from Denver.

I have been invited to make appearances at Yale's School of Journalism, the Harvard Law School and Rochester Tech sometime next spring, probably in April. I'm trying to pack all three visits into one week in April; perhaps I could visit bookstores in New Haven, Boston and Rochester at that time. Have you got an approximate pub date for *Beyond the Wall* yet?

I've also agreed to give a reading in San Diego sometime in April, and will sign at a bookstore there if you wish.

Here are some bookstores I'd be willing to visit (each is the best in each place):

Tucson: The Haunted Bookshop

Tempe-Phoenix: Changing Hands Bookstore

Sedona: Words & Music Store

Denver: The Tattered Cover

Salt Lake: The Cosmic Aeroplane (why must bookstores have such phucking cute names?)

Santa Fe? Austin? San Francisco? I don't know . . .

Tell your marketing mgr that he/she should be able to sell some of my books thru such outlets as health food stores (shameful but true) and the outdoorsy hiking-camping equipment stores. I told your sales mgr at Dutton about this several years ago but so far as I know they never acted on the suggestion. But those places sell a lot of books by Colin Fletcher, Barry Lopez, Annie Dillard—so why not mine?

Vanitas, vanitas, omni vanitas est . . .

Am now on page 871 of the novel [*The Fool's Progress*]—exactly where I was two months ago. Afraid I've been idling about—did I tell you that my new wife Clarke and I had a baby? 8 lbs 1 oz—same weight as my next novel. You still want to be the midwife?

I still think you should ask your artist to add a portion of a wall to the book jacket illustration; would triple its dramatic effect and clarify the book's title. You speak of subtlety—but is subtlety a strong point with my readers, bless their romantic hearts?

Received a letter a few days ago from a Mr "Lone Cone Karl" in Colorado, inviting me up on his mountain for dinner of poached elk but advising me to bring my .41 Magnum "just in case we don't hit it off." Me? him? or the elk?

I mention the .41 Mag because another fan sneered at my .357, calling it a child's toy, and recommending the .41 as the optimum "personal personnel weapon."

Dear Jack, what have I done? Where will it all end? How come I never get letters from Susan Sontag? "Susie Creamcheese"—what she always really wanted was to be a Frenchman. Or Roland Barthes?

Best regards, Ed A.—Tucson

Annie Dillard (28 DECEMBER 1983)

Dear Ms Dillard,

Please don't feel obliged to answer this letter. I'm writing it partly for your amusement, I hope, but also to attempt to clarify my own thoughts on certain questions of aesthetical theory. You write somewhere that you were a student (and obviously still are) of theology. I was once something similar, a philosophy major. A major? Well—a second lieutenant.

I understand and sympathize with your wish not to be labeled an environmentalist. In calling you that in my letter, I was trying to get a rise out of you. And hooked you too, with my barbless hook, just as you hooked me. I have probably suffered much more than you from hasty pigeon-holing by reviewers and other literary crickets. I am happy to be a nature lover, a crusader for virtue, a defender of those who cannot well defend themselves (like grizzly bears and crocodiles), but I really resent it when reviewers and librarians and booksellers almost automatically classify me as an "environmentalist writer" or a "nature writer" or even as a "naturalist." Most exasperating!

Merely stoning bunny rabbits, riling up ants and depositing my empty beer cans along major highways has not been sufficient to save me from the categories of the simple and the simple minded who are usually entrusted with the chore of reviewing books. It's ridiculous, and it's unfair, but somehow the label was pasted on me early and I've had a difficult time trying to acquire new and better bumper stickers for my books.

E.g., in going over my stuff in the preparation of a "Reader," I find that about 10 percent of what I've published deals directly with environmental issues, about 10 percent consists of amateur natural history, and the other 79 percent is a slumgullion stew of personal history, travel, bawdy jokes, old jokes (the best kind), politics (libertarian-anarchist), lit crit, character sketches, minor metaphysics (among metaphysicians I'm an unlicensed G.P.), prophecy both grim and starry-eyed and six novels concerned in various ways with the comedy of human relationships.

And the remaining 1 percent? Art: magic: wonder: the element that cannot be isolated. Or so I like to think. When I'm asked to categorize my work (I never am), I choose to place it in the bin under "L": Literature, Great. That delusion is necessary for all of us who write primarily for the pleasure of ourselves and, we hope, of others.

So. Krutch was a first-rate nature writer. (In his final role.) Ann Zwinger is a first-rate writer of natural history. Wisely, you have escaped such limiting identifications by infusing and suffusing your work with the magic of art, the radio-active glow of poetry—musick, we might call it.

I have tried, less successfully, to do what you are doing, and by means nearly opposite to yours; by writing big baggy vulgar books, throwing everything in but the kitchen sink and then adding the kitchen sink. I would like to evoke the sense of wonder and magic in the reader but without invoking the mystical, the supernatural or the transcendent. When I wrote once of "huge invisible wings vibrating across the sky," I felt and I knew that I was cheating a little, giving my readers a cheap thrill that in my own case was unearned. For other writers, for you perhaps, such a vision would be legitimate, but for me it was false.

But Barry Lopez likes that line so I guess I'd better leave it in. And who knows?—maybe I was being utilized by a higher power, God putting words into my typewriter against my will.

You mystics and transcendentalists have one clear distinct advantage over us naive realists: if your intuitions are correct, we shall all be forced to acknowledge it; later; if I am right, I will never know. For certain.

Enough of this beating about a smoldering bush. What is the true subject, or point, or premise, of literary art? Of fiction, to delimit the matter, of the novel, to delimit the matter more closely?

Well, how can you rule out any subject as a suitable one for the novel? The novel is the book of life, said Lawrence, and I agree. The novelist must be granted his premises, said Henry James; I agree with that too. And this above all, says Thoreau, over and over again, give me the truth, the truth however cruel rather than a comforting fabrication. And Solzhenitsyn asks, If the purpose of art is not to change the world, is it then any better than the barking of village dogs at night? And Sam Johnson ditto (see Preface to Shakespeare).

I find validity in all of the above attitudes. Very confusing. I'm beginning to be sorry I started this letter. What do I believe most deeply?

A good novel cannot be reduced to its "point," or to its theme, or subject matter, or central idea, or premise, or "hidden meaning," as you say. Okay. On the other hand, a novel without a point is pointless. Who wants to waste time reading a novel without a guiding theme? But reductionism is always fallacious, like the vulgar scientism so popular in our time (especially in California) that would reduce the whole world, all of reality, to a swarm of dancing Wu Li masters, to a mere idea in the mind of a cosmic subatomic physicist.

The editor of *Harper's* (that creep) once wrote, no kidding, words to the effect that human beings are really nothing but patterns of organic energy, nothing but mathematical equations on some kind of multi or non-dimensional blackboard. Talk about crude reductionism! Abstractionism! Gullible fake-scientific superstition! etc. Yet, his mentality is typical of the prevailing mentality of our time. Far more dangerous than nuclear bombs. (For which, how can we ever thank them?) A gross violation not only of sense and common sense and common horse sense but of our dignity as living breathing copulating human animals. Let Lapham and his semi-divine mathematicians show us how two coupling computations can result in one 8½ pound blue-eyed firm-fleshed squirming squalling baby named Rebecca Claire Abbey!

Anger! I'm foaming at the typewriter again. But of the seven deadly sins, wrath is the healthiest—next only to lust.

Pop! goes the pop-top. A can of Coors will calm me down.

Now. I'm all for art for art's sake. I believe in the unconditional freedom of the artist. I can enjoy the elaborate and refined artifacts of a Joyce or a Borges or a James or a Nabokov as much or almost as much as the next reader. The consubstantive equation of symbol with thing symbolized when artfully done can be a joy forever, or at least for a hell of a long time, until fashions change.

But getting right down, hurriedly now, to the cob of the corn, I want the novelist to tell the truth, all and nothing but, to the best of her ability. As well. In addition to the art, the magic, the formal wonder. Agreed, you cannot separate the truth of what is said from the way in which it is said, except in formal analysis, which is a waste of time, the sort of thing professors think they are doing in college lit courses.

Nevertheless, I ask the novelist to provide me with this abstract "both": art as art and art as truth. Truth-in-art.

What is truth? somebody said, thinking he could easily wash his hands of the sticky business. The answer to that is simple: in our free-thinking age the truth is what each of us thinks, feels, guesses or believes to be the truth. An unsatisfactory answer, I know, but—where all think alike, nobody thinks much. (Walter Lippmann.) You may even believe that there is no truth; if so, that is your truth.

And the arts, luckily, are quite different from one another. Music, for example (but not poetry), transcends the limitations of the novelist. Thus Palestrina, or Schutz, or Bach or Bruckner or Penderecki are much more satisfying for me than Dante or Milton or Racine or even Shakespeare.

The advantage of truth in the novel is that it reinforces the effect, enlarges the emotion, deepens the power. Thus I prefer, for example, Mann to Proust. Not that Proust falsifies or lies, but that for me there is more truth in Thomas Mann than in Marcel Proust. Much more.

Now I think I'm getting somewhere. (I can see you smiling over these sweating exclamations, if you're not already dozing.)

The novel should tell the truth, as I see the truth, or as the novelist persuades me to see it. And one more demand: I expect the novelist to aspire to improve the world. (I choose my banal phrase deliberately.) Like Solzhenitsyn, I want the novel to make a difference. As a novelist, I want to be more than one more dog barking at the other dogs barking at me. Not out of any foolish hope that one novelist, or all virtuous novelists in chorus, can make much of a difference for good, except in the long run, but out of the need to prevent the human world from relaxing into something worse. To maintain the tension between truth and falsity, beauty and ugliness, good and evil.

Therefore, while I am a libertarian in the arts, as well as in nearly everything else, I believe the highest duty of the serious novelist is, whatever the means or technique, to be a critic of his society, to hold society to its own ideals, or if these ideals are unworthy, to suggest better ideals. And so on. In this I sympathize with John Gardner's idea of moral fiction, though I think he had too narrow a notion of morality.

And for these reasons too I should dread seeing any novelist, especially the well-intentioned, assuming political power over the rest of us. But then, I'm opposed to anyone of any faction of any belief assuming power over the rest of us.

Anarchism? You bet your sweet betsy. The only cure for the ills of democracy is more democracy. Much more. Back to the "miserable cliché." Hardy or Dickens could not have written about the degradation of the natural world by human greed because the general idea of such degradation was unknown in their time. As I said, the idea is only a generation old—thirty years. I mean, the popular consciousness of such an idea. And no good novelist has yet attempted to embrace the general idea in a novel or series of novels. The many novels and films of a post-nuclear war period are something else, something different.

I do not see why a novel with environmental destruction as its guiding theme should be, as you fear, a "snooze." In fact, the idea contains the basic elements of classical Greek tragedy. Here we have this great powerful glittering engine, technology, created by and informed by (the ghost in the machine) the best and brightest minds of our century, and justified by its intention of doing good. Doing good! For the rest of us. For everybody! (Even the condors, they claim.)

And only one fatal little flaw: hubris, excess pride, the lust for power, the well-meaning desire to dominate both nature and human nature. Power corrupts: attracts the worst, corrupts the best.

The subject is too big, too complex, too tragic for our frivolous contemporary novelists, most of whom (Updike, for example, or Irving, or Bellow, or Percy, or Roth, or Oates, or Barth, or Gardner, or Mailer, to name but a few) cannot seem to go beyond the traditional themes of suburban hanky-panky, private spiritual angst, manners & morals, modernist and post-modernist aesthetical introversion, etc etc. Rich fields of artistic play, to be sure. But there's got to be more. Much more.

Why should it take a first-time filmmaker like Godfrey Reggio to show us, in *Koyaanisqatsi*, what is possible? Aided greatly by the marvelous music of Philip Glass. (I am glad to see, or rather to hear, that American composers are finally throwing off the dead weight of Schonberg & Stravinsky, that dreary serialism and that sterile neo-classicism.)

Ah well . . . I have rambled on much too long. Fun for me, a bore for you, since you have wrestled with these questions much more seriously than I would even care to try to do.

L'essais . . . I should have said, by the way, that *Living By Fiction* is not only elegant, simple and clear, but also subtle and witty. Subtle rather than simple; I really don't understand what you mean by symbol and thing symbolized becoming the same. Consubstantiation? or transubstantiation? which is the heresy? Men have died, and women burned, in disagreement over such syllables.

If you ever come to the Tucson area, give me a call and I'll buy you a Cowgirl Steak at the Redneck Cafe.

I hope that your baby arrives on schedule and that all is well. Ours did and is.

Fraternally

1984–1985

DURING THIS PAIR OF YEARS, Abbey remained firmly settled in Tucson with Clarke, Susie, and Becky. By this point, he had become painfully aware of his mortality, as his chronic pancreatitis spawned esophageal varices, the internal bleeding disease that would eventually kill him. "He's old," Ed liked to say, "but he ain't dead." Indeed, to most observers Abbey appeared vital and essentially unchanged physically or psychically. Yet reflections on death and mortality now became a common theme in his journals ("A canker of bitterness is gnawing at my soul." May 27, 1984), even as the unwanted grumpiness quotient in his correspondence increased. One book is published in 1984—*Beyond the Wall*—and one in 1985—*Slumgullion Stew.* Both are collections.

James Morgan, Articles Editor,
Playboy **Magazine, Chicago** (2 JANUARY 1984)

Dear Mr. Morgan:

Thank you for the Christmas card. Of course I would like to write something for *Playboy* again, if we can agree on a topic.

At the moment I'm on page 901 of another novel, this one a sort of picaresque Rabelaisian Appalachian hillbilly family saga farce and tragedy. If your fiction editor would like a look, I'll type up a chapter or two of it and send it along. Ask him/her to give me guidelines as to maximum length.

But I'm also interested in doing essays and journalism, altho' not in the field of environmental issues: I am still very much an eco-freak and wild preservationist but I have had nothing new to say on the subject for years. General travel is more my line now (see my Alaska piece in the March *Outside*, or my next book, *Beyond the Wall*, also due in March or April), and social and literary commentary.

E.g., I've been making notes lately for an essay on the subject "Great Living Bores," or "The Great American Bores" or some such title. My initial nominees for the list would be such folk as Jackie K Onassis, Henry Kissinger, Normal Mailer, William F Buckley and George F Will (because of their push-button opinions on any conceivable subject), perhaps Muhammad Ali (tho' he seems to be fading fast; should have thought of this several years ago), John Updike (for the rabbit story), maybe Ted Kennedy, maybe Susan "Creamcheese" Sontag (what she really wanted was to grow up to be a Frenchman), John Travolta certainly and other hack show biz types, Jesse Jackson and Walter Mondale, I'm sure, will be boring us silly in the months to come, the whole line-up of the Baltimore Orioles, Bob Dylan (changing his religion every six months), James Michener, Jesse Helms, Yasser Arafat, Hugh Hefner (oops!), Pope JP II (often pictured out here in the SW as a "Pope-alope," with pronghorns), Buckminster Fuller (tho' recently deceased), Carlos Castenada, Jerry Falwell, etc etc. Perhaps the list is already too long.

In any case, my emphasis would be a discussion of the qualities and nature of a great public bore, as opposed to merely minor, personal and "scintillating" bores.

And then, I'm thinking of going to Abyssinia next November for an exploration of the Omoo River. I know you're not particularly interested in any more river trip journals but I'm sure I'd find much of interest in Ethiopia to write about along with hippos, crocodiles & cannibals & black Reds. If I go I may take a look at South Africa, too, and even try to get into SW Africa and the sporadic guerrilla warfare said to be smoldering there.

I want to go to Australia one more time. Perhaps never to return. And if I ever finish this goddamn endless novel I plan to write a serious book about Mexico—*The Smoking Volcano on our Border*.

Say hello to Gonzo Gonzales for me. I've lost his address. I hear he's recently had published a novel about Mexico or something to do with Mexican revolutionaries. Ask him to send me a copy, I want to read it, and if he does I'll send him a copy of my next book.

Sincerely, Edward Abbey—Oracle

Don Congdon, New York City (3 FEBRUARY 1984)

Dear Don:

About the Viking anthology, *Writers of the Purple Sage*, I phoned the editor, Russell Martin, in Colorado and he agreed that he would use a chapter from *Abbey's Road* or *Down the River* instead of something from *Desert Solitaire*. However, he failed to call me back as promised to tell me what he and Gerald Howard at Viking did decide on. Would you please give Mr Howard a call, find out what they're using, and then—if it's anything but a chapter from *Desert Solitaire*—the deal is okay by me and you may deposit Viking's check for $200.

I returned Kaplan's MWG film option contract to your office Tuesday, Jan 31st by Express Mail, with a note suggesting how to contact my son Joshua, in NY, whose signature we apparently need on the papers. I also sent Josh a letter telling him to call your office, and to go there to sign the contract. Don't let him take the contract out of your office or sure as hell he'll lose it on the subway or something. He's a good, kind, intelligent, powerful young man but a bit careless, even reckless in some ways. E.g., I've seen him pound on the hood of a taxicab when the driver failed to stop exactly behind the white line at an intersection. And he usually vaults over the turnstiles rather than waste time buying tokens—a magnificent gesture, I agree. Don't let him wreck your office—call the PD if necessary.

Thanks for forwarding Jack Macrae's letter. I certainly do appreciate his expression of support. And perhaps we should give his offer serious consideration. I've been dawdling along on the novel, feeling I've got all the time in the world to complete it, and therefore wasting a lot of time. If Jack would agree to withhold all editorial suggestions and criticisms until I finish a typed-up first draft to my satisfaction (because, as I've explained, I'm easily confused by criticism while the work is in progress), why then— then—perhaps a contract, with partial advance, and a deadline, would be a useful incentive to me.

I don't mind typing up a portion of the book now, I'm going to have to do it sooner or later anyhow, and would be glad to send on to you and Jack some fifty or hundred pages, with a statement of intentions and an outline or synopsis of the novel as a whole. A twelve-month deadline at the time of agreement would be about right; I'd even agree to mail the ms to NY in monthly installments—that too would help me . . . say about sixty to seventy-five pages per month.

Regards, Ed A.

The New York Times   (15 FEBRUARY 1984)

Dear Op-Ed Page Editor:

Herewith is the bill for my article "Illegal Immigration and Liberal Taboos," written for your Op-Ed page on assignment from Mr William Meyers in May of 1982, condensed and rewritten on request from another Op-Ed editor, Mr Gideon Gil, during June or July of 1982, and finally rejected by Mr Gil in September 1982, no explanation given. Nor has my typescript of this article ever been returned to me.

Kill fee for solicited article . . . $500.00
Due & payable upon receipt.

Sincerely yours, Edward Abbey—Tucson

Governor Richard Lamm, Denver, Colorado   (20 APRIL 1984)

Dear Governor,

I've enjoyed reading about your impolitic public statements recently. You are absolutely right about the question of old age and medicated, technological survival beyond the point of a meaningful life. It's true, sooner or later, us old-timers have got to be willing to get out of the way of the newer generations. I tried to express this idea in *Desert Solitaire* in a chapter called "Dead Man at Grandview Point." But people don't pay much attention to writers—except in the long run, when the contest of ideas begins to determine the character of human society.

Anyhow—it's delightful and refreshing to hear of a man in public life speaking out boldly and honestly on such questions (most politicians are such craven temporizers!), and I congratulate you for doing it.

Now I want to urge you to stick your neck out even further on the media chopping block by taking up in public such issues as mass immigration from Latin America and differential birth rates in the USA. To even raise such questions arouses the reflex response of "racist, elitist, bigot" and so on—but somebody has to do it. If you don't I probly will; but it would be a lot more fun for all if you did it, since you command much more public attention than I ever could.

And write a book about it. I promise to give it a good review.

Your friend and admirer, Edward Abbey—Oracle

Don Congdon, New York City   (24 APRIL 1984)

Dear Don:

Thanks for your letter of April 20th.

I sent a note to Gibbs ("Shithead") Smith in SLC telling him to write directly to Jack Macrae about his, Shithead's, proposal to re-issue *Slickrock*. Whatever Jack wants to do about it should be our guide.

Whatever gave you the notion I regard ol' Shithead Smith as a pain in the ass?

Now, as to the novel-in-progress: What I suggested in my letter to you, about 2½ months ago, was that we should welcome Jack's offer of a contract and advance on the new novel. I am ready to provide Jack with a minimum of one hundred pages of clean, typed-up, more or less first draft samplings of the novel—probably several set-pieces like the baseball story—together with a detailed outline or synopsis of the book as a whole. I never suggested Jack should be asked to bid on a pig-in-a-poke. Gracious! The only condition I attached was that Jack agree to withhold any editorial advice until I complete the first draft of the novel, for reasons I've mentioned both to you and to him—i.e., because I am easily confused when offered advice in the middle of my creative throes.

Of course if Jack, or another publisher, after reading my outline and my sample chapters, should reject my novel-in-progress as unworthy of publication, that would constitute "editorial advice" all right. But that is a risk I am willing to risk.

As I also said in my previous letter to you, I believe I could deliver a complete first draft of the novel in about eighteen months after the signing of an agreement.

Regards, Edward Abbey—Tucson

Copy to Jack Macrae

PS: Dear Jack: I've told Smith that *Beyond the Wall* includes the three best chapters from *Slickrock*. Whether or not *Slickrock* is republished is a matter of indifference to me. This Smith is the fellow who published the new hardcover edition of *Solitaire* a few years ago.

The hand-written ms is about 990 pp long, in notebooks. I believe I'm about ⅔ of the way thru. Much will be discarded, but much should be added. It's gonna be a long book—not fat, but long. And good? I hope so.

Please ask the Sales Dept to send me ten copies of *Beyond the Wall* (five hard, five soft) and to bill me at author's rate.

Thanks. Ed.

Mr. Woodworth   (24 APRIL 1984)

Dear Mr Woodworth:

Thank you for sending me a copy of *Match!* I'm glad to see you're still in business. Or back in business.

A comment: I do think that anarchists should re-think their position on the immigration issue. I've been criticized by anarchists here and there for advocating a halt to illegal immigration from Mexico, some even accusing me of "racism" or "elitism" or "fascism," etc. But it is not a question of race: I myself am opposed to mass immigration, legal or illegal, from *any* source.

There are many good reasons—economic, political, social, cultural, environmental—for calling a halt to further immigration. (For a summary of my views, see my article in the *Phoenix New Times*, June 29, 1983—which you are welcome to reprint, in whole or in part, if you wish.) From an anarchist point of view, the essential argument against more immigration should be obvious: A crowded society is a restrictive society; an overcrowded society becomes an authoritarian, repressive and murderous society. And so on. See Garrett Hardin, *Naked Emperors*, for some very efficient dispatching of the "limitless growth" doctrine.

Carry on, Edward Abbey—Oracle

New York Times Magazine   (25 MAY 1984)

Dear Editors:

It is hard to see what Saul Bellow means by saying that the notion of humans having a spiritual life, conscious or unconscious, is an "impermissible thought." Since when? Bellow himself has been promoting an occult theosophical doctrine known as Steinerism in the pages of his own books for at least fifteen years.

In the United States the Me Decade goes on and on, with a whole supermarket of spiritual soulstuffs—mysticism, Orientalism, personalism, fundamentalism, transcendentalism, Yoga, Moon and countless others—available to the discriminating spiritualistical shopper.

In the world as a whole it is certain that never before have so many been so deeply engaged in one form or another of religious experience, from the most exotic and esoteric to the most orthodox, traditional and institutional—see the Ayatollah Khomeni's contemporary Iran for a good working example of the latter.

In Iran we have a society that incorporates those features Bellow most admires: a rigid hierarchy of powers and titles, firm authoritarian rule, and best of all an enthusiastic belief in life after death, a belief so strong that hundreds of thousands of young Moslems are being sacrificed in a crackpot sectarian war. Iran is Bellow's kind of country; he'd like it there.

Edward Abbey—Oracle

Karen Evans   (18 JUNE 1984)

Dear Karen,

Okay, I'll give it a go. If you have further questions call me, mornings or evenings—before 9 A.M. or after 6 P.M. Or come for a day or two in Tucson if you can; it's not likely I'll get out of here this summer.

1) Yes.

2) Yes.

3) The same only more so.

4) With DS [*Desert Solitaire*] (1968) I was only getting started. In later books, such as *Monkey Wrench, Abbey's Road, Down the River, Black Sun, Good News* and *Beyond the Wall*, I've attempted to make explicit what was only implied in that early work. I have also ranged across a much wider field of subject matter, going beyond strictly environmental concerns toward more general social, political and philosophical matters, or what I like to call the comedy of human relationships.

What I am really writing about, what I have always written about, is the idea of human freedom, human community, the real world which makes both possible, and the new technocratic industrial state which threatens the existence of all three. Life and death, that's my subject, and always has been—if the reader will look beyond the assumptions of lazy critics and actually read what I have written. Which also means, quite often, reading between the lines: I am a comic writer and the generation of laughter is my aim.

5) Well, I'm against some establishments and for others, I regard the human family, the human community, as basic and fundamental. I regard the modern nation-state as a grotesque distortion of human community. The same goes for most other big social institutions, such as organized religion, science, the military and—that vague beehive (like a geodesic dome) which looms a hundred stories high above our future.

6) I am a pessimist in the short run, by which I mean the next fifty or maybe a hundred years. In that brief interval it seems quite probable that too many of us humans, crawling over one another for living space and sustenance, will make the earth an extremely unpleasant planet on which to live. And this quite aside from the possibility of a nuclear war.

In the long run, I am an optimist. Within a century, I believe and hope, there will be a drastic reduction in the human population (as has happened before), and that will make possible a free and open society for our surviving descendants, a return to a more intimate and tolerant relationship to the natural world, and an advance (not a repetition) toward a truly humane, liberal and civilized form of human society, politically and economically decentralized but unified, perhaps on a planetary scale, by slow and easy-going travel, unrestricted wandering for all and face-to-face (not electronic) communication between the more adventurous elements of human tribes, clans, races. Instant communication is not communication at all but merely a frantic, trivial, nerve-wracking bombardment of clichés, threats, fads, fashions, gibberish and advertising.

7) See above.

8) I no longer have much interest in the supernatural, or what is mistakenly referred to as "mystical" events and experience. That kind of search belongs to the youthful stage of life, both in the individual and in the race. I now find the most marvelous things in the everyday, the ordinary, the common, the simple and tangible.

For example: one cloud floating over one mountain. Or a trickle of water seeping from stone after a twenty-mile walk through the desert. Or the smile of recognition on the face of your own child when she hasn't seen you around for several hours. These are the deepest joys, as we learn to understand when we go into the middle age of life.

The love of a man for his wife, his child, of the land where he lives and works, is for me the real meaning of mystical experience. Those who waste their whole lives hungering for fantastic and occult sensations are suffering from retarded emotional development and stunted imaginations. One world and one life at a time, please. I have no desire to be reborn until I have exhausted every possibility of this life in this time on these few hundred square miles of earth I call my home.

9) I've suffered from my share of personal disasters: the loss of love, the death of a wife, the failure to realize in my writing the high aspiration of my intentions. But these misfortunes can be borne. There is a certain animal vitality in most of us which carries us through any trouble but the absolutely overwhelming. Only a fool has no sorrow, only an idiot has no grief—but then only a fool and an idiot will let grief and sorrow ride him down into the grave. So, I've been lucky, as most people are lucky; the animal in each of us has a lot more sense than our brains.

10) Yes, there are plenty of heroes and heroines everywhere you look. They are not famous people. They are generally obscure and modest people doing useful work, keeping their families together and taking an active part in the health of their communities, opposing what is evil (in one way or another) and defending what is good. Heroes do not want power over others. There are more heroic people in the public school system than there are in the world of politics, military, big business, the arts and the sciences combined. My mother is a heroine—has been all her life. And if you take a good look, you may see that your brother is a hero.

11) I have no blueprints to offer anybody. Most human societies, especially the so-called primitive or traditional societies, have been organized (spontaneously, voluntarily, democratically and instinctively) on natural and therefore decent principles. It is only in modern times, as I see it, that is, in the last five thousand years, that the drive to dominate nature and human nature has perverted and now threatens to destroy the sound, conservative, sustaining relationships of men and women.

Our institutions are too big; they represent not the best but the worst characteristics of human beings. By submitting to huge hierarchies of power, we gain freedom from personal responsibility for what we do and are forced to do—that is the seduction of it—but we lose the dignity of being real men and women. Power corrupts; attracts the worst and corrupts the best.

So what should we do, here and now, as individuals? Well, see above, item 10. Refuse to participate in evil; insist on taking part in what is healthy, generous, and responsible. Stand up, speak out, and when necessary fight back. Get down off the fence and lend a hand, grab a-hold, be a citizen—not a subject.

12) Nothing worth mentioning. I've led mostly a furtive, cowardly, reclusive life, preaching loudly from the sidelines and avoiding danger. If I regret anything, it is my good behavior.

13) I see that we've skipped #13. I despise superstition—but why take foolish chances?

14) The worst thing I've ever done? My best is none too good.

15) Beer cans are beautiful.

16) Spiritual people like myself do not fret over diet. I eat whatever's handy, if it looks good.

17) The Glen Canyon Dam makes a handy symbol of what is most evil and destructive in modern man's attack on the natural world. But it is only one small example among thousands.

18) No.

19) My friends and my family share with me a whole constellation of similar and encouraging desires. They are the basis of my life, essential and indispensable. We don't clash with one another, we clash with our enemies, of whom we always seem to have enough. And we enjoy the clash. Goethe put it nicely (in this amateur translation): Only they deserve liberty and life / Who earn it in the daily strife.

20) My personal life is an ordinary life, of no particular interest to others.

21) I don't know what McGuane means by calling someone a "cult hero." Maybe he knows. Most writers give public readings now and then—what of it? But of course you have to be invited.

22) I'm not interested in the technique of art or the art of technique. When I want to write something I just sit down (or stand up) and do it. Scribble, scribble, nothing could be easier. It helps, naturally, to have something to say.

23) Fiction is my primary interest. I've published six novels so far, have written a couple of others not yet published, and am presently halfway through a novel about life and death. Most of my effort has gone into fiction. Saving the world is only a hobby. Most of the time I do nothing.

24) Publisher's hype and reviewer's cant. By sticking a writer in a convenient mental box, the reviewers and critics save themselves the trouble of actually reading, understanding and thinking about the writer's work. But there are too many writers, too many books, too much glut and gluttony.

25) See above.

26) I've enjoyed the love of some pretty good women, the friendship of a few good men, and made my home in the part of this world I like best. What's left? I desire nothing but more of the same.

27) I took the other road, all right, but only because it was the easy road for me, the way I wanted to go. If I've encountered some unnecessary resistance that's because most of the traffic is going the other way.

28) About two years ago a herd of doctors gave me six months to live, because they believed what the C.A.T. scanner told them. As usual, the machine was wrong. My first thought, when they brought me the news, was that I wouldn't have to floss my teeth anymore. Then I wrote out a will and made a large deposit in a bank (a sperm bank) for my wife, who wanted a baby, just in case the six months remaining might not be sufficient to insure the success of the usual procedures. Then I wondered if I might have time to write one more book—a short one. I'm afraid I forgot all about Glen Canyon Dam.

Those were interesting times, but now it appears that, barring accidents, I'm in for the long haul: my father, at age eighty-three, is or should be flossing a few teeth of his own. And he still spends several hours every day out in the woods cutting down perfectly normal, healthy, pine trees—he's got a one-man logging business. But his eye is off a bit; a few months ago he was felling a tree, trying to lay it down as close as he could at the side of a flatbed truck; instead he dropped the tree into the front of the truck, smashed the bejesus out of both the cab and engine. He needed a new truck anyway.

Well Karen, this is fun but it's much too easy. If you wish to revise and colloquialize the more formal and sententious parts of my response, please do so—if you can make it read like a real conversation please do so. And if there's anything more you need, call me.

Regards, Ed Abbey—Oracle

David Petersen, Durango, Colorado (29 JUNE 1984)

Dear Dave,

I've read your article on sheep vs. coyotes and I like it, very much. As straight honest journalism I can't think of anything I'd add to it or take away. It's fair, objective, succinct and complete. Says enough but not too much.

Now, as to make a literary essay of it, something people would read for fun, pleasure, emotional thrills, as well as information, you'd have to go far beyond the neat journalistic format. You know how I'd do it; I'd inject a few anecdotes or stories based on personal, physical experience w/ coyotes & sheep. But there are many other techniques, such as talking w/ various people involved in the wool business. Etc.

As for my writing for T-MEN [*The Mother Earth News*], no; am too busy right now w/ other projects. But you are welcome to reprint anything you wish (except from *Solitaire*); contact Don Congdon for terms.

Good luck & best regards.

Ed A.

John Macrae, New York City (5 JULY 1984)

Dear Jack:

I've been pissing around for months now, doing interviews, reviews and introductions to books by other people, and delaying the hard moment when I must get to work on my own book. But I swear I'll be sending you the hundred sample pages of this new novel within the next three or four weeks.

In future reprintings of *Beyond the Wall*, would you please have the production department correct a few more misprints, as follows:

page 2, line 5, change "late November sun" to "early December sun"
page 9, line 23, change "Geological Service" to "Geological Survey"
and of course the awful misprint on page 34: delete the "Jay," please!

I like the blurb from Larry McMurtry, even though I am weary of being categorized as another regional Thoreau. But do we have to have it on the front of the book? I know it's partly my fault, but can't you slide it around to the back of the book?

Had dinner with McMurtry only three evenings ago, here in Tucson. He and Leslie Silko are writing a screenplay together. He thinks the misspelling of his name is amusing and appears to feel no annoyance about it whatsoever—he is a genial, relaxed and happy man—but feels sorry for his part in branding me as one more goddamned Son of Thoreau. So I let him do all the apologizing.

Onward.

Regards, Edward Abbey—Tucson

Arizona Daily Star (10 JULY 1984)

Dear Editor:

The gun control controversy goes on and on, with both supporters and opponents failing to deal with the central issue. The central issue is not the relative safety of handguns versus shotguns, or automobiles versus rifles, or pistols versus burglars, but rather the purpose and significance of the private ownership of firearms in general.

In a free society, the citizenry insist on their right to own weapons not because they wish to attack one another but because they must possess the means to defend themselves against the ever-present danger of police oppression and an authoritarian state. The slogan "If guns are outlawed, only the Government will have guns" may sound simplistic, but it states the essential truth: authority loves power; and power attracts the worst, corrupts the best.

Look around you. Does anyone think that our government officials are immune to such temptations, especially when they have to deal with a rapidly growing population, leading to more social conflict, leading to more demands for regulation and centralized control. The abuse of handguns is a false issue (ban handguns and the shotgun in the closet will become a more popular instrument for resolving family quarrels); the real issue is democratic freedom. As Citizen Tom Paine (a good man) once said, "Our liberties we prize; our rights we will maintain."

Edward Abbey—Oracle

John Macrae, New York City (22 SEPTEMBER 1984)

Dear Jack:

Don Congdon has forwarded on to me your note to him dated Sept 13th in which you apparently say that you will not offer a contract for my novel "at this stage." Naturally, I am very disappointed by your reaction, and greatly surprised; you'll recall that last Spring you urged me to show you a sample of the novel, along with a detailed outline, in return for a contract and an advance which you felt would aid me in completing the book. I took you up on the offer because by that time I had come to feel the same way.

Adventures of the Barbarian, or whatever I finally call it, is a complex and lengthy work. With a little over nine hundred longhand pages in ms now done, I have reached a point where the encouragement of a contract and the incentive of a deadline is exactly what I most want. Furthermore, I need the money.

I don't know why you think I'm "resisting" a contract. O! contraire. So I'm asking Don to show my samples to a few other NYC publishers. If, like you, they all turn it down, I will be forced to reconsider the whole project, maybe even drop it for the time being. Perhaps there is something fatally wrong with the basic idea and structure of the novel—though I don't think so. Or if New York doesn't like the book, I can easily get some small press, like North Point or Capra in California, to at least put the book in print. With a full year's work ahead of me on that book, I don't intend to go on without the certainty of some kind of publication and readership.

Of course the novel will be long—probably six- to eight-hundred pages in final form. But that is not an unusual length. Nor will it all be "late night Abbey," as you seem to fear. Essentially the book is a comedy, about surviving with laughter despite the worst that life throws at you. Sure, there are a couple of death scenes in the novel—but this is the story of fifty years in a man's life: how could it be otherwise? You must have noticed by now that my heroes never die—anymore than I do. This novel too will have a happy ending. Guaranteed.

Anyhow, if nobody wants to publish this novel, there are two other books I've got in mind for the near future: a book about the growing disaster of contemporary Mexico—*On the Edge of the Volcano: Mexico Today*—and a sequel to *The Monkey Wrench Gang*—*Hayduke Lives!*

And maybe a book about Australia, if anyone's interested—*The Luckiest Country*—and a short novel about the life and times of ordinary "blue collar" working people, like my brother Howard and his family, and my neighbors right here in Tucson—*Country Blues*.

Let me know if you're interested in any of these other ideas.

Sincerely, Edward Abbey—Tucson

cc to Don Congdon

American West Magazine, Tucson (27 OCTOBER 1984)

Dear Sir:

The October-November issue of *American West* is first rate; I like especially the splendid article by Douglas Peacock on his life among the GRIZZER, and I look forward to reading his book on the subject.

About the Navajo people and their perennial problems, I would like to make the following no doubt unwelcome comment: If the Navajos truly want to preserve their cultural integrity as a tribe (which I'm inclined to doubt), they must face up to the truth that their basic problem is not economic, political or social, but biological.

Consider the facts: In 1890 when the Navajos were resettled on their present reservation, they numbered about 15,000; today the tribal population is something over 160,000 and growing fast, at a rate greater than any other American sub-group except the Hispanics and the Mormons. In brief, the Navajos have greatly out-bred and exceeded the carrying capacity of their range; the land cannot support one-tenth their present number.

Industrialization is not the answer: Transforming the reservation into a Greater Newark, N. J., would merely compound their troubles by encouraging even faster population growth, completing the destruction of their land and traditions, confirming the majority in their passive acceptance of Federal hand-outs for survival and condemning the employable remainder to a helpless dependence on our screwball boom-and-bust planetary economy.

What is the solution? The solution is obvious but I am not going to spell it out in this letter. If the Navajos really want to regain the pride, dignity and freedom of an independent people, they must stop feeling sorry for themselves, and stop looking to outsiders for aid. Let them confront the facts of their situation and act upon it. What they need more than anything else is the strong tonic of self-reliance.

Sincerely, Edward Abbey—Oracle

Carroll Ballard, Hollywood, California (26 FEBRUARY 1985)

Dear Carroll,

Your phone call of last night leaves me feeling baffled and a mite discouraged. I wrote that screenplay to your specifications, following step by step the sequence of scenes as listed in your outline of Feb the first.

And now you tell me you don't like it.

Take the bridge-blowing scene: it was your idea, not mine, to have the attempt fail because of Bishop Love driving onto the bridge. In my own outline, or "treatment," as you can see, the bridge is destroyed, albeit inadvertently, by gunfire, setting off Hayduke's charges—and then the pursuit begins in earnest.

Also, in my original version, the bridge is a railway bridge, and a supply train is partially destroyed by the blast. But you wanted to make it a highway bridge, I forget why. Now you think it should be a railway bridge again—which was my plan all along: the nuclear railroad.

What we do not need is a bridge-blowing scene in either the prologue or epilogue of the movie: that is bound to give the movie-goer a misleading notion of what is to follow, setting up false expectations. *The Monkey Wrench Gang* is a comedy about a bunch of amateur saboteurs; the violence should be kept to a minimum to avoid falling into cinematic clichés. One big blast ⅔ thru the film, followed by the shootout near the end, should be sufficient.

As to establishing Doc and Bonnie's motivations for engaging in industrial sabotage, I don't see how I can do more than I've already done: or why I should. Like Smith and Hayduke, they are dedicated conservationists, wilderness lovers, eco-freaks. Why belabor the point? The fact that they are shown participating in illegal and risky actions in defense of the canyonlands establishes their convictions; everybody knows by now what environmentalism is all about, whether they sympathize with the cause or not. (And most Americans, if we can believe the polls, do sympathize.)

I can't remember what else you think is wrong with the script, but I'd be happy to confer with you again, if you want to come to Tucson. Anytime. Spend a week here, if you wish, and we'll try to revise the script together. But I'm not going to spend another three or four weeks writing a whole new screenplay unless Paramount comes across with more money. I have other work to do.

Regards

PS: Think some more about the GEM: the ideal villain!

Outside Magazine, Chicago   (28 FEBRUARY 1985)

Dear Editors:

As "Outsider of the Year," I want to nominate Mr David Foreman, chief organizer and unofficial leader of the conservationist group known as Earth First! (Always spelled with the exclamation mark.)

Ably assisted by a number of friends, of course, who should also be named (and I do not include myself, since my role has been largely passive), Mr Foreman has given the nearly moribund environmental movement new life, renewed vigor, a sense of humor, and perhaps most important, a sense of conservationist activism as a manly, womanly endeavor requiring direct personal participation, physical as well as moral courage and the willingness to risk injury, arrest, even public scorn (of a kind) for the sake of preserving what remains of the great and original American wilderness.

I could cite many examples of Mr Foreman's brave risk-taking for a cause he believes in, but one will have to suffice here: In the effort to preserve the Kalmiopsis Wilderness of northern California/southern Oregon from a Forest Service logging-road project, Dave Foreman was deliberately hit and run over by somebody driving a pickup truck owned by the Plumley Construction Company. This happened during a planned, open, well-publicized protest demonstration with local police observing. As usually happens in such incidents, the police arrested the victim, not the culprit.

Because of internal injuries suffered from the attack, Foreman has not fully recovered his health. Nevertheless, he continued and still continues his leadership role in Earth First!, organizing acts of civil disobedience (in the tradition of Martin Luther King), editing the *EF! Journal*, traveling around the country in support of the conservationist cause and taking full part in the tedious but essential work of lobbying politicians and bureaucrats.

Whether the new tactics and attitudes raised by EF! will be enough to save our wilderness remains to be seen; it is clear that conventional political methods have failed. At least Earth First! is making an heroic final effort. Dave Foreman is an authentic American hero.

Edward Abbey—Oracle

The Bloomsbury Review, Denver, Colorado (7 MARCH 1985)

To the Editor:

Reading your "Brave New Visions of Science," I was reminded of Samuel Johnson's remark, "Whatever is remote from common appearances is always welcome to vulgar, as to childish, credulity."

Your science reviewers, like many of today's American writers, suffer not merely from vulgar, childish credulity in regard to science-and-technology, but from a serious streak of moral servility. The majority gape at the activity of our scientific technicians in the attitude of genuflection. On your knees, commoners!

Meanwhile, the obvious, inescapable, simple truth of American life is that we are surrounded by gibbering electronic machines that make daily existence a neurotic ordeal, while overhead, undergoing constant refinement, hangs the nightmare of total annihilation. The one great gift of modern scientists to humanity is the nuclear bomb. (How can we ever thank them?)

Recent history demonstrates that scientists, as a class, are as happy working for a Hitler or a Stalin as for the oligarchs of the USA. Most scientists work their specialized niches as servants for commerce, industry, government or war. (And what's the difference?) These millions of little men in white smocks, busily torturing atoms and animals in their laboratories, are generally up to no good, and should be kept under strict public control.

Sincerely, Edward Abbey

Linda Hagen, Manager, Cabeza Prieta National Wildlife Refuge, Ajo, Arizona (7 MAY 1985)

Dear Ms Hagen:

The Cabeza Prieta is the best desert wilderness area left in the USA. Along with the Tinajas Altas range, and the adjoining Pinacate region in Mexico, the whole region should be made an international wilderness preserve. Mexico's Highway 2 would be sufficient to provide motorized access to the center of it, together with roads presently in use in the adjacent Organ Pipe Cactus [National Monument] and the US Interstate highway on the north. The old jeep track known as El Camino Diablo, together with the connecting network of jeep trails to Charlie Bell Well, and in the Tule Valley, Mohawk Valley, Growler Valley and Cabeza Prieta mountain range, should be permanently closed to all motorized traffic.

Developing this splendid region for tourism by re-opening the old jeep roads would be a tragic mistake, and must not happen. There is no need and no demand on the part of the motoring public for such development. The Organ Pipe Cactus NM road system is already in place, in use, and provides more than adequate access to the desert for those who are willing to travel only in cars and trucks.

As for the bighorn trophy hunters, they should be encouraged to pursue their hobby by means of the horse, the mule, the burro and on foot. Such truly primitive style hunting would make success in the area a much more satisfying achievement.

The ORV users have done so much damage to the American desert already, it would be a crying shame to invite them into the wonderful Cabeza Prieta Wildlife Refuge. I am shocked that such a change in management is even being considered, especially since we had thought that the Cabeza Prieta was going to be included in the Wilderness Preservation system. What happened?

Please give full consideration to my suggestions and put me on your mailing list: I want to be informed of all proposals for policy changes in the Cabeza Prieta NWR.

Sincerely, Edward Abbey—Oracle

Copies to Rep Morris Udall
The AZ Daily Star
The AZ Republic

John Macrae, New York City   (31 MAY 1985)

Dear Jack:

Thank you for your letter of May 22nd. Sorry I missed you in New York but I was overcome by nostalgia, homesickness etc., and had to clear out sooner than planned. However, I did get to see my son perform in *Midsummer Night's Dream*; we also saw a performance of Shepherd's *Curse of the*

Starving Class. (The first good, the second only fair.) My lecture at Harvard a few days earlier was attended by about 150 proper Bostonians; not bad, they said, for a night in "Reading" Week. I talked about the writer's role in America, his duty to be a critic of society etc., that sort of thing. The audience laughed at most of the right places. Only a few people walked out.

I am glad that you have decided to publish my *Confessions of the Barbarian*, and I look forward to completing the book. This will be a major effort on my part; and if it fails to be my best book, then I'm going back to horseshoeing and cattle stealing. Of course, I want your editorial help and advice in revising and reshaping the work as a whole, but, as I've said before, it would be easier for me to finish the first draft of the book and then to hear what you have to say about improving it. An extra $15,000 in the advance would be a strong inducement to making the opening, as you say "more accessible" and "less rough," and I am naturally eager to learn exactly what you mean by those terms. Certainly, I want to capture the reader's attention from the beginning and hold it until the end: that is half the purpose of my art. The other half must be to tell my story in the most honest way that I can.

Best regards, Edward Abbey—Tucson

Jim Harrison, Lake Leelanau, Michigan (6 JUNE 1985)

Dear Jim,

Just recently read *Sun Dog* and cannot forebear making a few comments, tho' I know I shouldn't do this.

First, I admire, more than ever, the power and grace of your style, the vivid rendering of the physical scene—you manage to make even Michigan sound like a land of splendor and mystery.

But why for godsake why did you have to make the hero of your book this goddamn Bechtel Corporation type, this sleazy asshole of a construction engineer who flies (first class, always) around the world building more and more useless, destructive, ugly and wasteful dams? Why?

These people are the worst vermin in modern society; they are parasites; they do more damage than the nuclear bomb builders. Surely by now you've read about the effects of the Aswan Dam in Egypt, for example: the flooding of ancient homelands and temples, the downstream ruin of the fishing and farming communities in the Nile Delta, the schistosomiasis that infests the irrigation canals, all this to generate electrical power to glorify the already swollen power of a few militaristic oligarchs who run things in that miserable country. The dam doesn't solve anything; population growth among those benighted A-rabs has already outstripped the limited agricultural benefits of the dam.

As with Aswan, so elsewhere: in the Amazon, in the Zambezi, in North America; lands destroyed, communities ruined, ancient and beautiful networks of life submerged, to create huge stagnant playgrounds for the speedboat tourist and motorboat fisherman and suchlike scum. All for the sake of Power. POWER! P O W E R!

Good God, Jim, there are terrible things going on in the world today. Why are writers like you and McGuane so afraid to stick your necks out, to touch anything controversial, difficult, dangerous? Why toady to the rich and powerful? You don't need them. Why pander to the East Coast literati? You don't need them either. (The best publisher in the country today is North Point Press in Berkeley.)

No more YUPPIE heroes. Please.

Yours fraternally, Edward Abbey—Oracle

Carroll Ballard, Hollywood, California   (26 JUNE 1985)

Dear Carroll:

Just received your letter and screenplay for MWG. I've been camping out in the hills for the last three weeks, didn't get into Salt Lake until day before yesterday.

So, I've read your screenplay and like everything about it except the title. To me it seems like a good script, ready for shooting. I especially like the opening and closing scenes with turtle (even if I did think of that myself).

However, if you and Bob Kaplan want me to write another version, I'd be glad to take a crack at it, following the general guidelines you suggest. I'll send a letter to Don Congdon today, ask him to contact Kaplan and make some kind of deal. Once I brood on this problem for a while and get a good basic idea, I think I should be able to type up a new screenplay in about six to eight weeks.

I'll be in Berkeley, San Francisco and Palo Alto July 12–14th, signing the new R. Crumb edition of *The Monkey Wrench Gang* (and other books) for something called The Nature Company, a Bay-area bookseller. Perhaps we could get together for a few hours on one of those days. I expect to spend most of the rest of the summer here in the Salt Lake area, returning to Tucson sometime in September.

I'm sure the best strategy would be for you and Kaplan to hire a hotshot professional screenwriter, and get some big-name movie star interested in a film of *Monkey Wrench Gang*, but if that is not in the cards then I will do my best to help out. If this connection with Paramount really is, as you say, our last good chance to see a film made of my book, then I must help out—if I can.

Best regards, Edward Abbey—Salt Lake City, Utah

cc to Don Congdon

Northern Lights, Missoula, Montana (24 AUGUST 1985)

Dear Editor:

The long, tedious and rambling "speech" by Edward Abbey reads as if it were based on notes scribbled on a memo pad by a drunken author during a bumpy airplane ride from Pocatello to Lewiston, Idaho (so it was), and then further mangled, garbled, expurgated and redacted by a baffled stenographer trying to make sense of a tape recording of that same interminable lecture (she did the best she could). This explains the curious elisions and such solecisms as "chick grass" for "cheat grass." (Or maybe there really is such a thing as chick grass up there in Montana.) None of these imperfections can be blamed on the editor of *Northern Lights*; author Abbey was given an opportunity to proofread the galleys of "On Truth, Cattle and Cowboys etc.," but never got around to it.

Although my official policy is NEVER APOLOGIZE NEVER EXPLAIN, I will make an exception to the rule this one time and hereby humbly apologize for the generally meek mild temporizing tone of my address to the citizens of Montana. Why? Because, on returning to Arizona, I learned that the Forest Service ("our" public servant) is planning to spray some kind of

Union Carbide poison on several thousand acres of mesquite in order to benefit three or four beef ranchers. And this despite the fact that hundreds of people now live in the area and thousands more use it for recreation. Is there no limit to the greed, arrogance and stupidity of the livestock industry? No: there is not.

Regards, Edward Abbey—Oracle

Doug Peacock, Glacier National Park, Montana (OCTOBER 1985)

Dear Dugles,

You're not the only one who's wacko. I've been in a deep purple funk for months and for no good reason at all. I used to be a happy manic-depressive: no matter how depressed I might get, at least I had the manic phase to look forward to. (Like the end of tourist season at the Parks.) Now, nothing but sloth, torpor, lethargy and a weird bleak black melancholia that stinks of despair.

Why? Don't know; that's the most depressing thing about it. Some chemical imbalance, maybe. Probly should start popping lithium tabs.

I got a contract for this fat novel, and an advance which I've already spent, but haven't written a word on the God damned book since last April. Why not? Sloth. Indolence, Acedia. Stagnation. Wrath. Envy. Pride. (Too proud to work anymore.) Gluttony. Lust. Avarice. All the Seven Deadly Sins and I'm hooked on at least five of them. Six.

For no good reason. I've got a good wife and my little Rebecca is pure delight, and even Susie and I get along fairly well, and my body is holding up to its normal crimped flabby model and I've got a book to write and the world by the tail with a downhill pull and everything is hunky-dory and every morning I wake up thinking I should stick a pistol in my belt and start walking west . . . and never come back.

Transmission problems. Can't get my ass in gear. I did climb a couple of 13ers near Durango [Colorado] last August and wrote a couple of magazine articles and finally made it down the Salmon River, but that's about all I've done besides brood and stew and piss and shit for six months. And you think you got troubles. In the art of self-pity, you're a rank amateur.

Poor old Alan H. is worse off than either of us. His wife went back to NYC, both his kids hate him and are also in NYC, his novel was rejected by every publisher he showed it to, his agent is an alcoholic, the IRS is auditing his 1982 tax returns and his doctor won't even allow him to drink anymore—nothing but Chablis! And I think I've got troubles.

Spiritual death . . . Well Doug old buddy, I'm doing my best to cheer you up. As some Frenchman said (Voltaire?): "It is not sufficient that we be happy; it is necessary that others be miserable." Your struggles to get your book through that S&S digestive system are maddening, exasperating, infuriating: in your place I'd be contemplating REDRUM. As no doubt you are. Did you ever get any help from Congdon? I'm sure that once your book is actually published it will be a hit, maybe a big hit, and your name will be in neon and you'll get enough invitations for this and that to drive you insufferable with arrogance. So don't let up on them.

Meantime—you should probly look for a job.

No, no, I'm only kidding. But you should let Lisa and the kids come home. The weather is nice down here now, temp in the eighties, huge vast roiling cloudscapes and obscenely lurid sunsets and sunrises (being an insomniac, I seldom miss a sunrise) and the owls are hooting, the javelinas clacking their tusks at two in the morning, the coyotes yodeling, the crickets chanting their autumnal dirge etc etc.

Read a book called *Naples '44* last night and I've been wallowing in nostalgia all day, thinking of Italy, Amalfi, Capri, Sorrento, Vesuvius, the sweet young whores, the cornutos and pizza and scugnizzi and my Harley 45 with the 88mm brass cannon shell for a tailpipe, and all my cunt-crazy buddies in the 349th Infantry Regiment who are probly dead by now, or in prison for life, or wearing Pacemakers or getting transplants or still paying alimony or lined up outside the Salvation Army or beating their heads against rubber walls in some VA hospital or—who knows?—maybe a few of them actually marching into late middle age with dignity, in good mental and moral health, doing socially useful work and patting their grandchildren on the head. Who knows? I haven't heard a word from any of them now for twenty-five years.

The madness of our chaotic, improvised, desperate lives . . .

Thanks for the note from Benson. Tell him that, by my standards, it still looks like a needle-dick to me.

Don's been here a coupla times. He and Ann now officially legally "finally" divorced but still good friends. Don's living in a condo-pad on River Road and helping somebody build a hourse—I mean house. Hope to get him started on a cabin for me up at Cliff Dwellers sometime this winter. The Developers are closing in around us here. Hope to move out in a year. I still love the Sonoran Desert but Tucson is a foul mess. Don seems no more wretched, lost and discontented than usual. Like Alan H. he's already got a new girlfriend. Life goes on!

Grandma Pepper bought my Susie a brand-new car—Nissan and red—for her birthday. I never owned a new car in my life, except that Datsun pickup, which I sold two weeks ago for $1300. Shoulda kept it.

We miss you, Doug. (You too Lisa.) Come back!

David Petersen, Durango, Colorado (1 NOVEMBER 1985)

Dear Dave,

You ask, Why do I support Earth First!?

Let's say it's because I see Earth First! as precisely the sort of spontaneous, anarchic, extemporaneous uprising I most admire. Beginning at bedrock bottom, where all authentic rebellions must find basic footing, it has nowhere to go but onward and upward, for some as yet undetermined distance, before it is clubbed down and smashed like all of its predecessors have been in the modern era. By "modern era" I mean, of course, the last ten thousand years—or since the invention of agriculture, serfdom, urban living, the standing army, hierarchy, oligarchy and Tyrannosaurus Rex: the State.

How's that for wild-eyed rhetoric? Best regards from

Your brother, Ed—Oracle

Sierra Club, San Francisco (19 NOVEMBER 1985)

Dear Sierra Clubbers:

I wish I could be there for your December 5th "Celebration," but I probably won't be.

Please pass on my best regards to Dave Brower and Stewart Udall; I wish them nothing but victories from here on out—and a few good laughs if things don't quite work out that way.

And if you wish, read the following message to those who attend the "Celebration":

To my fellow river rats, peak baggers, desert freaks and canyon cranks:

The canyonlands country of southern Utah is the most weird, wonderful, magical place on earth—there is nothing else like it anywhere. We must make an all-out effort to save not part of it but all of it. No more compromise—no more giving away three quarters in order to save one quarter. These public lands are the property of every American from Maine to California, and if necessary we should make the saving of them a national issue.

Personally, I support the Earth First! proposal for Utah: not 3 million acres, not 5 million acres, but all 16 million acres of BLM roadless areas should be preserved, permanently and forever, as a wilderness home for the mule deer, the turkey buzzard, the bighorn sheep, the faded midget rattlesnake, the mountain lion, the whiptail lizard and all other citizens, of whatever genus or species, who love the land—for God's sake, for its own sake, and for our sake.

Cheers, Edward Abbey—Oracle

PS: Contribution enclosed.

Newsweek, New York City (1 DECEMBER 1985)

Dear Editors:

George Will gloating over the failure of the Geneva conference to curb the suicidal nuclear arms race must raise a serious question about your columnist's order of values. In fact he would appear to be morally irresponsible—and it shows in his face: he looks like one of those mean, gelid, teacup-pinching women in Grant Wood's painting *Daughters of Revolution*.

Why not replace Mr Will and his stale predictable push-button opinions with somebody new, or at least different, who might offer us a fresh point of view? With Gary Wills, for example; or Kurt Vonnegut; or Wendell Berry; or Noam Chomsky; or the historian William Appleman Williams; or Governor Richard Lamm; or that famous unknown author from the Wild West, young Mr Edward Abbey?

Sincerely, Edward Abbey—Oracle

Arizona Daily Star   (5 DECEMBER 1985)

Dear Editor:

In your editorial, "War Remembrance," you chide Terry Choate for proposing to build a memorial honoring those who fought against the Vietnam War. You base your objection on the grounds that such a monument would "reopen old political wounds."

That is precisely the point. Those wounds have not healed, and they never will heal until we as a nation find the moral courage, as the Germans have done, to face up to and acknowledge the truth that our Government committed not merely a blunder but a vast crime against the people of Vietnam and against the young Americans who were conscripted to fight there. The war against Vietnam was an unjust war—criminal, cowardly, atrocious, dishonorable. As in our many other imperial wars against the American Indians, against the Mexicans in 1848, against the South in 1861–65, against the Filipinos in 1899–1901, against Nicaragua, Guatemala and El Salvador right now, the driving purpose was expansion of American power. There are two evil empires fastened on our planet at present and the Soviet Union is only one of them. Men and women of honor must oppose both.

Edward Abbey—Oracle

Gerald Marzorati, Harper's, New York City   (11 MARCH 1985)

Dear Mr Marzorati:

Herewith my reply to the critics of "Bad Guys in White Hats":

It's good to know that so many people share my interest in cowboys, ranchers and our public lands. In addition to the letters shown above, about a hundred others were sent to my home address, many of a highly personal nature and most too enthusiastic to be printed in a decent family magazine like *Harper's*.

Now to the business at hand.

Mr Beer agrees with my central thesis, that the public rangelands are overstocked and overgrazed. He differs from me in placing primary blame on the responsible government agencies. I agree with him that the Forest Service, the Bureau of Land Management and the Fish and Wildlife Service have done a poor job, but I think they do a poor job because of the undue political power exercised by the livestock lobby and its hired politicians here in the West.

Mr Beer raises the question of wildlife exploiting private property. Indeed that is a problem for many ranchers; it is not the problem I was attempting to deal with. He also accuses me of speaking only for some elite group of "sports." Wrong: I was speaking for myself, the wildlife and the general health of the land.

Lee Hollingsworth thinks my college buddy was only another urban cowboy. Not so. My friend "Mack" now owns and operates a working cattle outfit in New Mexico.

To Mr Eppers I say this: All citizens should enjoy the privilege of living on, with and for the land. When the American population is reduced to a sane and rational number (say about 50 million), we can do so. Until then, however, the public lands should be reserved for the pleasure of everyone and for the livelihood of our most underprivileged minority—the native wildlife.

Georgia Jones suggests making an open-season range of Manhattan Island. From what I hear, Manhattan—like Los Angeles—has already become exactly that.

Barbara Myers is mistaken. In the West as a whole, nearly all forms of wildlife have lost habitat and declined greatly in numbers since the advent of livestock grazing. The elk, the buffalo, the bear, the lion, the bighorn sheep, the wolf, the pronghorn antelope do not need electrified water wells—they need room to live.

Governor Herschler is partly right: As a place to live, Wyoming is still more pleasant than New Jersey or California. But he and his fellow promoters, developers and empire builders—throughout the West—are doing their best to change all that.

Sid Goodloe is correct: the abuse of public lands by "recreational vehicles" will soon equal and surpass the damage done by a century of overgrazing. We should stop it.

To Robert A. Jaynes—always talk back. Don't let an old desert rat like me buffalo a young cattleperson like you.

Finally, again, do cowboys work hard? Of course they do—part of the time. And they love it.

Edward Abbey—Oracle

1986

VACATIONING IN MEXICO . . . summering in Moab . . . Clarke announces she is pregnant again . . . medical problems worsen . . . hard at work on *The Fool's Progress* . . . a relatively quiet year.

Ms. Shute (12 FEBRUARY 1986)

Dear Ms Shute:

Thinking about your request for suggestions on great four-wheel-drive trips, I find that I cannot really help you much. There were some good ones: down Baja California before the Mexicans paved the road; from coast to coast through central Australia; from Algiers to Capetown in Africa; and into the many odd corners of the Great American Desert in our own Southwest.

But now I find that I am weary of such adventures. Not because I'm sinking deeper and deeper into my Late Middle Age—arthritic joints make mechanical travel more tempting, not less—but because the Jeep, the Blazer, the Bronco, the Land Cruiser, the Ram and all their many four-by-four cousins have become a plague upon the land.

The ideal off-road journey? I'll tell you: under water. I would like to see every four-by-four on earth, every three-wheeler, every dirt bike, trail bike and Big Foot truck driven straight into the Marianas Trench, three thousand feet below the surface of the Pacific Ocean, and parked there—left there—for the duration.

For the duration of what? For the duration of this techno-industrial-commercial slime-mold that is transforming our planet into one vast battleground of Cretins against Nature. With the Cretins winning.

What's wrong with the horse? Or the burro? Or the bicycle? Or even, God help us, the human foot? Why should not Americans especially learn to walk again? There is this to be said for walking: it is the one method of human locomotion by which a man or woman proceeds erect, upright, proud and independent, not squatting on the haunches like a frog.

Little boys love machines. Grown-up men and women like to walk.

Sincerely, Edward Abbey—Oracle

Mr. Austin (14 MARCH 1986)

Dear Mr Austin:

Much thanks for your letter. I was away for three weeks and only got your letter yesterday, however, so I suppose it's too late to help you with your college paper on conservation or whatever it is. I tried to telephone you last night but you were out; I left my phone number with your wife (or daughter?) but you didn't call back.

Anyhow—I enjoyed your letter and certainly appreciate your interest in my books. (They are all available, by the way, at Ken Sleight's bookstore in Moab.) As to my role in the Earth First! outfit, or "radical environmentalism" in general, well, about all I do is contribute a little money now and then (my tithe), and on rare occasions make a speech for them. Otherwise I'm no help at all: I don't go to meetings, lobby politicians, write to bureaucrats (any more) or even engage in any practical night-shift work, other than accidentally stumbling into a survey stake now and then when I'm trying to find a place to lay my bedroll.

Old Cal Black is not a bad guy, I've met him a couple of times, and I like and respect him as a person, as an individual. Of course his dedication to industrial development, whatever the cost to other values, sticks in my craw. There we disagree: directly but not—I hope—violently.

I hate and fear violence myself, have always avoided barroom brawls, and tho' I'm a bit of a gun-nut, and a member of the NRA, I never shoot at anything but beer cans and mule deer. (In season.) And seldom hit either, except by accident.

Well, this is too late to do you any good, but what the hell, I like your letter and next time I come through Blanding I'll give you a call and maybe we can have a talk, if you wish. If you ever come down to the Tucson area give me a call.

Say hello to Cal for me and give my best regards to Sheriff Wright—a good man.

Sincerely, Edward Abbey—Oracle

Ann Zwinger, Colorado Springs, Colorado   (MARCH 1986)

Dear Ann—

Just been looking thru the new edition of [Zwinger's] *Wind in the Rock* from U of A Press.

What a rich & lovely book it is—rich in information (all the details I keep forgetting), and lovely in its graceful style, luminous tone and quiet reverence for that land we love.

Fraternally, Ed Abbey

Carroll Ballard, Hollywood, California   (17 MAY 1986)

Dear Carroll,

Rec'd your long letter of May 15th and have considered your many suggestions for a new version of our screenplay. Sounds good to me and I think somebody should type it up as you propose—but not me. When this latest version is ready, then I will go over it, as agreed, and touch up the dialogue when and if needed—the final "polish."

You'll probly think I'm malingering but Carroll, I've already spent over three months on this screenplay—these several screenplays, actually—and I must get back to work on my goddamn novel. I have a contract for this book, it will be published—if I finish it—and I have an October first deadline to meet. And there's an advance . . . awaiting me when I complete the job. And a real, tangible book; an *objet d'art*, I hope, which will fit nicely (like a cocked and tumescent torpedo) in the right hand.

Frankly, it seems to me I've already earned my $25,000 from Paramount. In January, I wrote a twelve-page treatment, attended the first conference, came home and wrote a complete 133-page screenplay which I still think is the best version anyone has done so far. I was finally paid for that . . . some three-four weeks ago.

Then you came to Tucson and we spent four or five days revising or "polishing" my/your screenplay. I have still not been paid for that job, which we did—when?—back in early April sometime. Early March!

And two weeks ago I flew to L.A. for another conference, which was largely a waste of time; that business could just as easily have been done through the mail. And then I came home and wrote two more entirely new scenes for you. And I am ready, willing and happy to do the final "polish," whatever that means, whenever you and Kaplanax and Paramount agree on what the final screenplay should be. But I am not willing to write what amounts to another new screenplay, on speculation, especially since, so far as I can tell, the moguls at Paramount are not really committed to this project yet.

Furthermore, most of what you ask for in your letter has already been done, in one form or another, and I don't feel like re-doing it all in one more version. The only thing you want which I have not already provided is a speech by Doc attacking the nuke waste dump in Canyonlands, a speech which I think is unnecessary, redundant and from a cinematic point of view not very interesting.

Meanwhile, Paramount has obtained what apparently amounts to an indefinite option on my *Monkey Wrench* book for a measly $10,000, while the Screenwriter's Guild duns me for their $1000 initiation fee. (I gave them a $100 option on it.)

So now what? Okay, I'll write Doc's speech to the hearing, right now, and send it along with this letter. But I simply cannot afford to do all the cutting and pasting and re-typing which your continual and repeated visions and revisions require. I can't afford the time. To do all that you ask would take me at least two weeks, with most of it more or less merely altered versions of work that you and I have already done.

Do I sound a bit exasperated? Weary? Discouraged? Put upon? Yes I do—and I am. My wife thinks I'm being bitchy about this, and maybe I am. But that's truly the way I feel.

I don't blame you for these complications. My agent should have got me a better deal in the first place, and I could've done the whole job last summer, when I had the time free. I have complete faith in you, Carroll. I know that when some producer gives you the money to get going you will make a great and resounding movie of this story. And Christ, if I had nothing else to do at this time, no other job to complete, I'd be willing to tackle the project again, from the beginning, even without a contract. But my first obligation now is to my publisher; I'm already three months behind on my promised delivery of the book to him. (Jack Macrae at Holt.) I mean I had promised him a complete first draft of the novel by May Day—1986!

Now: a slug of cough syrup and I'll get into Doc's speech.

Regards, Ed—Tucson

Cliff Woods and Family (22 MAY 1986)

Dear Cliff and Family,

I hear from Douglas that you people were offended, maybe even hurt, by some of the things I said in that article about the beef industry that was reprinted in the *Arizona Star*. Well, I guess I can't blame you and I'm not surprised. I was attacking the beef industry (and the woolgrowers); I really would like to see domestic livestock eventually removed from our public lands—especially the national parks, national forests and national (BLM) rangelands—where other uses, such as hunting, fishing, camping, human recreation and habitat for wildlife—seem to me more important and in conflict with the traditional grazing business.

But the beef industry tends to try to hide behind the great American love affair with the cowboy; therefore I could not resist the temptation to poke a little fun at the Marlboro Man and the old cowboy image. My notion of "fun," I suppose, looks like ridicule to others, and I can understand why some of my friends (not ex-friends, I hope) were annoyed by my remarks.

It would do no good to apologize for what I said about cowboys and ranchers. Too late to take it all back or eat my words. Furthermore, it would be false on my part, because I really meant what I said. All that I can do then is to remind you that I did allow for "a few honorable exceptions" in my attack on ranchers and I had people like you in mind when I spoke of exceptions. (I enclose the original script of the speech I made at the University of Montana; the speech was transcribed on tape and parts of it printed in a Montana magazine called *Northern Lights*, then reprinted in *Harper's* Magazine, then reprinted in various newspapers around the country—so I've made at least ten thousand new enemies. Something I hardly needed.) Anyhow, if you read the enclosed script, perhaps it will ease your minds a little bit concerning my attitude.

If not, I would regret it very much, for I have always admired and respected you people—all of you, the whole family—and hope that we can continue to be friends. I still want to see you again, from time to time, and get Uncle Cliff's stories down on tape—as soon as I finish this goddamned novel I'm working on. But if you don't want to see me anymore I guess I could not blame you one bit. Or if you'd like to tell me face to face what you think of me and that article I would certainly oblige; I'll even buy the drinks. Let me know.

Regards–Tucson

Cormac McCarthy (15 JUNE 1986)

Have just read *Blood Meridian*. A beautiful terrible splendid book. You must have made a compact with the Judge Hisself to write such a book. I envy you your powers, salute your achievement and dread not a little for the safety of your soul.

Luckily, altho' wholly true, your book is not the whole truth—which you know as well as I. Now I must read your other books while looking forward to your next.

Good fortune . . . E.A.—Tucson

The New Yorker (20 JUNE 1986)

Dear Editors:

Please include me out of your "Am. Best" celebration. The nat'l parks which you imagine as havens of wilderness have been largely taken over by the profit-minded developers of industrial tourism. Those venture capitalists you praise are the types who'd sacrifice all human & natural values to the god of commercial avarice (a mortal sin). The technologists you cite as the envy of even the (robotic) Japs are the servants in the main of big business, gov't & war—not of human well-being.

The end result of this orgiastic self-aggrandizement has been the reduction of the majority of Americans to the status of indentured employees—helpless dependents on gov't & industry. They may be the best cared for & most lavishly entertained serfs in history but they are serfs all the same.

That pop. culture of TV, rock "music," home video, mechanical recreation & plastic architecture—from Sinatra to Springsteen, from Disney to . . . ?—is the culture of helots. Whatever became of Jefferson's vision of a society of self-reliant, independent freeholders? Of Lincoln's dream of a true democracy—gov't by the people? Lost, crushed, buried beneath an avalanche of greed and garbage.

Yrs., Edward Abbey—Moab

Moab Times-Independent, Utah (SUMMER 1986)

Dear Sam:

Please allow me to respond to critics of my recent letter, etc. In return I promise to shut up forever on the subject of the Sacred Cow and kindred matters. At least in the vicinity of Moab.

In regard to the beef rancher and his cow, I must stand by my original statement: the beef cow on our public lands is a public nuisance. Worse, beef cattle eat up forage and browse which could be used to support a much larger population of elk (especially elk) as well as mule deer, bighorn sheep and pronghorn antelope. And buffalo. Everyone who cares about hunting should ponder this fact. And everyone I've talked to about it agrees with me—in private. Beef ranching on our public lands is a taxpayer-supported industry whose time has come and gone. Let's give it a decent Christian burial and be done with it.

As to the charge that I am a cranky old man, I plead guilty. Born in 1927, I am therefore fifty-nine years old at this point in time. Tragic but true. That's what happens when you keep hanging around. And if I seem cranky it's because I first came to the canyon country in 1949 when it was still free, wild, undamned and beautiful. So for thirty-seven years I have been forced to witness the gradual destruction of this land by commercial greed, by a blind brutal industrialism which cares for nothing but corporate profits and leaves here, as it did in my native Appalachia, ravaged hills and an embittered people.

Finally, the matter of Moab the town. On this point I truly feel apologetic. When I said in that TV interview that Moab was "ugly," I was referring to the commercial strip which runs through the heart of it—the Atlas mill and slime pit, the cobweb of powerlines, the sheet-metal warehouses, and so on—not to the old residential areas, which are as lovely as any such in any other American town. I don't object to junkyards; junkyards are fascinating. And I have lived in enough trailer houses myself to know that with a little care an immobilized mobile home can be made as pretty as any $150,000 house on a hill. Usually prettier. More important, there are many beautiful people living in Moab, some of whom are friendly acquaintances and a few of whom are old good reliable friends of mine.

The one thing about Moab (and southeast Utah) which is truly ugly is the climate of hate and intimidation, created by a noisy few, which makes the decent majority reluctant to air in public their views on anything controversial. This is bad for Moab, bad for Utah, bad for the future of democracy. Where all pretend to be thinking alike, it's likely that no one is thinking at all. Diversity of opinion must be welcomed, even encouraged, if Moab is to achieve the one kind of growth it needs—moral growth—and become a beautiful small city in a sweet green valley worthy of that which surrounds it: the most magnificent landscape on planet Earth.

Cheers! Edward Abbey—Moab

The Nation, New York City (11 SEPTEMBER 1986)

Dear Editor:

What can Douglas Crase mean by calling Auden's moon poem "disagreeable"? (*The Nation*, September 6, 1986). Auden was not denying that the moon landings took place; he was merely expressing for many our relief that no trace of that shamefully expensive and crassly exhibitionist techno-stunt is visible from Earth. Like Auden, most people still admire the grace and loveliness of the moon, night after night, without ever giving a thought to that fading incident of fifteen? sixteen? years ago. As a friend of mine says, "What was Armstrong doing up there anyway? You can't play the trumpet in a vacuum."

Exactly: The idolatry of science is the grossest superstition of this gross decade, right in there with creationism, astrology, the *Dancing Wu Li Masters* and the "Tao of physics." The more we learn of outer space and inner space, of quasars and quarks, of Big Bangs and Little Blips, the more remote, abstract and intellectually inconsequential it all becomes. In this respect, George Bradley's drab flat prosaic poems serve as an apt reflection of their subject. Or in the view of Sherlock Holmes: "Whether the earth goes around the sun or the sun around the earth matters not a tinker's damn to me."

The Earth is where we live. Our growing awareness of humankind's progressive destruction of this gracious planet (thanks largely to scientific technology) is the one great tragic discovery of our time. Now there is a mighty theme for a mighty book—but a challenge to which no modern poet or novelist has yet adequately responded. Where is our Melville our Milton our Mann when we need him most?

Sincerely, Edward Abbey—Oracle

High Country News, Lander, Wyoming (4 OCTOBER 1986)

Dear Editor:

Sorry to intrude upon your columns once again, but I would like to correct a few errors in the account of my remarks at the Telluride "Ideas Festival."

About growth, I said that "Growth is the enemy of progress." (Figure that out for yourselves.) I said, furthermore, that "every normal, healthy organism, plant or animal, human or otherwise, grows to a certain optimum size (not "space," a meaningless notion); and then, having reached maturity, stops growing physically." Anything which grows without ceasing we call a monster—or a tumor.

As to reason and common sense, I believe in both. What I said at Telluride was that, judging from human history, so far, I have little hope or faith that reason and common sense will be applied in our attempts to resolve our ever-growing problems. (One more example of the self-contradicting nature of "healthy growth.") What will probably happen, I said, is that nature will solve our troubles for us in the traditional manner: through plague, famine, civil war, earthquake, flood and climatic changes. Since we humans choose to breed and multiply like rabbits, mule deer, fruit flies or bacteria in a culture dish, we must expect to enjoy a similar fate—over and over again, as in the past. Nothing to regret here, it's simply one aspect of the grand pageant of life. I merely wish to insist that we must stop pretending that we are somehow different from, or in some fashion superior to, the other animals on this planet.

Did I really say that "an ice age would be nice"? Actually, I'm in favor of expanding desertification. I'd like to see North America become a dry, sunny, sandy region inhabited mainly by lizards, buzzards and a modest human population—about 25 million would be plenty—of pastoralists and prospectors (prospecting for truth), gathering once a year in the ruins of ancient, mysterious cities for great ceremonies of music, art, dance, poetry, joy, faith and renewal. That's my dream of the American future. Like most such dreams, it will probably come true. That is why I'm still an optimist.

Sincerely, Edward Abbey—Moab

Barry Lopez, Finn Rock, Oregon   (25 OCTOBER 1986)

Dear Barry,

I've just seen the "Nature" issue of *Antaeus*. I liked your piece and the one by Jim Harrison but the rest is awfully turgid turbid upstream wading. What solemn and severe types these official nature writers are!

(I saw the stone horse once, about ten years ago, guided to the spot by a lovely young BLM ranger named Linelle. Alas, I was so interested in the ranger that I paid only official attention to the intaglio.)

My feelings are hurt, naturally, that you guys couldn't find anything of mine worth including in your anthology. All those dozens of essays I've written on outdoorsy subjects—don't they qualify as "nature writing"? I'd told Daniel Halpern he was welcome to reprint anything of mine he wished. I know that Gretel doesn't like me anymore, since she became a cowperson, and Dillard has apparently only read one book of mine, but I thought that you and Hoagland were interested in my stuff.

And not a thing by Peter Matthiessen? What did he do wrong? Or Wendell Berry. Or David Quammen. This literary politics is a strange business. Or maybe this is simply what happens when you have six or seven people all trying to edit one issue of one magazine—a peculiar jumble. One man can make some silly mistakes—but for pure confusion there's nothing like a committee.

Ah well, to hell with all that. There are cheerier things on my mind. Finished another novel a month ago and mailed it off, all 915 pages, to New York. My wife is pregnant again: I'm going to become a father, once more, about next April the first—April Fool's Day. I will then be sixty (60) years old. I'll be raising two teenagers in my seventies. If I survive that long. And since my father, age eighty-five, and my mother, age eighty, are still puttering about the farm back in Appalachia, I suppose—barring accident—I will survive that long. The biologists assure us that longevity, like intelligence or good conformation, is essentially a matter of heredity, and maybe they're right.

And I'm still enjoying the "golden glowing on the mind" of two weeks spent alone wandering through the canyons of southern Utah—moonlight, storm clouds, wind and sun. Finally got to some places I'd been meaning to visit for the last forty years—Pritchett Arch behind the rocks; Cheesebox Canyon west of Bridges; the summit of Mount Ellsworth; Poison Spring near the Dirty Devil River; lower Muley Twist Canyon in the Waterpocket Fold; and some other places so remote, obscure, rainbow-colored and beautiful they don't even have names. A land of marvels!

Write me a letter when you get the time.

Best regards, Ed

John Macrae, Henry Holt & Co.,
New York City (21 NOVEMBER 1986)

Dear Jack:

Tried to phone last Friday, about 5:45 your time, but nobody home. Called all three Holt numbers in my book.

Anyhow: I've read *The Fool's Progress*, all 901 pages, straight through from beginning to end, and this is what I think. Almost every page requires some re-writing. There are entire scenes and passages in the book that should be re-written word for word or discarded. The early love scenes between Lightcap and Honeydew Mellon are embarrassingly bad—sappy, foolish, silly. The tone of that section in the chapter "Comforters," where Lightcap visits Van Hoess and goes to bed with Valerie, is all wrong. Lightcap himself appears as an unattractive character in that scene and in many others, especially in the middle of the book.

There is, as you said, too much hasty careless self-indulgent writing throughout the book, again especially in the early and middle chapters. Some of the anecdotes, like "Dynamite Dawg" and "Billy McClain shooting up his own suit," probably belong in a different book I have in mind—*Tonopah Tales*. There are too many little political mini-editorials (a la John Updike). There is too much repetition of certain words (like "sequestered"), certain phrases and certain jokes (I was trying them out in different places).

Lightcap's tour through the center of Albuquerque (in "The Comforters") is too rhapsodic, silly, even ugly in places. There are too many hints of racism and sexism here and there in the book, which I know will lead to much trouble with the reviewers.

The chronology of scenes and chapters is sometimes confusing and must be clarified, rearranged and perhaps identified by month and year. There are several loose ends to be tied up, e.g., how many children does

Lightcap have anyway? How many marriages? Somewhere late in the book his first meeting with his last wife—Elaine—should be described or at least mentioned. Perhaps—but I'm not sure of this—the whole book should be written in the third person. Perhaps—but again I'm doubtful—the prologue and epilogue, the two brief chapters at beginning and end by the "Editor," should be dropped. I would like to see how they look in galley form, however, before deciding.

By now you should have received the little Capra Press back-to-back book which I sent you last week. There you can see how the "Editor's Preface" and the opening chapter, "Confessions of a Barbarian," look in print. In my opinion, and in that of others who have read this part, they look good. And if you'll get a hold of a copy of Dutton's Abbey Reader, *Slumgullion Stew*, you can see how the baseball story, "Rites of Spring," appears in print. That too has received a favorable reception (review enclosed).

Both of those chapters, as well as some from other parts of the book, I've been reading to college audiences during the past twelve months; they've been generally received with much and most gratifying laughter, which is what I hoped for.

As for the novel as a whole, I think it is sound. I am quite pleased with it. In fact, I think there is greatness in it—author's delusion, perhaps. I know it is the best thing I've been able to write so far and I am proud of it and eager to see it in print and published. I am not disturbed by the wide range in tone and tenor, from the farcical to the semi-tragic, from hillbilly comedy to black comedy to simple seedy red-dirt realism. That aspect of the book fits in with a long and honorable tradition in American fiction. It also corresponds to life itself, as I have known and experienced life.

What kind of novel is it? Well—it really is, among other things, a sort of shaggy dog story. I see nothing wrong with that. It is also of course the tale of a *picaro*—a picaresque adventure. It's about a fool and his progress from birth halfway to the grave. It's a semi-autobiography. It's the story of fifty years in a man's life—and to some extent, the distorted perhaps grotesque reflection of fifty years in our nation's life.

Certainly, Henry Lightcap is an eccentric, obnoxious, arrogant bastard—but he also learns, toward the end, some humility, becomes capable of love and sympathy for others. Yes, Henry is a whiner, a coward, a sneak, a cheat, among other things, but he suffers too, he pays for his many crimes, and I think that most readers, while unwilling to identify with him, will see enough of themselves in him to sympathize and even root for his survival.

(Many readers, of course, and reviewers, will hate this character, hate this book—but that's nothing new; I've had to endure that sort of reaction to every book I've published, including the semi-popular *Desert Solitaire* and *Monkey Wrench Gang*. I can take it. I'm accustomed to it. My books never win prizes—but they have won many and loyal readers, God bless them.)

So: let's get on with it. I believe that I can do the re-writing job within three or four months, assisted by my corps of able typists here in Tucson. I hope that we can publish the book before all the leaves fall in '87—if not next Spring, then next Fall. As you know, I'll be in San Francisco for the next two weeks. . . . I'll phone you sometime next week, when I think you've received this letter. Please return the original typescript with your notes and editorial suggestions to my Tucson address.

Best regards, Edward Abbey

1987

BENJAMIN CARTWRIGHT ABBEY is born (March 19). After a lifetime of feeling snubbed by the "East Coast literary establishment," Abbey receives a letter from Irving Howe of the American Institute of Arts and Letters, offering him a $5,000 honorarium and the Institute's "achievement in writing award." But both baits are contingent upon coming to New York to accept, and Ed bluntly declines, remarking to friends that it was "too little, too late." Abbey's health continues to slip, straining his capacity for humor, as per this journal entry from April 19: "I am becoming a cranky old man. Quite. Extremely contentious. True. Quarrelsome, petulant and exceedingly irritable. Right. I have less and less patience with fools, bores, pedants and crooks. . . . I fear for the lives of my children. I regret and am outraged by the systematic destruction of the natural world for the sake of human greed. Exactly." Another summer spent "cooling off" in Moab (when my wife and I visited the Abbeys there in July of '87, the daytime temperatures were over 100°). Plenty of magazine work this year, but no new books.

**Senior Vice-President, Paramount Pictures Corporation,
Los Angeles, California** (JANUARY 1987)

Dear Sir:

I have received your letter dated December 16th, 1986, regarding further work on a screenplay based on my novel *The Monkey Wrench Gang*. After due consideration, I have decided not to sign the agreement nor to perform any more work on the aforesaid screenplay until the following obligations are met:

1) that I be reimbursed for my trip to Los Angeles last June for a conference on the *Monkey Wrench* screenplay (about $150);

2) that I be paid the $3750 due me on submission of the third "final polish" of the screenplay, which I delivered to Robert Kaplan in early October 1986;

3) that the option on my book *The Monkey Wrench Gang* be renewed at once for the agreed-upon sum of $20,000; note that the ninety-day period between my submitting the final "polish" and the option renewal has now elapsed;

4) that before doing another revision of the *Monkey Wrench* screenplay, we agree on a fee of at least $25,000, one half to be paid in advance and the other half to be paid upon my delivering to you such a revised screenplay. I prefer not to enter into any more open-ended agreements; this current one, as your letter makes evident, has been dragging on since September 12, 1985—nearly seventeen months!

By "fee" I mean a professional fee, such as any other professional writer would be paid for doing this kind of difficult creative work. Larry McMurtry tells me, for example, that $25,000 is not unusual for a ten-page treatment of a screenplay.

I am a professional writer; *The Monkey Wrench Gang* has been continuously in print since 1975 and has sold about a half million copies, with an influence and reputation far greater than that figure might suggest.

Yours sincerely, Edward Abbey—Tucson

cc: Don Congdon
Carroll Ballard
Robert Kaplan

City Magazine, Tucson   (22 FEBRUARY 1987)

Dear Editor:

City Magazine gets better and better. The entire February issue was good; I liked especially the articles by Tom Sheridan, Byrd Baylor and J. P. S. Brown. However, when old-time cowperson Brown complains that sportsmen shoot up water tanks and leave pasture gates open, he should be reminded that those water tanks and gates are on public land, that those cattle are eating forage that belongs to our elk, deer, pronghorn and bighorn (and the desert tortoise), that the entire public-lands beef industry continues only through public sufferance and welfare subsidies of various kinds, and that in fact those cattle and those beef ranchers are our guests, exploiting our resources on our lands and have long since worn out their welcome.

Myself, I always leave gates open—and I urge everyone else to do the same. Once we get those stinking cattle out on the highways, where they belong, we can herd them all back to Texas, where they come from. Cheers!

Edward Abbey—Tucson

Don Congdon, New York City   (10 MARCH 1987)

Dear Don:

Herewith copies of letters to Macrae and to Martha Lawrence of Harcourt Brace in San Diego. Self-explanatory, mostly. Jay Dusard, in case you haven't heard of him, is a newly arrived young photographer whose book *Portraits of the North American Cowboy* was a big hit (out here, at least) a couple of years ago.

Check from *Harper's*.

Sent you the contract from U of A Press a few days ago. If it appears okay to you, mail it back to Steve Cox. U of A Press is also interested in reissuing an Abbey Reader.

Phone call from Carroll Ballard last week. He says I've been fired as writer on the *Monkey Wrench* project but that Paramount is going ahead, investing a hundred thousand or more in a real screenwriter, sending a scout team to Moab, Utah, rolling out the old casting couch etc. Ballard retained as probable director. He sounded gloomy about it all but that's Carroll's style. Says the chances of Paramount doing a *MWG* film are now 60–70 percent positive. Said he'd hire me during the shooting for a cameo role in some mob scene. Must alert my son the actor!

Maybe we should propose a sequel to *MWG* to Avon Books? Call it— *Hayduke Lives*. Actually, I've had such a book in mind for years, contingent upon somebody really making a film of the original book. It's time I made some real goddamn money; my wife is having another baby near the end of this month. Claims I'm the father.

Had a letter from Am Academy of Arts & Letters yesterday. They want to give me $5000—but I have to come to New York to pick up the check. Well . . . too little, too late.

By the way, I'd still like to see your comments on the World War II scenes in my *Fool's Progress* novel. Are they credible? Plausible? Any factual errors? Old Major Doctor Brendan Phibbs is reading it now.

Cheers! Edward Abbey—Tucson

John Macrae, Henry Holt & Co.,
New York City (10 MARCH 1987)

Dear Jack:

Received your latest communiqué yesterday and my response remains the same. I cannot agree to this hybrid book of half new essays, half old, which you propose. It's not a matter of defrauding the public—I realize that we can make the contents of the book perfectly clear on the jacket copy—but [I object to] my appearing to be unable to come up with a new book, completely new, three years after *Beyond the Wall*.

Again I say, why not reissue the Abbey Reader? That was your original idea. Or better, put out an entirely new collection of essays, namely those I sent you eight weeks ago, under the title *A Writer's Credo and Other Essays: 1984–87*? Or better yet, why not do both?

(*Merely Circulating* is not acceptable to me, as a title, for anything over my name. Of all modern American poets, that prissy precious aesthete Wallace Stevens is the one I most dislike—except of course for his one great poem "Sunday Morning.")

If you do not want to publish a new Abbey Reader, please let me know. Both Sierra Club Books and the University of Arizona Press are willing to do it, and I've got to give one of them a decision soon.

Rolling right along with the novel, slashing and revising and rearranging with gay abandon. Should have the complete new book back to you sometime in April. About 700 pp in typescript, I'd estimate. No prologue. Maybe a brief epilogue showing Henry returning west, still alive, in a red convertible, with his daughter Ellsworth at his side.

Cheers and best regards and a kiss for the new Mrs Macrae!

Same difficult old Edward Abbey

Copy to Don Congdon

Irving Howe, American Academy of Arts & Letters, New York City (20 MARCH 1987)

Dear Mr Howe:

Thank you for your letter of March 4th in which you inform me that I am to receive an award from the Academy. I appreciate the intended honor but will not be able to attend the awards ceremony on May 20th: I'm figuring on going down a river in Idaho that week. Besides, to tell the truth, I think that prizes are for little boys. You can give my $5000 to somebody else. I don't need it or really want it. Thanks anyhow.

Yours truly, Edward Abbey—Oracle

Edward Hoagland (22 MARCH 1987)

Dear Ted—

Thanks for your recent letter. Yes, we had another baby, Benjamin Cartwright Abbey (named after my wife's family), born two days ago, eight pounds, twelve toes, one nose etc., all normal and healthy and pink as a boiled shrimp. I've got five children now, ranging in age from thirty-one to two days, not out of "boldness," as you like to fancy, but from passive complaisance on my part, the wish to please. It was the women who exhibited the will, the means and the courage.

So now I'll be raising two teenagers in my seventies. Madness! (But I rather like it.) We'll manage somehow.

I've about finished rewriting another goddamned novel and hope to see it in print about a year from now. Apparently those NYC publishers can't get a book out in less than a year anymore, acc[ording] to my agent. I've got three possible titles for it (it's sort of a contemporary picaresque): *The Fool's Progress*, or (2) *Adventures of a Tall Dog*, or (3) *Confessions of a Barbarian*. Tell me which you like the best.

André Bernard sent me the first four books in your new Nature Library series. Nice design, interesting introductions, but why the one by whatshis name on crabs? I thought this series was to consist entirely of classics, i.e. dead authors. I hope you include, anyhow, one of Krutch's books, such as *Voice of the Desert* or *The Grand Canyon* or his one about Baja California.

Why do you claim I misquoted you in my "preface" to *Down the River*? I've still got that postcard in my files. Also, Horgan's book about Gregg really does read like a parody; Gregg's life seems like a parody.

Halpern did invite me (twice) to contribute something to that *Antaeus* anthology but said it had to be "non-controversial." How could anything non-controversial be of intellectual interest to grown-ups? He didn't explain so I didn't contribute. To tell the truth, I find most nature writing, like that of Muir's and McPhee's, very dull. Unreadable. Rhapsodies put me to sleep. Especially when, like Dillard, they keep sneaking in references to some hypothetical entity named "Gawd." Bring back Occam's razor!

Enclosed is a copy of my letter to Irving Howe and the Academy, which should amuse you. I suspect that you or Peter Matthiessen or Wallace Stegner was behind that offer. Or Susan Sontag? The river I allude to is the Owyhee, which starts in Idaho but runs through Nevada and eastern Oregon also (I believe)—Claude Dallas country. No, Claude is not a hero of mine; but anyone who shoots two game wardens and then escapes from prison is of interest to me.

Regards, Ed A.

Jon Krakauer (CIRCA EARLY 1987)

Dear Mr Krakauer:

As requested, here is my list of the ten most significant events in the American West during the past decade:

1. Revolting Development: 487 literary exquisites, flycasters, coke sniffers, horse lovers, movie actors, hobby ranchers, Instant Rednecks and other jet-set androids from the world of *Vanity Fair* move into Santa Fe, Tucson and the Livingston, Montana area.

2. Hopeful Development: Congress finally passes an Immigration Control Act—but two hundred years too late.

3. Revolting Development: Beef ranchers murder 155 grizzly bears in Montana and Wyoming.

4. Hopeful Development: Grizzlies harvest twenty-two tourists.

5. Revolting Development: US Forest Service lays plans and obtains funds to bulldoze a road to within at least one/quarter mile of every pine tree in our national forests.

6. Hopeful Development: Teton Dam collapses in Idaho.

7. Revolting Development: Hemlines go down on park ranger skirts.

8. Hopeful Development: Earth First! founded in the Pinacate Desert by Dave Foreman, Howie Wolke, Mike Roselle and Bart Kohler.

9. Revolting Development: Howie Wolke arrested for pulling up survey stakes in Little Granite Creek, Wyoming.

10. Hopeful Development: Chief Engineer killed by lightning at dam construction site on Dolores River in Colorado.

11. Hopeful Development: Drunken shotgunner killed by falling gut-shot saguaro cactus near Phoenix.

12. Hopeful Development: 565 range cattle killed in Utah by little green men in UFOs (Unidentified Fucking Objects).

13. Hopeful Development: Benjamin Cartwright Abbey born March 19, 1987, vows eternal resistance against every form of tyranny over the soul of man (and woman).

Edward Abbey—Tucson

John Macrae, Henry Holt & Co.,
New York City   (3 APRIL 1987)

Dear Jack:

Finally received the contract from Don [Congdon] for the new book of essays. Before going on with this, however, I want to make certain that you and I are in agreement on the title and the contents of the book.

In my letter to you of March 24th I suggested four titles, any one of which would suit me, i.e. *Vox Clamantis in Deserto*, or *Keeping It Up* or some combination of *Rock Salt and Apple Pie* or *Buckshot and Cherry Pie*, together with an explanatory subtitle viz., *Seventeen* (or whatever the number) *New Essays* (or *Pieces*) *by Edward Abbey*.

Keeping it Up comes to me in a letter from Peter Matthiessen in which he urges me to "keep it up"—whatever "it" may be—and if you prefer that as a title we could use a line or two from Peter's message as an explanatory epigraph.

One Life at a Time, Please is a good suggestion; I like it but would prefer to use one of the four listed above. Of the four *Vox Clamantis* is my favorite; you'll object that the kind of people who read my books lack a classical education. True; but a little brain tickler might attract interest on the part of a wider public while not being so esoteric as to offend Abbey's redneck fans. Of course I would slip a translation of the phrase into my introduction to the book. Anyhow, please give it serious consideration. (Think of the cachet, prestige, high-toned old Christian color such a title would lend to book, author, editor and the grand old house of Holt.)

Now as to contents of book. We are agreed, I trust, that this collection of pieces will not include any essay, chapter or portion from any previous book of mine (a new Abbey Reader remains a separate project).

About the introduction, I could easily make it as long or as short as you wish—whatever length needed to complete the book—and would be happy to touch on most of the topics you mention in your letter of March 23rd. I see the intro as a free informal essay dealing with literary journalism in general, nature writing in particular, together with a bit of background information on some of the essays in the book. (E.g., "Immigration & Liberal Taboos" is a piece originally commissioned by the *New York Times*, for their Op-Ed page, then rewritten to Op-Ed's specifications, then rejected—and never paid for—by the *Times*, then rejected in succession by *Harper's*,

Atlantic, Texas Monthly, New Republic, Mother Jones and of course *The Nation*, then finally published by the *New Times* where it was lambasted in the following issue by one Jaime Gutierrez—an ambitious young *jefe* politico in the Arizona state legislature; this being an unusual maneuver by any periodical publication, indicating how touchy the whole subject is, especially in states with a large and growing "Hispanic" population.)

So. Please let me know if you are agreeable to the above plan for the book and I will hustle the contracts back to Don by Express Mail. Also, give me a deadline for the introduction, and the number of words required.

Best Regards, Ed Abbey—Tucson

Abbeys, Home, Pennsylvania   (4 APRIL 1987)

Dear Mother and Dad,

Seems like I haven't writ you two a real letter for a long time, so here goes. First the news:

As you know, Benjamin Cartwright Abbey was born on March 19th. A healthy normal baby, about eight pounds, with all the usual appurtenances. Now, two weeks and two days later, he seems happy and healthy, sleeping most of the time, nursing at his Mommy the rest of the time. An easy baby so far—not colicky as Rebecca was.

Clarke's mother Carolyn has been here since March 22nd—a big help. She's a fine woman, always kind, patient, considerate, energetic. I wish she could stay with us much longer but she's going home in a few days.

Becky's a bit jealous of the baby, of no longer being sole attention getter, but I guess that's unavoidable, inevitable—she'll simply have to adapt to having a baby brother.

Clarke is blissfully happy with her new child. She takes motherhood so seriously and enjoys it so immensely. Me, I'm all right, although when I look forward to raising two obnoxious teenagers in my seventies—I try not to think about it. I'll probly be spending more and more time out in the desert somewhere.

Susie is now halfway thru her second term at the University, doing well. She is going to London in September for four months as a student, and does seem properly excited about that. I'm hoping that four months away from us and her grandmother will give her some independence and bring her more fully alive.

Got a wedding invitation from Abbi. We can't go, of course, but if you do, I hope you can stop in Tucson for a few days either on the way there or the way back. We'd sure love to see you: either of you; both of you.

This summer we expect to be in Moab again, at the Pack Creek Ranch. Someday soon we've got to start looking for a new home; the land developers and real estate sharks are threatening to surround our place here with 2500 new "housing units," as they call them. 2500! Good Gawd. Tucson is becoming a squalid mess; half a million people living here now. Time to clear out. If I were young again I'd head for Australia.

What else is new? Well, I've nearly finished revising another novel, to be called *The Fool's Progress*, or maybe *Adventures of a Tall Dog*. If all goes well, it should appear in print about a year from now. Am also putting together another book of essays which is scheduled for publication this coming October. I think I'll call it *Buckshot and Apple Pie*. Or perhaps *Rock Salt & Cherry Pie*. How do those grab you?

Paramount Pictures has renewed the option on *Monkey Wrench* for another year, so there's still a possibility that book may become a movie in a year or two. But where Hollywood is concerned, you can't count on anything for certain. Some of my stuff is being recorded on [audio] tape cassettes; when those are ready I'll send you copies.

The weather here is windy, balmy, sometimes wet. Desert springtime, with flowers popping up all over the place, trees leafing out, streams gushing down from the mountains. Great time of year for hiking, camping, exploring, sleeping under the new moon and the old stars. At dawn and at evening we hear the coyotes howling with excitement—mating season. And lots of fresh rabbit meat hopping about to feed the young ones with.

Enough of us. We're healthy and busy and as reasonably happy as mortal humans have any right to be. I hope that all is well with both of you: that you've survived another Appalachian winter without hardship, that your bodies are functioning, the furnace working, the cars still running. Same goes for Hoots and Iva. Give them both my love.

I think about you often, you two old-timers, with unlimited admiration, respect and—naturally—love.

Write us more letters when you get the chance.

All the best from your son

Edward Hoagland (11 APRIL 1987)

My Dear Hoagland:

On March 22nd I sent you a genuine letter, answering your queries about our new baby and my current novel-in-progress. In return I receive the attached note dated 3/31, which baffles me.

"I liked Saroyan too, though he wasn't a personal friend."

What does that mean? I said nothing whatsoever about any Saroyan in my letter. Did you get my letter confused with somebody else's letter? What is going in your head? Who cares whether he was your friend or not?

You're "fond of me," you say, and anything I do is okay with you. What in gods name does that refer to? Was I supposed to consult you before begetting another baby? Another novel?

In one respect your note does appear to be a kind of reaction to my letter, in that you say that you like *Adventures of a Tall Dog* best. That statement makes a kind of sense except that I doubt if you even know what a "tall dog" is. Do you? What does the expression "tall dog" mean to you?

And why should $5000 seem like "peanuts" next year? Next year? What about this year? I've got two children to support, plus a wife, a teenager in college, a dog, a cat and an unreliable pickup truck.

In my letter I asked you about several things. Why, for example, did you include that book about crabs in your Viking-Penguin *Nature Lovers* Series. A simple question, easy to answer, I should think, but you say nothing about it. I suggest including a Krutch book in the series. No response. I ask why you accused me of misquoting you in my preface to *Down the River*: no response. I sent you a copy of my letter to Irving Howe, which I thought would interest you: no reaction. (Aren't you a member of the Am Academy of Arts & Letters? I think you once told me you are.) I tell you about my brief exchange with Daniel Halpern of *Antaeus*, to which I know you contribute: no reaction. I mention your heroes Muir, McPhee, Dillard—no reaction. I mention Claude Dallas and the Owyhee River: no reaction. Not a twitch of interest.

Trying to correspond with you, Hoagland, is like trying to converse with a zombie, a jellyfish, a bucket of lard. You seem to be an inert mass, dead from the neck up. And if my letters bore you so much, why do you persist in contacting me from time to time? Those phone calls, which always turn out to be about nothing at all, or almost nothing: postcard trivia. And your bland postcards, concerned with even less. What's the point?

I was ready to abandon this futile non-correspondence a year ago; then I get your cards . . . so I reply, trying to buck you up: can't let a fellow writer go down the drain without making some effort to rescue him. But this leads to nothing.

The only reason I ever maintained contact with you is because you're the only member of the East Coast literati who has ever indicated the slightest interest in my books. (Altho' that was long ago: 1970, to be precise, when you wrote that friendly review of *Black Sun* for the *New York Times Book Review*; since then, so far as I can tell, you haven't read a thing of mine.) Like many writers who live in the West, I sometimes imagine that possibly I am missing out on something by not being intimate with the Manhattan Literary Club. My contact with you was my only contact with that privileged circle. Think of the brilliant talk that must go on back there! Why is *The New Yorker* so dull? *Vanity Fair* so sleazy? The *New York Review* so conservative? These are examples of things I'd like to talk with you about in our letters—but what's the use. I can't even get the time of day out of you—the simplest question is greeted with nothing but viscous evasions.

E.g., why are you always fawning over Updike? What did he ever do for you? And is he really the only contemporary American writer of fiction that you read? What about Don DeLillo? Pynchon? Barry Hannah? Or Cormac McCarthy—have you even heard of him?

To hell with it.

You keep protesting too much that you are my friend—trying to make explicit that which, if it were true, would best be allowed to remain implicit—but I don't believe you. And never have. Friends are those who willingly share. Even the most casual of my friends at least make an effort to respond to my letters—to answer them. Gretel Erhlich says that you write letters to her; why won't you write me?

Yes, to hell with it. Let's call an end to this inane, pointless, worthless pretense at communication. If you're not bored with it, I certainly am.

So long, Abbey—Tucson

Edward Hoagland (17 APRIL 1987)

E.H.:

Hey! finally got a rise out of you.

I retract my accusations. Some of them. But you still insist on refusing to answer my letters, while persisting in pestering me with trivial inquiries. It is that, my dear fellow, which so exasperates me.

(There is no such verb as "savage." Never was and never will be if I can help it.)

No book of mine has rec'd a favorable review in the *NYTBR* since 1968-70. [*Monkey Wrench Gang*] was never reviewed there at all. *Abbey's Road* was denounced as racist because I described the Abos as they are, not as they should be. [*Beyond the Wall*] was dismissed as aestheticism. Who are these protégés of yours? Not that I have the slightest hope you'll answer a simple, direct question . . .

John Macrae, Henry Holt & Co., New York City (22 APRIL 1987)

Dear Jack:

Rec'd this package by Federal Express from Holt, yesterday, a portion of but not all of our book of essays. In fact, it's a jumble. Several chapters are included in duplicate but with whole pages totally illegible. Other chapters we agreed to include in the book are missing—not here.

None of the stuff has been copy-edited. Okay, I'll do it myself. Better that way.

But I must have the rest of the stuff. I cannot put the book together until I receive the missing chapters. Please, therefore, mail me the entire batch of essays etc that I sent you last January, including the one I sent you under separate cover. (i.e., "All Vigor Spent," the *Geographic* essay on the Rio Grande.)

Send back everything, including the book reviews. Altho' I don't want to include them in this book, I do want them back. As I said in my covering letter, I have no copies. So mail the whole mess back to me, I'll sort it out, and make a book of it. It'll take a lot of work but I should be able to get a book ms back to you in ten days or so, together with an introduction, as requested, of about twelve hundred words. (You sure that's enuf?)

Too bad we didn't get started on this project a couple of months ago. Like you, I hope this book can be published this Fall. But it's going to be tight now, because of all the confusion and delay.

For the love of God, Jack! why don't you hire some help? I get the impression you're trying to do everything yourself. Even your assistants and secretaries don't answer my letters or return my phone calls. Which causes more delay and more confusion.

I like your choice of *Rock Salt and Cherry Pie* as a title. Catchy. People here like it. I think it'll sell.

I still think we should publish the novel first. Except for proofreading about six hundred pp of retyped ms, the novel is ready to go. But if you prefer to publish the book of essays first, I'll defer work on the novel for a couple of weeks and get to work on *Rock Salt* etc. Think about it.

Regards, Edward Abbey—Tucson

cc: Congdon

Superintendent, Saguaro National Monument, Tucson (6 MAY 1987)

Dear Sir:

This is a complaint. Several times in the past few months, while attempting to enjoy the west side of Saguaro NM with friends, we have been pestered by officious, arrogant, ignorant men with guns, Mace cans and radios who wear the badge, uniform and hat of Park Service rangers.

But they are not rangers. They are merely cops, of the most typical, insolent, bullying, low-grade sort. The first occasion took place last January when we were having a picnic at one of the picnic areas called—Eskimini? Something like that. Anyway, although none of us were violating any park regulation in any way, this cop—wearing a ranger's uniform and attempting to impersonate a park ranger—came swaggering among us with his gun and other heavy equipment for no other purpose than to nose around, see what we were doing. After making everyone annoyed and uncomfortable, he finally left, unable to cite us for any violation. His name badge, as I recall, identified him as one [name deleted].

The second incident took place a month or two later. My friends and I were having another picnic at the same place when two of these cops in ranger uniform drove up and starting shouting at us from about a hundred yards away. (We were up in that stone shelter on top of a little hill; they stayed below in the parking lot.) After considerable yelling back and forth—they made no pretense at simple courtesy—we learned that one of our cars, parked in the thirty-foot-wide turnaround, was "illegally" parked, although there was enough space for two other cars to pass abreast of it. I did not get the names of the two cops in this case.

The third incident occurred two or three weeks ago. Two friends and I were taking photographs along the dirt road west of the above-named picnic area when your policeman appeared, stopped and demanded to know if we had a "permit" to take pictures. Of course we had no permit. He insisted that we stop taking pictures. We obeyed—as before, he was armed with revolver and Mace and that tin badge which apparently makes him a little autocrat.

So that's the gist of my complaint. But I also have a more general complaint: What kind of people are you hiring as rangers these days? Where do you find them? They look and act like cops—not rangers—and the next time one of these armed and uniformed goons bothers me I'm going to try to find out if he knows anything about the history, wildlife, plant life or geology of Saguaro National Monument. Or if he knows anything about the purpose of the national parks, or the traditional role of rangers in the protection and interpretation of national parks. Somehow I'm inclined to doubt if they do. I think these guys would be much more at home in some urban slum, bullying drunks, transients, prostitutes and children.

Why do they carry guns, anyway? I worked as a ranger for the NPS for sixteen seasons, from the Everglades to Mount Lassen, and never had to carry a sidearm. (Yes, I kept a .38 concealed in the glove box of my patrol vehicle but never once, in all of those years from 1956 to 1970, did I find a need to use it or even exhibit it.) The ranger's job, as I was taught, was to defend and preserve the parks in as close to a natural state as possible, to assist visitors in trouble and to provide information, when asked, about the flora, fauna, rocks, history and so forth of the park or monument in which I worked. We were not cops and never thought of ourselves as cops.

So my final question is, What the hell is happening to the Park Service? If you now need cops rather than rangers, it suggests that something is seriously wrong with the administration of the park system. If traffic control takes up more time than wildlife observation, it suggests there is too much motorized traffic where it does not belong—in a park. If police work takes precedence over ranger work, that suggests that the parks are losing their original character as nature preserves and being transformed—and malformed—into something like urbanized recreation facilities—a violation of the original, traditional, central and essential purpose of national parks.

Sincerely, Edward Abbey—Tucson, AZ

cc: Bill Hoy, NPS regional director, *Arizona Daily Star*, Nat'l Parks Association, Park Rangers Assoc, *Washington Post*, *New York Times* . . .

Arizona Daily Star (10 MAY 1987)

Dear Editor:

Too bad about Gary Hart. Just another hack politician. If he were a brave and honest man, he could have stood up before the media and said something like this: "Yes, I like pretty women. So what. All normal, healthy, living men desire many women. What of it. Now I'm going to continue my campaign for the Presidency and if you don't like it you can go to hell."

If he'd had the courage to talk like that, 90 percent of the men in America would have backed him. And maybe even half the women. In any nation but the USA, it is taken for granted that a man of distinction, ability, wealth or power will keep a mistress and a few girlfriends on the side. Only in America, still suffering from its grotesque, hypocritical Puritan heritage, do we persist in attempting to deny and repeal a million years of basic primate biology.

Edward Abbey—Tucson

Earth First! Journal, Tucson (11 MAY 1987)

Dear Editor:

Your journal gets better all the time. In the May (or "Beltane" issue—what is this exotic jargon?) I liked especially the article on the "First Ecologists" by George Wuerthner. Exactly on the mark. When I mentioned these matters in an article in *Outside* Magazine in 1983 and at greater length in the book *Beyond the Wall* in 1984, I received nothing for my pains but the usual reflex abuse from white middleclass liberals with their queer and perverse racial guilt neurosis. "Reverse racism," as they call it nowadays.

"Them there knee-jerk liberals," says my neighbor Foster Bundy, "they cain't say the word shit even when their mouths is full of it." True fact, Foster. But it is a writer's duty to write and speak and record the truth, always the truth, no matter whom may be offended. The Alaskan natives have no more right to immunity from criticism than any other group, faction or interest in our society.

In reply to certain letters from readers who ask for the basis of my optimistic belief that the military-industrial state will begin to disintegrate in about fifty years, I refer them back to my response to A. B. Schmookler in a previous issue of the *EF! Journal*. There I wrote, plain for any reader with eyes to see, as follows:

". . . the whole grandiose structure is self-destructive: by enshrining the profit motive (power) as our guiding ideal, we encourage the intensive and accelerating consumption of land, air, water—the natural world—on which the structure depends for its continued existence. A house built on greed cannot long endure . . ." And so on. Read with some care, lads.

Incidentally, I am still waiting for Mr Schmookler to reply to my response to his critique of "anarchy" and anarchistic theory. The one reply he made does not touch on the principal points in my little essay.

Edward Abbey—Oracle

Tom H. Watkins, Editor, *Wilderness* Magazine,
The Wilderness Society, Washington, D.C. (18 MAY 1987)

Dear Tom,

I am surprised by your letter of May 14th: does that mean you will not print my rebuttal to Wendell Berry? If not, please return it and I'll peddle it elsewhere. Nevertheless, I am surprised. If you won't give me a chance to reply to Berry, then you should ask Stegner or A. B. Guthrie or somebody to do it. You're going to have a lot of unhappy members in the WS if you leave the impression that Berry's Gifford Pinchot view of the world is the official ideology of the Wilderness Society. I've heard half a dozen people complain about it.

Too bad Krutch is not still alive. Maybe you should reprint his essay "Conservation Is Not Enough." Meaning, of course, that "stewardship" is not enough. Or almost anything from Aldo Leopold's *Sand County Almanac* would serve as proper rejoinder to Berry.

I should not have to repeat myself in this letter, but I will: Simply because humankind have the power now to meddle or "manage" or "exercise stewardship" in every nook and cranny of the world does not mean that we have a right to do so. Even less, the obligation. In principle, there is nothing in Berry's essay that would disturb Watt, Hodel or Reagan: they too believe in "wise use" or "stewardship"; they too believe that overpopulation is a myth; they too believe in the antique Hebrew doctrine that everything on earth was placed here for the convenience and appetite of humans.

Berry is a farmer. His notion of wilderness, as he says, is a weedy fencerow between plowed fields. He is not really interested in the idea of large-scale, regional wilderness and never has been. He makes a strange spokesman indeed for an organization that calls itself The Wilderness Society. If his views are now the views of the Society's present management, then I prefer to disaffiliate. Please return my essay, if you're not going to publish it, and also my $100 [contribution].

Sincerely, Edward Abbey—Tucson   ·

Wendell Berry, Port Royal, Kentucky (24 MAY 1987)

Dear Wendell,

Attached is a copy of a letter I wrote to T. H. Watkins at *Wilderness* Magazine in attempted rebuttal of parts of your argument in your essay "Preserving Wildness." As you will see, I disagree sharply with some of your opinions, a reaction, I'm sure, that will not surprise you, any more than I was in any way surprised by what you wrote. Nothing in your essay is at all inconsistent with many essays on similar subjects that you've written before. What did surprise me was seeing your views presented as more or less approved Wilderness Society doctrine.

Anyway—this is all a laborious preamble to my real question: Do you think I am unfair to you or to your words in my response? For the sake of brevity, I dispensed with the usual fraternal amenities etc, and as is my habit, pursued my various points with what I like to think of as "vigor" but others call "harshness." Watkins, in his letter back, accused me of being "plain not fair" to you. Perhaps I was. If you think so, I would be happy to revise the piece, or throw it away, before trying to get it published anywhere. I was hoping Watkins would offer to publish it in *Wilderness*, but I guess he won't.

So, let me know what you think, if you care to trouble yourself about this. I would not want to risk endangering the kind of feelings you've shown me in the past for the sake of mere polemical spleen. Your friendship is far more important to me than striving to win points in a formal debate.

Fraternally, Ed A.—Tucson

John Macrae, Henry Holt & Co.,
New York City (24 MAY 1987)

Dear Jack:

I sent you the complete, revised and edited typescript of *One Life at a Time, Please* (or *Rock Salt and Cherry Pie* if you prefer) two weeks ago, via Congdon's office. I trust the book has by now found its way into your hands.

Is it long enough? If not, let me know at once and I'll send you two or three more short essays. I do hope it comes out to at least two hundred printed pages. Anything less tends to look like a (ugh) book of verse.

A woman in your office named Amy called here last week wanting to know if I would do some drawings for the book. I called her back last Friday but she was gone. Tell her my answer is No; not enough time. I'm already back at work on my novel. Also, as I suggested in my letter to you of March 24th, I would prefer to see the artwork done by Elissa Ichiyassu, the woman who did the beautiful job with *Beyond the Wall*. If there's not enough time for her to do new art, you could use the same drawings for this new book— merely juggle them around, and change the color of the cover, of course. Or else have the book decorated by the artist who did the skull on the jacket proof you sent me. Consistency.

As for jacket copy, I enclose the proof you sent me with requested changes. If you want a quote, this is my favorite:

"What entertains many and exasperates others is Abbey's unique prose voice. Alternately misanthropic and sentimental, enraged and hilarious, it is the voice of a full-blooded man airing his passions."—Peter Carlson, *People* Magazine.

Or this one:

"We are living . . . among punishments and ruins. For those who know this, Edward Abbey's books remain an indispensable solace. His essays, and his novels too, are 'antidotes to despair.'"—Wendell Berry, *The Whole Earth Review*

Best regards, Ed—Fort Llatikcuf, Arizona

Jim Harrison (24 MAY 1987)

Dear Jim—

I liked your piece in the current *Outside* very much. Good tough boisterous writing as always. I liked especially your nice words about Doug Peacock; he was delighted when I told him about it, rushing right out to buy a copy. (I read my *Outside* in the supermarket magazine racks; except for [David] Quammen's column the magazine has become, generally, too sleek and rich for my taste: the nature lover's *Vanity Fair*.)

I was surprised, however, by your calling Kerouac a "great soul." Jack Kerouac?—the author of *On the Road, Dr Sax, Visions of Gerard* and other juvenilia? Surely not! Your words waggled before my eyes. Have you tried to read *On the Road* lately? Unreadable. In the same class as *Franny & Zooey* and *The World Acc to Krap* and any one of the current two hundred scribbling women that have taken over, as they did in Hawthorne's time, the literary racketplace. But Kerouac—you mean that creepy adolescent bisexual who dabbled in Orientalism and all the other fads of his time, wrote stacks of complacently self-indulgent, onanistic books and then drank himself to death while sitting on his mother's lap, down in Florida somewhere? Surely not so. Say it ain't so.

I don't really give a damn about the Kerouac cult one way or the other, except that it accompanies the total neglect and/or abusive Indexing of some real modern American authors. Tom Wolfe, of course, who died at thirty-eight—younger than the ever-teenager Kerouac. Or Nelson Algren.

Or Steinbeck or Wallace Stegner or William Eastlake for that matter. Our literary critics are like a herd of sheep, or a school of fish, or a flock of ducks, always facing in the same direction, relying for security on the perfection of their unanimity, the telepathic unison of their current opinions. You don't need them.

Your list of favorite musicians was also conventional. Be daring sometime. Stick your neck out. Take a chance. Say a good word for Mahler, Waylon Jennings, Roy Acuff—or Shostakovitch—his quartets and late symphonies are as interesting as anything Mozart or Stravinsky (the current idols of the pussywhipped) ever wrote. Do you really worry that much about keeping up with fashion? To hell with the *Vanity Fair* mob. (See attached correspondence.)

Best regards, Ed A.—Fort Llatikcuf

Rowohlt Verlag, Hamburg, West Germany (14 JUNE 1987)

Dear Editors:

Thank you for sending me the five copies of *Die Universalschrauben-schlussel Bande*. (Great title for a movie!) I am delighted that my innocent little book, after twelve years of often frustrating delay and evasion, has finally found a good publisher in Germany. Though I myself am not competent to judge the translation, some friends who know Deutsche assure me that yours is a good one; please convey my gratitude to Fraulein Sabine Hedinger.

With this note I am sending you a copy of the 10th Anniversary edition of *The Monkey Wrench Gang*. Please note that this edition, the only true and complete one, includes a chapter (#21) called "Seldom Seen at Home." This chapter was inadvertently left out of the original Lippincott edition (1975), which is why, I suppose, your translator also did not include it; she was, I suppose, working from the original—but slightly mutilated—edition. If you do additional printings of *Die Bande*, I do hope that you will restore this chapter to its proper place.

Although brief, I regard it as thematically central to my novel. For what is *The Monkey Wrench Gang* really all about? Yes, it is about the domination and industrialization of Nature, the natural world (as we say); but—it is also and fundamentally concerned with the domination of human nature by our excessive, uncontrolled and inhuman technology. (A la Heidegger—a man whom I come to see, more and more, as the most important philosopher of the 20th century.)

If you publish a hardcover edition of *Die Bande*, please send me a couple of copies. And if the book is successful in Germany, I would urge you to consider publishing it in a larger format (what we call, in the USA, a "trade paperback") with illustrations by Robert Crumb. I've heard that his work is quite popular in your country.

Best regards, Edward Abbey—Moab

Barry Lopez, Finn Rock, Oregon   (14 JUNE 1987)

Dear Barry:

Enjoyed your article in the current *Harper's*. Reinforces my intention to visit soon the beautiful, tragic, divided land of South Africa.

Amusing to find us both in *Life* Magazine this month, trying to say about the same thing in widely—and wildly—divergent ways. I ask people to stay home; you ask them to change their wicked attitude.

But it's wrong of us both, I think, to adopt the lofty stance, the wise man's tone, and do nothing more. Of course, in the long run, humans must regain a sense of community with nature. (If we ever really had it.) But in the meantime, the hard work, the important work, is that of saving what is left. I despise the role of guru, or leader, or remote philosopher, earning easy money writing the right thing while the "troops," the hundreds and thousands who actually stand before the bulldozers, spike the trees, lobby the politicos, write the tedious letters, lick stamps, staple leaflets, organize committees, attend meetings, hire lawyers and sometimes go to jail, do what they do with no fame, no public credit, certainly little or no pay (except Sierra Club bureaucrats etc), and no reward but the sense of having opposed the rich and powerful in the name of something more ancient and beautiful than human greed and human increase. The writer's job is to write, and write the truth—but he also has the moral obligation to get down in the dust and the sweat and lend not only his name but his voice and body to the tiresome contest. Part of the time, anyhow. I once asked Tom McGuane why he lets others fight his battles for him in Montana; "don't want to get mixed up with those counterculture types," he said. Asked Annie Dillard the same thing; "don't want to be known as an environmentalist," she said. Asked Edward Hoagland and Jim Harrison something similar; "Don't try to bully me into doing what you do," Hoagland replied; and Harrison never replied at all. And so on.

What these people are most concerned about, I guess, is their literary reputations, not the defense of the natural world or the integrity of their souls. But how far can you go in objectivity, in temporizing, in fence-straddling, before it becomes plain moral cowardice? I admire these writers as writers; lovely prose style, all of them; but I can't fully respect them as citizens, that is, as men. As women.

A. B. Guthrie, Jr. on the other hand, doesn't worry about his standing with *Esquire* or *Vanity Fair*. Neither does Wallace Stegner or Wendell Berry or Farley Mowat or Charles Bowden. Me, I do worry about it—but not much. That is, I gave up a long time ago and have resigned myself to my simple role as village crank. It pays good and it's easy. In fact it's genetic, bred in the bone: my old man, eighty-six now, talks pretty much like I write. He's outlived all of his poker-playing whisky-drinking tree-cutting friends and should be lonely as that pine snag on yonder point of the mountain. But he's not. Rich in memories and pride, and still cutting trees (selectively), he seems to enjoy his old age more than he ever did his youth. Or so he says and so my mother agrees.

Where was I? What was it I really wanted to tell you in this letter? Senility—I forget. If you come through Moab Utah this summer, look us up; we're renting (in July) a house near the City Park while searching for a new home on the red rock (the developers threatening to force us out of Tucson); can't tell you what our phone number will be if any, don't know the street address, but you can always find us through Ken Sleight's Bookstore.

Best regards, Ed A.—Tucson

The Nation, New York City   (14 JUNE 1987)

Dear Editor:

There's always something worth reading in the *Nation*, even in the grimmest of its weekly periods. But I've not often come across two essays in one single issue which I found as inspiriting and restorative as Edward Hoagland's "Up With Spring" and Bill Kauffman's defense of traditional American isolationism—or self-reliance, as I would call it. Hitch the two together, like a span of mules, and they read Up with Spring: Down with Empire. Now there's a war cry you could win elections with.

Regards, Edward Abbey—Moab

Ms. Margonis, Books Editor, The Nation, New York City   (23 JUNE 1987)

Dear Ms Margonis:

I wonder if you could do me a favor? I would like to obtain a copy of a book review published in your magazine back in 1982 or 1983. The book reviewed was *Down the River*, by Edward Abbey (Dutton, NY 1982); the name of the reviewer was Denise [Dennis] Drabelle. Back issues of *The Nation* are not available here. I enclose a SASE and a check for $100 to cover your clerical expenses. If this is more than needed, please have your subscription manager apply the balance to a subscription to *The Nation* for the Grand County Public Library, Moab, Utah 84532; if not enough, bill me for the difference.

I would much appreciate it if you could have a copy of the requested review sent to me by July 15th. (And if you're wondering why I want it, I'll tell you: I'm thinking of contributing Drabelle's review of my book to the Pushcart Press's forthcoming book, *Rotten Reviews*.)

I'm sorry you could not use my review of Charles Bowden's two books. He really does deserve some national exposure and so far has got none; the *NYTBR* and the *Chicago Sun-Times* also turned down my review. Perhaps because one of the books was published last year.

Anyhow, I'd be happy to review more books for you, any time. Fiction is my primary interest, but if you wish I'll review books about the American Southwest, Indians, natural science, what the hell, I'm interested in everything. Note my new summer address below. I'll be back in Tucson in October.

Regards, Edward Abbey—Moab
(and similar to *New Republic*)

**Director, Bureau of Land Management,
Washington, D.C.** (11 JULY 1987)

Dear Sir:

As a hunter, fisherman and camper on our public lands, I strongly object to your proposed new regulations concerning livestock grazing on BLM lands. Your regulations go in exactly the opposite direction of what is needed: i.e., we need far more restrictions on cattle grazing, not less.

In fact, the grazing of domestic livestock—cows, horses, sheep—on our public lands (ours, not the ranchers') should be phased out completely during the next ten years. Those taxpayer-supported parasites have been abusing our public property for over a century now: it's time to call a halt to it. In every western state human recreation, or tourism, is a far bigger money maker for local people than ranching, mining and logging combined, and even aside from mere economic considerations, the health of the land requires that we give first priority to wildlife habitat, watershed protection and ample opportunity for the public enjoyment of what is a public treasure: the free and open spaces of our western states, especially the vast areas under BLM administration.

Those cows are eating grass that belongs to our elk! And most hunters out here are getting fed up with that unjust and destructive situation. Your new regulations would be a big step in the wrong direction. If you don't soon start reducing the number of cattle on our public lands, then we hunters are going to begin a stock reduction program without your help. I feel, and most of my friends agree, that every domestic cow found stumbling around on our public lands should be regarded as a game animal. Open season, no bag limit.

Sincerely, Ed Cartwright—Oracle

cc: Arizona Wildlife Federation, National Wildlife Federation, National Rifle Association, Trout Unlimited, Big Game Hunters' Trophy Association

The Bloomsbury Review, Denver, Colorado   (12 AUGUST 1987)

Dear Editors:

I enjoyed reading the interview with John Nichols in your July-August issue. But why does Ray Gonzalez label me "right wing"? Unfair—and absurd. True, I am in favor of closing our borders to further immigration. From any source. But this is a position supported not only by 80 percent or more of American citizens, but also by such conventional liberals as Morris Udall, Richard Lamm, most labor leaders and almost all environmentalists.

The strongest opponents of immigration control are the industrial farmers of the Southwest, the U. S. Chamber of Commerce, the *Wall Street Journal*, the R.C. church and a few Hispanic politicos eager to enlarge their power base and become U.S. Senators.

As for American meddling in the affairs of Central and South America, I'm against that also. I'm not greatly impressed by the Sandinistas, but I'm sure they're better than Ronald Reagan's *Somocista* mercenaries. Let's stop supporting dictators, police, torture and militarism in Latin America and allow those miserable, starving, overcrowded nations to carry out the revolutions (democratic and demographic) that they so desperately need.

Me, I look forward to the collapse of both the Soviet and American empires. Does that make me a right-winger or a left-winger? Who cares and what's the difference?

Edward Abbey—Oracle

James Cohee, Sierra Club Books,
San Francisco   (7 SEPTEMBER 1987)

Dear Mr Cohee:

In reply to your note of September 2nd, I can offer only guesses as to total sales of my books so far. None of the NY publishers ever include cumulative sales figures in their royalty reports—at least mine don't. But since all have stayed in print (except *Jonathan Troy*) since first publication, and gone through many printings, I suppose the numbers might be somewhere as follows:

The Brave Cowboy, four different editions, thirteen printings, 200,000 copies? 300,000? Who knows?

Fire on the Mountain, four editions, eleven printings, 150,000;
Desert Solitaire, five editions, thirty printings, 500,000 or more;
Black Sun, four editions, six printings, 100,000;
The Monkey Wrench Gang, three editions, nineteen printings, 600,000;
The Journey Home, two editions, sixteen printings, 100,000;
Abbey's Road, two editions, ten printings, 75,000;
Good News, two editions, eight printings, 60,000;
Down the River, two editions, ten printings, 75,000;
Beyond the Wall, two editions, four printings, 40,000;
Slumgullion Stew, two editions, two printings, 15,000;
Etc. The above do not include sales of some of these books in Canada, the U.K., West Germany, Australia and other foreign countries. (Very small.) For accurate and up-to-date numbers you'd have to contact all the many different publishers, some large, some small, here and abroad. I've probably had more different publishers than any other American writer. Why? It's a complicated tale and I don't understand it myself.

Here's an author's biography:

Edward Abbey was born and raised on a farm in northern Appalachia but has lived since 1947 in the American Southwest. He was educated, more or less, at the University of New Mexico, Edinburgh University, and Stanford University. He is the author of many books, including *Desert Solitaire, The Monkey Wrench Gang, Down the River*, and a forthcoming novel, *The Fool's Progress*. At present, he lives with his wife and two children near the town of Oracle in Arizona. Current literary projects include *Hayduke Lives!*, a sequel to *The Monkey Wrench Gang*.

Sincerely, Edward Abbey—Moab

Outside Magazine, Chicago (18 SEPTEMBER 1987)

Editor:

Mr. Alston Chase, in your October issue, alludes to Earth First! and the Sea Shepherd Society as "eco-terrorist" groups. Mr. Chase, as a writer and philosopher, should consult his Oxford dictionary of common usage. "Terrorism" means the deliberate killing of human beings in pursuit of a political end. (E.g., as in Nicaragua by Reagan's mercenaries.) No one in EF! or Sea Shepherd, so far as I know, has ever preached, practiced or condoned such policy or tactics for any purpose. Civil disobedience, yes; sabotage, perhaps—but violence directed at human life, never. Anyone unable to grasp such simple distinctions has no business fooling about with a typewriter. Mr. Chase owes EF! and Sea Shepherd a complete, abject and public apology.

E.A.—Moab

Donn Rawlings   (10 NOVEMBER 1987)

Dear Donn:

Going over my novel *The Fool's Progress* one last time. Scheduled for publication in September 1988. Last chance to get it right and again I would like to ask for suggestions from you.

I'll send you copies of Macrae's letters, altho' most of what he says will be of no assistance to you since the basic ms is now two hundred pp shorter than the one you have in your possession and the pagination therefore different. But his letters—and Congdon's—will give you an idea of what they think could be improved thru cutting.

1) My first question to you, then, is: Do you agree that the novel could be improved by cuts here and there? And if you agree, what scenes, incidents, passages, dialogues, seem in your opinion to drag, to slow the narrative (not always or necessarily a fault, of course), to be repetitive? I like the idea of motific repetition myself, in the manner of a musical imposition, but if such repetitions appear to the reader as careless mistakes by the author, then of course they will not work. I'm not asking you to cite page and paragraph; just general scenes. E.g., is the love affair between Henry and Claire too long?

2) Are some parts too short? Do you find important bridge scenes missing? E.g., the termination of the marriage between Henry and his painter-wife Myra? In your version of the ms there's a long chapter about Henry's adventures in NYC, his wife's infidelity, the final breakup of the marriage: partly at Macrae's urging, partly as experiment, I deleted the entire New York City chapter from the book—i.e., Henry's jobs at Western Electric and the public welfare office, his reunion with Myra, his last fight

with her. Maybe I should restore at least part of that material. No doubt the business at the welfare office—the documents, phone calls etc, go on too long—but I'm rather fond of Henry's conversation in bed with Myra, the job episode at Western Electric.

How about the ending of the book? I'm throwing away the fake "editor's" preface and epilogue—but perhaps I should have some sort of final epilogue, after Henry's meeting with brother Will in the woods. E.g., a very brief scene showing Henry in a car speeding thru Texas toward El Paso, returning to the West, apparently in good health, and with his daughter, his only child, twelve-yr-old Ellsworth, seated beside him. He has kidnapped her from her grandmother and is headed for—Moab? Baja Cal? Vancouver? Sydney? What do you think of that?

3) Questions of technique: Does the switching back and forth from present tense to past tense, from first person to third person, bother you? Does it help the story? In general, as you've no doubt noted, the scenes or chapters in the novel's "present time" (1980) are told in present tense and first person, and most of the flashback scenes (half the book?) in third person and past tense. Not a daring device, or one likely to cause any difficulty with the average reader—but is it annoying? Irritating? Confusing? Clarifying? Useful? Interesting? Should I be, must I be, absolutely consistent in this juggling act?

Punctuation: I dislike it, except where needed for clarity of meaning. I prefer dialogue, e.g., without quotation marks, where I can get away with it. In this novel, you've seen, I have done without quotes in the flashback scenes, used them in the present-time scenes. Does that work all right? Does it create occasional confusion? Irritation in the reader?

4) Old jokes. Most of my jokes are old, stolen from others or from *pissoir* walls. If you've heard some of them or too many of them before, tell me so. Sexism and racism: Is there too much of it in the novel? Henry really is somewhat of an Archie Bunker type, in some ways; does that bother you very much? (I'm not concerned with the reaction of doctrinaire liberals, feminists, minority advocates—few of them will read the book and of those few all will hate it anyway; and I'm weary of bending the knee to all of our many current taboos in this area.)

5) What else? Well, there are many other problems with this novel. As you've said, however, it's the "baggy type" of book—a kitchen sink novel—and my hope or faith is that what would be serious mistakes in a

conventional novel may pass as picaresque libertinism in this book. They've got to or I've got nothing here at all; it's too late to rewrite the entire book, too late to make a different kind of book of it, and furthermore, on the whole, I like *The Fool's Progress* very much as it is. Pretty much as it god-damned is and to hell with the reviewers and the critical torpedoes.

So please, give me a few words if you can. I take full responsibility for the final product; don't hesitate to tell me what you think is clearly bad, or too careless, and don't worry about hurting my tender feelings. As one who has been called an "eco-fascist," "genocidal racist," "creeping fascist hyena" and such, I've developed a fairly thick skin. The only response I cannot bear is—silence. No response. Coarse laughter in all the wrong places would be better than more of the silent treatment.

Best regards to you and Carol, Ed A.

Mildred Abbey, Home, Pennsylvania (15 NOVEMBER 1987)

Dear Mother,

Much thanks for the very nice handmade dress you sent for Becky's birthday. She loves it and has already worn it to several kiddies' parties. Thanks also for the two items from Goodwill.

Benjamin is now eight months old and doing well. He's still a fussy baby, waking up several times every night and keeping us both very busy, but he seems to be perfectly healthy and most of the time very happy—he has a wonderful smile. We'll send you some new pictures soon. Or maybe I can find some to enclose with this letter.

I finished two books this summer. The first, a collection of essays to be called *One Life at a Time, Please*, should be in the bookstores by Christmas; the second, a long, five-hundred-page novel, won't appear until next September. That one I'm calling *The Fool's Progress*. It's a novel about love and marriage, work and play, life and death—everything. What else is there?

Clarke is busy looking after our two new children. I'm writing a couple of magazine pieces and getting ready for my teaching job at the U. in January.

Susie is now in London, attending a University of Arizona field school on British literature, history and politics. She says that she loves London and may stay there for the whole winter. The bad news is that she's fallen in love with some punk rock musician—my worst fears realized! But I guess it was inevitable. And she has to learn sometime what life can be like.

I telephone Johnny now and then; last I heard, he was still undergoing chemotherapy, feeling miserable, but hoping for the best. We used to think that Hoots had all the bad luck—but now look what's happened. He consoles himself—Johnny does—with his doctor's assurances that he will probably live for at least five more years. Some consolation! But at least he's not alone; Nancy visits him occasionally and he has a girlfriend, a Filipino woman named Sonia, who appears to adore him and who stays with him all the time.

I hope that all is well with you and Paul, that you're both keeping active and out-of-doors and fully engaged with life and work. I deeply regret that we all live so far apart. Send me a letter, tell me the latest news. Give my best to Hoots and Iva.

Love, Ned

Meredith Maran, Banana Republic, Inc. (27 NOVEMBER 1987)

Dear Mr. Maran:

Thank you for the nice letter and the seductive invitation to test-wear some charmingly pre-worn (but not pre-owned?) garment from the Banana Republic catalogue. However—I've already got more goddamned clothes around here somewhere than I'll ever wear and besides, when I do need a pair of socks or a clean shirt I go to Bob's Bargain Barn or Yellow Front or K-Mart where everybody knows me and there's never any problem about credit. (Always carry your MasterGun.) But thanks again anyhow.

Truly, Edward Abbey—Oracle

PS: You're welcome to print the above if you want to. And yes, I remember *Talpa* and *El Grito del Norte* and poor old Rini Templeton who was apparently murdered in her hotel room in Mexico City about a year ago, did you know that? As for John DePuy, he and I are still good friends. He now lives in Bluff, Utah and is still painting huge mystical landscapes of the American desert.

City Magazine, **Tucson**   (13 DECEMBER 1987)

Dear Editor:

As my old friend Larry Powell should remember, when I wrote that piece called "The BLOB Comes To Arizona" (*NY Times Magazine*, 1977), I attached Tucson—as an integral part of the BLOB—to its big sister Phoenix. The two cities, in my mind, were and still are one and the same, a slimy palpitating smog-colored greed-begotten ever-expanding commercial-industrial slum. Except for the shrinking stretch of Interstate between them, how tell one from the other?

As for this urbanizing organism eventually convulsing its bowels to produce another "great novel" (whatever that is), who cares? I would not sacrifice a single living mesquite tree for any book ever written. One square mile of living desert is worth a hundred "great books"—and one brave deed is worth a thousand.

Edward Abbey—Tucson

Alston Chase   (16 DECEMBER 1987)

Dear Mr. Chase:

Saw your reply to my letter in the January *Outside.* You ought to be ashamed of yourself. Such cowardly and dishonest weaseling. You're supposed to be an educated man; you know very well that sabotage and terrorism are two widely different things. Any dictionary makes the distinction clear; the public knows very well what "terrorism" means, tho' probably not familiar with the word "sabotage." But you know the difference and therefore your attempt to defame and slander the brave young men and women of Earth First! and the Sea Shepherd Society by calling them "eco-terrorists" is intellectually dishonest and morally base.

This kind of sloppy language, whether employed through ignorance or—as in your case—through an intent to discredit, is exactly the kind of thing that puts you media people in such an unfavorable light in popular opinion. You are no better, in that respect, than the dogmatic leftists and doctrinaire liberals who call me a "racist" or "fascist" or "genocidal elitist" because I happen to oppose mass immigration into the USA. Irrational name-calling in place of rational argument—the *ad hominem* approach—

tends to reduce all public discourse to the level of Trotskyites and John Birchers screaming at each other at a Berkeley street fair.

Shame. If you were a man, or even merely a gentleman, you would have the decency to apologize to Dave Foreman and Paul Watson—and to the readers of *Outside* for attempting to insult their intelligence.

If you ever come to the Tucson area, give me a call; it would be a pleasure to say these things to you face to face.

Sincerely, Edward Abbey—Oracle

Don Congdon, New York City (22 DECEMBER 1987, THE SOLSTICE)

Dear Don:

Thanks for your letter of December 16th. Thanks also for the check from Holt and Sierra Club.

I'm not counting on Macrae's $15,000 "bonus," but I do have some leverage, as he's quite anxious to cut the novel *Fool's Progress* down to five hundred pp. However, the artistic integrity of the novel must come first; I am making all the cuts I can (like Brutus and the boys did to Julius Ceasar), but I will not wreck the rhythm or methodical madness of my book for the sake of a lousy 15G's. (Do they still call them "G's"? or is it "K's"?)

What kind of novel is *The Fool's Progress*? Well, hard to explain. It is not an autobiographical novel; it is not a slice of life novel; it is not even merely a picaresque novel. It is an Edward Abbey novel! Yes, goddamnit, that's what kind of novel it is! And the goddamned reviewers and critics are going to have to accept it like it is—or reject it—I don't give a fuck. (There is a time and place for everything—including arrogance.)

About Avon Books and their dog-in-the-manger attitude toward a trade paperback edition of *Monkey Wrench Gang*. Does Avon really have exclusive rights to such an edition? I don't have a copy of the contract here; in fact I don't think I ever got one, since the deal was made between Avon and Burlingame originally; but my contracts with Avon for their mass-market paperbacks of *Brave Cowboy, Black Sun,* and *Fire on Mt* refer to "rack size paperbacks" only. What does that mean? Perhaps I do retain author's rights to a trade paperback edition of *MWG.* Perhaps you could obtain a copy of the contract from Matson or Burlingame and check up on this point, if you think it's worth the trouble. It'll be at least two years before *Hayduke Lives!*

appears in print, and the people at Avon are being unfair both to me and to themselves, it seems to me.

What about Joseph Pierson of Modular Movies? (What's a modular movie?) Is he going to renew his option on *Good News*? And that other guy, Chris Shelton, who took the option on the "Rocks" episode in *Desert Solitaire*—is he the one who declined to renew? Or was it the other guy?

Guess I need a better filing system. Or a better secretary. (My wife complains she's overworked and underpaid already but what did she expect? This is not a union shop. Arizona is a right-to-work state. Life is not fair.)

Merry Christmas and Happy New Year, Don.

Ed—Fort Llatikcuf

Jim Carrico   (29 DECEMBER 1987)

Dear Jim:

Thanks for the card and the note. Yes, I was only kidding about a seasonal ranger job but this ranch caretaker deal sounds interesting. Tell us more about it: Exactly where is the place? What are the living accommodations like (I've got a wife and two small children again, you know, ages four and one)? Does the job include transportation devices—4×4 truck, saddle horses, trail bike—or do I have to supply my own? Could I get away now and then if I provide a satisfactory alternate caretaker? somebody like maybe Bill Hoy, for example? and so on. No salary attached, I presume? And what exactly would my duties consist of?

Yes, old Hoy never quits. I guess we'll never get him out of Fort Bowie now. I'd like to move to Ajo myself, live in one of those old miner's shacks; you and Bill ought to join me there. It's becoming a retirement town, you know, since the mine and smelter shut down, apparently for keeps. We ought to get some of us good people in there before the Californians and Minnesotans buy up the whole place. DePuy, for instance—I'm trying to get him interested in spending the winters there.

Well, it's good to hear from you. I trust you're having a good time at Big Bend; I always did love that place myself and have always regretted passing up a couple of opportunities to work there as a seasonal [ranger] back in the early '60s.

All my best to you and Ginny,

Ed A.—Tucson

1988

ED'S "FAT MASTERPIECE" of a novel, *The Fool's Progress*, is finally released, followed shortly by his final self-edited essay collection, *One Life at a Time, Please*. Meanwhile, he is hard at work on one last fast novel: *Hayduke Lives!* A glory of camping, alone and with friends. Mother Abbey, 83, dies in a traffic accident and Ed goes back to Home for the funeral. As his esophageal varices (an internal variation on varicose veins) worsens, Abbey's "bleeds" come more often, hitting harder and harder, occasionally sending him to the emergency room for transfusions.

Phoenix New Times   (JANUARY 1988)

Dear Editor:

I am disappointed to see that *NT* has apparently discontinued its book review column. Altho' most of your readers have doubtless probly not opened a book since they dropped out of high school, many of us do still care about ideas, the close scrutiny of life and the literary art. A concern with books gave your periodical a touch of intellectual class, compensating for excess attention paid to trash movies, glutton eateries and junk music— i.e., "rock" music to hammer out fenders by, or vomit with while hugging yr toilet bowl.

E.A.—Oracle

Henry Kisor, Books Editor,
Chicago Sun-Times   (18 JANUARY 1988)

Dear Mr Kisor:

Thank you for sending me a copy of the review of *One Life at a Time, Please*. Tell Sam Curtis I liked the review but don't understand why he accuses me of "gratuitous meanness" in the essay on public-lands beef ranchers. My audience at Missoula thought the lecture was funny; most of them laughed, only a few got mad, yelled, walked out, fired off guns etc. Also, the joke about failing to insult everyone "present" was meant, well, as a joke; most people seem to find it humorous, as I do, and as Brahms (from whom I stole it) did.

And the part in "Immigration . . . " which he views as "overkill" I see as simple straightforward fact: If it appears hyperbolic to reviewers it is only because most American writers have allowed themselves to be muffled by the bland, suffocating, self-censoring politesse of our hypersensitive taboo-ridden decade. I think we need some plain speech and blunt talk and a facing up to the truth in this guilt-neurotic country. And some tolerance for humor: Like most of my reviewers, Curtis seems totally unaware of the author's humorous intentions. Of course, if I have to point this out it means I failed; but in reading these essays to various groups around the country, most people responded, as I intended, with laughter. (A little nervous, in some cases.)

Ah well—us writers never get enough love. And the more we do get, the more we want.

If you still wish to do that interview, I'm willing. If you ever get to the Tucson area, call me . . . otherwise, just send me a bunch of questions on paper and I'll answer them to the best of my ability. The fat novel, *The Fool's Progress* (five hundred pp or so), is scheduled for publication this coming September. Knowing NY publishers, however, it'll probably be at least two months late.

Regards, Edward Abbey—Tucson

Ann Zwinger, Colorado Springs, Colorado (21 JANUARY 1988)

Dear Ann:

Sorry I didn't get a chance to talk w/ you at that writer's shindig last— Nov? I was abducted by Donn Rawlings and never got back.

Anyhow, I hope your work is going well. Tell your publisher to send me an advance copy of your next book & I'll give it a plug. (Tho' that might do you more harm than good . . .)

Best regards, Ed A.

The Nation, New York City (22 JANUARY 1988)

Dear Editor:

Thank you for publishing the review of the new Jeffers anthology. Dana Gioia's bold brave defense of the poetry of Robinson Jeffers was much needed, long overdue and brilliantly presented. Jeffers is one of our great and basic Am poets, right in there with Walt Whitman, Emily Dickinson (a sop to *les femmes*), Robert Frost, Wallace Stevens & WC Wms. (Who else? Can't think of any others.)

Jeffers in fact was more than a great poet, he was a great prophet. Everything he predicted about the corruption of empire, the death of democracy, the destruction of our planet and the absurd self-centered vanity of the human ape has come true tenfold-over since his time. The work of Jeffers makes us realize how comparatively petty is that of Eliot, Pound, Stevens & all their many imitators.

Let justice be done! Tho' Parnassus fall . . . even in the literary world. Now will some daring critic come forward to rehabilitate the name of Thomas Wolfe?

E.A.

The Tucson Weekly   (22 JANUARY 1988)

Dear Editor:

If C. J. McElroy's Dead Animal Museum is not the world's largest, as his attorney Alfred Donau says, it is certainly the world's ugliest. Here is one place where bulldozers and dynamite could be employed, for a change, in a truly constructive way. Meanwhile, the county should condemn the building and use it as a jail (which is what it looks like) for trophy hunters, Off Road Vermin and all others convicted of molesting our wildlife. Dr Donau expresses concern for what he calls the "sanctity" of life; if he is sincere, he should mention that concept to his boss. In my opinion, one living oryx, ibex, jaguar or leopard is worth about ten thousand C. J. McElroys.

(Ah! Do I smell the odor of smoking particle board? Yes, it's Conrad Goeringer, brains steaming with fury, leaping at his typewriter, about to accuse me of criminal hypocrisy. Save your steam, Conrad: I plead guilty: I really do believe that the lives of such endangered mammals as mountain lion, grizzly bear, bighorn sheep or desert pronghorn are of more importance, in the larger scheme of things, than the survival or non-survival of a few million humans here and there on a planet already grossly overcrowded with more than five billion ((5,000,000,000)) of us naked apes.)

Sincerely, Edward Abbey—Tucson

Playboy Magazine, Chicago   (23 JANUARY 1988)

Dear Playboy:

Your "Forum" article on the handgun controversy by William J. Helmer is interesting but does not touch upon the central issue: the right of the people to own, possess and bear arms. As I wrote in Playboy several years ago, a well-armed citizenry is the best defense, the final defense and ultimately the only defense against tyranny. Rifles and handguns are the weapons of democracy; if we allow them to be taken from us, we retreat one more big step back from the great American tradition of self-reliance and decentralized power. As I said then and believe now, When guns are outlawed, only the Government will have guns. The Government—and a few outlaws. If that happens, you can count me among the outlaws.

By the way, I also enjoyed the bright, clever story by young Aaron Abbey. Is he any relation to the great American novelist and essayist Edward Abbey, of Oracle, Arizona?

Sincerely, Edward Abbey–Oracle

Barry Lopez, Finn Rock, Oregon (25 JANUARY 1988)

Dear Barry—

Thank you for the thoughtful letter. Of course it's not easy to speak of the free writer's obligations. Art first? or the community (meaning all life, not only human life)? Or first one, then the other? *Both*, I say, in any case. Somehow. (Enjoy your travels while you can; the world, I think, is becoming nastier, uglier, meaner every year. Take care: survive: we need you.) Come visit when you can. Fraternally,

Ed A.

Susie Abbey, London, England (14 FEBRUARY 1988)

Dear Sooze:

Enclosed are some Am Express travelers cheques for your amusement and delectation. Have fun. Be sure to keep the record slip; you'll need it for refunds if you lose any of the cheques.

Clarke and I have given careful consideration to your desire to enroll in that applied arts school in London and—we do not think it a very good idea. The school's Los Angeles main center has no accreditation, none of our artist friends ever heard of it and the tuition costs are higher than those of a real college or university.

However, I sympathize with your wish to stay in London for another two or three months and am willing to help you do that. I wish you were

going to a good school there, or to a school in Israel, but since you're not—
you're not.

But I will not finance your stay in England beyond this coming Spring
unless you enroll in a real English (or Scot) university, with a good academic reputation both in Britain and the USA. You are a very bright and
able young woman, you've already built up a good academic record, you're
ready to begin your junior year in college—and that's what I want you to
do. Return to a good university next August, either here or there, preferably
here. If you are determined to live in a big city, you could go to Los Angeles
or San Francisco or maybe even NY if we can afford it. But you must go to a
good school. I will not pay out a lot of money to put you through some kind
of trade school or vocational school or commercial arts school; you are too
good for that. Too smart. Too promising.

I'm not sure how much talent you have for art. I know that you are good
with words and ideas and would probly do well in English, journalism and
literature, which in turn could ease your way into the glamorous worlds of
the magazines, of publishing, of free-lance writing. And if you are good at
art, you could major in art in college in the two years you have remaining.

But a commercial art school? No. *Nein. Non. Nyet.* (Do I make myself
clear? Yes. Am I a snob where you are concerned? Yes. Do I expect great
things from you? Of course. Will I be disappointed if you do not become
famous, rich, highly admired? No—but I will be somewhat surprised.)

So, you get the picture. Basically, we all want you to come home pretty
soon. We love you and miss you. I'm glad that you're enjoying London and
England and a little of Europe, but I don't want you to stay over there much
longer unless you go to a good school. And even then, we want you to come
home for at least a month, soon, for vacation. You should be applying, right
now, for admission to a good school somewhere, anywhere, unless you
want to drop out and work or travel for a year, which I also think would be
a nice idea. But the next two years in a school of "applied arts"? Negative.

So come home for a while. Love and a hug from your

Dad

The Tucson Weekly (12 FEBRUARY 1988)

To the Editor:

Left-wing dogmatists like Carlos (Conrad G.?) Portela think I'm a right-winger ("fascist! sexist! racist!") because I oppose immigration and massive taxpayer-funded nursing for the terminally sick. The right-wing dogmatists think I'm a left-winger ("terrorist! anarchist! bleeding-heart liberal!") because I oppose Washington's murderous policies in Latin America and because I'm against humankind's planetary war on Nature.

What neither wing can grasp is that the bird of truth—like the falcon! the eagle! the yellow-bellied sapsucker!—flies on two wings. Not one. Two.

"The hero of my tale," wrote Tolstoy in his memoirs of the battle at Sevastopol, "is truth." This is a notion beyond the rigid ideologies of both our political Right and Left. Enraptured by their visions of Heaven in Space or Heaven on Earth, neither faction has time to concern itself with anything so crass and vulgar as experiential, verifiable, irrefragable, empiric fact. It's an old and common human failing; we must be . . . understanding.

Sincerely,.Edward Abbey—Tucson

John Macrae, Henry Holt and Co. (9 MARCH 1988)

Dear Jack:

The jacket copy you sent me is not "brief"—it goes on and on for a page and a half. Please: let's keep it truly brief (one paragraph), modest, simple. No hyperbole, no quotes from unknown Midwest reviewers, no extravagant claims. Lots of blank space on the jacket flap looks good. Remember, the author is assumed by most readers to be responsible for everything on as well as in the book. And the author should be!

That goes for the art also: I want to see your proposed jacket illustration but unless it's very good, I'd prefer to stay with my Tarot fool, which is exactly right for the novel; a crude ("harsh"?) cartoonish effect is exactly what I want; the medieval look gives the suggestion of universality, which is also what I want; the less contemporary it looks, the better. If you don't like my version of the Fool, let's get Robert Crumb to do it.

Anyhow, this book is very important to me, my first and perhaps last attempt at a serious novel, and I want everything just right. Appropriate.

Perfect! The figure of the Fool, emblem of the novel, should appear on the jacket and again on, or opposite, the title page. Please! Have a heart for your poor anxious author. All you have to risk is a measly hundred thousand dollars or so: while I have my reputation for impeccable good taste at stake! See you in the Fall; and if you don't do this book right, I'll be accompanied by my friends Lacey, Hooligan and Igor, fully armed.

Love, Ed A.

Arizona Daily Star (13 MARCH 1988)

Dear Editors:

Why has no one in Arizona come out against the absurd Hyper-Destructing Super Collider scheme? I understand of course that we could not expect any such opposition from our hack politicos or media magnates, with their usual mindless appetite for what they call "Growth." But where are the middleclass taxpaying citizens who will have to finance this multibillion dollar boondoggle? Where are the conservationists who should be defending what little remains of our open space and besieged wildlife? And where (but I mention this group only for laughs)—where is the community of Arizona writers who might be expected, when no one else will, to speak up for moderation? Common sense? A slight pause in our mad rush into technological horror?

Why does not someone ask the question that must always be asked in respect to these industrial-science proposals, namely, *Cui bono*? Who benefits? Who gains from these super-colossal industrial science projects? A moment's reflection and the answer is obvious. The gainers will be that same little pack of land speculators, construction contractors and assorted Chamber of Commerce types whose only apparent motive for living is money-profit-greed. Plus a few janitorial positions for high school drop-outs.

And, oh yes, finally, among the principal beneficiaries will be the witch doctors of modern physics, whose greatest gift to humanity so far has been the nuclear bomb.

Edward Abbey—Oracle

John Macrae, Henry Holt & Co.,
New York City (20 APRIL 1988)

Dear Jack . . .

How's our novel proceeding? I hope that you're willing to agree by now
that the Tarot pack Fool makes an appropriate symbol for Henry Lightcap
and a good motif for the jacket illustration. I agree that my own drawing is
crude, harsh, cartoonish (deliberately so), but of course a professional artist could produce something more elegant, no doubt. But maybe not quite
so appropriate.

Anyhow, I have been counting on the Tarot fool as visual symbol for my
novel for over two years now. To me it seems perfect. Please don't discard
the idea unless you can convince me you've got something better.

One Life . . . got a nice review in *Outside* Mag. Brief, but generous. I suppose, as usual, those scum at *Time*, *Newsweek*, What Else?, will choose to
ignore the book. As always. In thirty-four years—my first book was published in 1954—in thirty-four years I have never had a review in *Time*,
Newsweek, Or—*Wall St Journal?* Well now, what of it.

My best regards to you, Amy, Sarah and all,

Ed A.—Tucson

Robert Houston (27 APRIL 1988)

Dear Robert:

Here's a list of my own favorites. Or two lists, actually, of the best that
come immediately to mind.

TEN GREAT MODERN NOVELS
The Death Ship, by B. Traven
The Bridge in the Jungle, by B. Traven
The Treasure of the Sierra Madre, by B. Traven
The Magic Mountain, Buddenbrooks, and *Dr. Faustus*, by Thomas Mann
Growth of the Soil, Hunger, and *Pan*, by Knut Hamsun
Independent People, by Halldor Laxness
Journey to the End of the Night, by Céline

Nausea, by Sartre
Zorba the Greek, by Kazantzakis
The Underdogs, by Mariano Azuela
The Cancer Ward, by Solzhenitsyn
Light of the World, by Jean Giono
Seven Red Sundays, by Ramon Sender
The Skin, by Curzio Malaparte
Of Time and the River, and *You Can't Go Home Again*, by Thomas Wolfe
The Grapes of Wrath, by John Steinbeck
A Walk on the Wild Side, by Nelson Algren
Tropic of Capricorn, by Henry Miller
Stalingrad, by Theodor Plivier
Darkness at Noon, by Koestler
Molloy, by Samuel Beckett
(twenty-six, actually!)

CONTEMPORARY FAVORITES
(mostly American and English, skimmed off the top of my head,
    with a cautious avoidance of U of A and Tucson writers):
Kingsley Amis: *Lucky Jim, That Certain Feeling, Stanley and the Women,
    The Old Devils*
Evelyn Waugh: *A Handful of Dust, Black Mischief, Scoop, Vile Bodies*
Wm Gaddis: *The Recognitons, JR*
Wm [Kurt] Vonnegut: *Slaughterhouse Five, Player Piano, Galapagos*
Wm Kotzwinkle: *Doctor Rat, The Fan Man*
Wm Eastlake: *The Bronc People*
Katherine Porter: *Noon Wine, Ship of Fools*
Joan Didion: *Play It As It Lays*
Jos Heller: *Catch-22, Something Happened*
Don DeLillo: *Ratner's Star, White Noise*
Thomas Pynchon: *V, Gravity's Rainbow*
Cormac McCarthy: *Blood Meridian, Suttree, Child of God,
    Outer Dark, The Orchard Keeper*
John Barth: *The Sot-Weed Factor*
Robert Coover: *The Public Burning*
James Jones: *From Here to Eternity*
Norman Mailer: *The Naked and the Dead*

Carlos Fuentes: *The Death of Artemio Cruz*
Gabriel-Marquez: *Love in a Time of Cholera* (tried but failed to labor
    through *100 Yrs of Solipsism*)
Graham Greene: *The Quiet American*
Chas Bukowski: *Women, Notes of a Dirty Old Man*
Wm Faulkner: *Mosquitos, Spotted Horses, The Wild Palms*
Ernest Hemingway: *To Have and Have Not, For Whom the Bell Tolls*
Tom Wolfe: *The Bonfire of the Vanities*
Richard Wright: *Native Son*
Donald Barthelme: *Snow White*
Thomas Berger: *Crazy in Berlin, The Feud, Who Is Teddy Villanova?*
Walter Clark: *The Ox-Bow Incident*
Larry McMurtry: *Lonesome Dove, Horseman Pass By*
E L Doctorow: *Ragtime*
J P Donleavy: *The Ginger Man*
John Fowles: *The French Lieutenant's Woman*
Bernard Malamud: *The Natural*
Peter Matthiessen: *At Play in the Fields of the Lord*
Nabokov: *Lolita, Pnin, Bend Sinister*
J C Oates: *Son of the Morning, Them, Angel of Light*
Charles Portis: *True Grit*
Philip Roth: *Portnoy's Complaint, Our Gang*
Robert Stone: *Dog Soldiers, A Flag for Sunrise*
Nathanael West: *Day of the Locust*
Virginia Woolf: *To the Lighthouse* (well, 20th C.)
Wallace Stegner: *The Big Rock Candy Mountain*
Malcolm Lowry: *Under the Volcano*
Wendell Berry: *A Place on Earth, Old Jack, The Wild Birds*
Edward Hoagland: *Seven Rivers West*
etc etc. . . .

GREATEST BOOKS OF ALL TIME, SO FAR
Montaigne: *Essays*
Burton: *The Anatomy of Melancholy*
Thoreau: *Walden* (and other essays)
Shakespeare: *Collected Songs, sonnets and soliloquies*
Selected poems of Shelley, Keats, Blake, Burns, Skelton, Byron,

Marvell, Herrick, Edward Thomas, Dylan Thomas, Thomas Hardy,
E. A. Housman, Auden, Wilmot, Waller, Marlowe, Dekker, Larkin,
Yeats, Wyatt and, best of all, Anon.
Certain books from the Elizabethan Bible: *Genesis, Exodus, Song of Songs,*
Job, Psalms, Proverbs, Ruth, Ecclesiastes, Isaiah, and the *Gospel*
According to Matthew
Selected poems of Whitman, Frost, Stevens, Lindsay, Masters, Jeffers,
Williams, Pound, Eliot, Kinnell, Bly, Ferlinghetti and . . . ?
Mark Twain: *A Connecticut Yankee, The Mysterious Stranger* and
Huckleberry Finn
Tolstoy: *The Cossacks, War & Peace* and *Hadji Murad*
Chekhov: collected stories
Conrad: *Victory, Heart of Darkness, Lord Jim*
Joyce: *Ullysses, Portrait of the Artist* . . .
Hugo: *Les Miserables*
Zola: *Earth*
Proust: *Swann's Way, The Past Recaptured*
Among the ancients: Diogenes, Heraclitus, Lucretius, Catallus . . .
Among *les philosophes*: Lucretius, Epicurus, Bruno, Spinoza,
Schopenhauer, Santayana, Russell . . .
Lao-Tse: *The Way*
Melville: *Ahab the Arab*

And so on and so on, but this is getting ridiculous; what I really like,
better than any book, is the sound of a girl singing to herself in a distant
melon patch, of a small boy playing "Red River Valley" on his new har-
monica while dangling his bare feet in the muddy waters of Crooked Crick,
West Virginia, of a raven on the canyon wall.

Mike Roselle   (29 APRIL 1988)

Dear Mike:

Thanks for your note of April 13th. Of course I'd been planning to write
to you for months, ever since I heard about your latest capers and incarcer-
ations, and as usual, through sloth and indolence, didn't get around to it.

Anyhow, I'm glad to hear you'll be out of there by June. Indeed, both women and wilderness will now seem even more delightful to you. I never spent more than a few days in jail myself, and not once for an honorable cause—the charges against me were things like vagrancy, reckless driving, public drunkenness and "negligent" driving—but even those few days were enough to greatly enhance the pleasures of freedom.

I hope to read all about your adventures soon. In the *EF! Journal* perhaps? Thanks for the kind remarks about my books. I've always admired you too, much more than I admire myself: People like you and Howie and Dave and friends actually get out and practice what I only preach. Yours is the better role. My excuses are various: I'm too old, too lazy, too cowardly, too bogged down in family life, etc., but whatever the reason, the fact is I do my best to stay out of legal trouble. Tho' God only knows the temptations to do otherwise can be powerful.

Have a good time in Hell's Canyon and keep on raising hell. You're a hero to me and to many others also. Give my best to your *companera* Karen.

Fraternally, Ed—Tucson

Alexander Cockburn, c/o *Zeta* Magazine   (CINCO DE MAYO 1988)

Dear Mr Cockburn:

I'm a regular reader of your column in *The Nation*, always with interest, usually with general agreement. You can easily imagine then, how deeply you have wounded my feelings by calling me (and my good friend Dave Foreman) "fascist," "racist," etc. I am accustomed to such childish name-calling from sectarian fanatics like Murray Bookchin, but I would have assumed that you would adopt a more rational tone.

Opposition to mass immigration, legal or illegal, from any source, does not make one a fascist or racist. It merely makes one an opponent of mass immigration, as are the overwhelming majority of American citizens, including most Mexicans, blacks, Indians etc. (If we can believe the polls. And the response of Congress to years of complaint.) Most labor leaders and unions are against more immigration, for good and obvious reasons; almost all conservationists are against immigration, for reasons even more good and obvious. The basic fact is that America is sinking under an overload of political, social, economic and environmental problems; we are in no position to take on those of Latin America, Asia and Africa as well. Of course much of the Third World's misery is caused by European and American imperialism. Among our many moral obligations is to bring that infernal meddling to an end. E.g., no more loans, no more weapons, no more medical missionaries, no more CIA chicanery. Agreed. But it's merely a white middleclass liberal guilt neurosis to imagine that our domineering arrogance is the sole or even the central source of mischief. Africans were murdering, eating and enslaving one another long before Vasco de Gama appeared off the Angolan coast. The endless horrors of Mexico go back at least to the Mayan and Aztec empires and their culture of war, massacre, slavery, torture, human sacrifice and cannibalism. To most Mexican Indians, Cortez probably appeared (at first) as a liberator. And Asia: India and its caste system, China, Japan. . . . Ah well, you see my point.

If you hope for any sort of dialogue and unity with all factions on the vaguely leftist or radical side of politics, you must cease from silly verbal abuse. If you don't want it, then we go on as we are, fractious and impotent.

Edward Abbey—Oracle

Zeta Magazine   (6 MAY 1988)

Dear Sirs:

I'm willing to shrug off sectarian political abuse ("racist! elitist! sexist! fascist! terrorist! redneck! Democrat!") because over the years I've become fairly accustomed to it. But what does Alex Cockburn mean by his remark in your April issue that I advocate "marching middle-aged tourists on foot into wilderness areas"? Is that what the Khmer Rouge did, the swine!?

Cockburn says that he's read some of my books but he cites no source for his allegation. I can't recall ever writing such a thing myself. It violates my principles. I'm in favor of preserving the wilderness, not crowding it with more tourists, middle-aged or whatever, on foot or in Winnebagos.

Merely out of curiosity, please: What is Cockburn talking about?

Yours fraternally forever, Edward Abbey—Oracle

Lewis Lapham, Editor, *Harper's* **Magazine,**
New York City (7 MAY 1988)

Dear Mr Lapham:

Letters such as that by Mr Steve Gallizoli (*Harper's*, May 1988), attacking my "stinking environmentalism," remind us that functional illiteracy is a serious problem in our United States, perhaps more of a threat to the republic than ORVs, AIDS or the CIA.

On the one hand, Mr Gallizoli accuses me of urging feedlot beef upon the American public as preferable to hunting wild game. But I wrote no such thing. What I said in "Hunting in Earnest" is that killing merely for sport is morally wrong. On the other hand, Mr Gallizoli accuses me of condemning the "entire" beef industry in a previous *Harper's* article, thus finding me guilty of hypocrisy. But I did not condemn the entire beef industry—only that tiny 3 or 4 percent of subsidized welfare ranchers who turn loose their private cows upon our public lands. The two arguments are not contradictory but complementary.

The inability to grasp such clear and simple distinctions is a symptom of functional illiteracy, a common malady among high-school graduates (like Mr Gallizoli) from the arid wastelands of Arizona.

Edward Abbey—Oracle

Joan Tapper, *National Geographic Traveler* (10 JUNE 1988)

Dear Ms Tapper:

My apologies! It appears that I badly goofed. Since I wrote that story "River of No Return" back in 1985, I had assumed that it was published in your magazine the same year. (Or was it 1986?)

Of course, both my book publisher and my agent should have contacted you for permission to reprint the articles first published by the Geographic Society. That is customary, I believe, and they have always done so in the past. Or at least I think they have. At any rate, I have never had to perform that chore myself—and I have now published six or seven collections of magazine pieces.

As for failing to credit original publication to the *Traveler*, that is strictly my fault. I should have caught the omission in proofreading the galleys; I did not. Again I apologize.

How can I make amends? I will return the money paid me for the "River" story, if you wish. . . . And you may publish my confession of negligence in your magazine, if you wish. Anyhow, I am very sorry and much embarrassed by these breaches of our agreement and of editorial courtesies.

Finally, I hope I haven't so disgraced myself that you never ask me to do something for *Traveler* again. Right now I'm bogged down in the writing of one more novel—*Hayduke Lives!*, a sequel to *The Monkey Wrench Gang*—but expect to be free for travel and journalism again by next Spring. How about a piece on Western Australia? Or the Fish River in SW Africa? Or the Quinn River in northwest Nevada—a river that runs for only about a month each year, and disappears into the sands and alkali of a sinkhole lake?

Sincerely, Edward Abbey—Oracle

The Tucson Weekly (12 JUNE 1988)

(In reply to Jeff Smith's attack on "stupid cheerleaders")

"Stupid"? They're cute, soft, bouncy, sweet, sexy, beautiful, the only things worth watching in the dumbest dullest most repetitive simpleminded game ever devised.

"Stupid"? I'll bet any one of those girls has an I.Q. twice as high as the ten giant burrheads thumping and a-thundering back and forth, to and fro, up and down that tiny piece of hardwood floor, dumping a leather beachball thru a net funnel over and over and over again, in what always seems like the longest thousand-minute hour in all of organized sports.

Unfortunately, the TV cameras have evidently fallen into the control of a gang of feminist prudes, thus giving us only rare and tantalizing glimpses of the only part of this silly game that most male viewers give a damn about.

(Printed? Hah! Never mailed, never written, never even dared!)

Editor, *Stinking Desert Gazette* (11 AUGUST 1988)

Dear Bob:

Would you please convey the following response to The Wild Wonted (Wanted?) Women of Moab. They forgot to print an address in their "Slinking Desert Glace"—a charming little broadside, by the way. Hmmmmm:

To: Wild Wonted Women, Moab, Utah

Dear Sirs:

Your "Open Letter" to me was noted and much appreciated. Believe me, I have been trying for years to get a vasectomy, but my public simply will not permit it. Last time I even reached my physician's operating table, but as she examined me, wondering why I'd never been circumcised, and then going further to make sure everything was in good functioning order, at that climactic moment another mob of tearful young women burst into the room and carried me off, begging to "have my baby," as you ladies say.

So—what could I do? I haven't even been allowed to make a deposit in a sperm bank; flinging their skirts in the air, the tellers hurl their bodies in my path, causing me to stumble and fall—once again. Over and over and over again.

Sincerely, Edward Abbey—Oracle

Editor, *City Magazine*, **Tucson** (18 JUNE 1988)

Dear Iggie:

Anyone who takes a radical stand on public issues will receive hate mail. I get my share, including threats on my life and against my wife, kids, dog, cat, etc. Until recently all such mail reached me only through my Oracle P.O. box. Now, however, it begins to appear in the letters columns of the *Tucson Weekly*, the *Tucson Citizen*, the *Arizona Daily Estrellita* and even in the much esteemed *City Magazine*. All of these public letters, written in the same hysterical incoherent sub-literate style, are attributed to a certain "Carlos Portela" or sometimes "Portillo." Who this person is or why he is so displeased with me I can't say, but obviously he (she?) has never read a book of mine (or likely any book at all) and has only the dimmest, third-hand notions of what I've written. None of this should matter to anyone but me, except that it seems unfair, "not cricket," as we say, that *City Magazine* would allow its letters page to be used for the pursuit of what seems to be a monomaniac vendetta.

Sincerely, Edward Abbey

Jim Fergus   (26 JUNE 1988)

My dear Mr Fergus:

The papers you sent to me c/o [Ken] Sleight finally arrived. I have read your essays and like them very much, especially the terribly moving piece about the gutshot bear. That essay should be anthologized. Perhaps it has been. Please send me copies of your essays on McGuane and Harrison if convenient; I'd love to read them. And if you ever need an agent, or a better agent, try mine, Don Congdon, at 156 5th Ave NYC 10010. Mention my name. Good luck with the novel. You are a gifted writer and I'm certain you will have many books published in the years to come.

No more questions? Please be sure to let me know if you want to quote anything from what you may have found of interest in the Abbey "archives." I might allow you to quote things from some of the private correspondence if I'm sure it won't hurt anyone or violate any confidances. Confidences?

If you'd like a recent photograph of the celebrated author, write to photographer Mark Klett, Tempe AZ. He was a member of our Grand Gulch expedition in May.

Just got back from a week in Cabeza Prieta Nat'l Wildlife Refuge, where I spent many many hours inside a saguaro-rib blind counting bighorn sheep and other beasts for the government. Temp 116 degrees F. in the shade. Humidity about 5 percent. Got my truck bogged down in the sand for forty-eight hours on the way in, nearly perished from exasperation and sheer terror. Of course, I had plenty of water with me, i.e., thought I did, enough for a week—fifteen gallons—but I was ten miles from Eagle Tank, sixteen miles from Papago Well and fifty miles from the nearest human habitation (Ajo, Arizona).

The desert, always sublime, really can be sublimely terrible as well. Finally had to deflate my rear tires to 5 psi to get out of the sand, then reinflate them with a hand pump. Took me the two days to think of that, after nearly killing myself with jack, shovel and cutting brush. But finally made it through, got to Eagle Tank, set up camp, ate a whole watermelon to celebrate. And saw four sheep. One fox. Several coyotes. Thousands of doves and millions of bees. And got stuck in the sand again on the way out. But only for two hours that time.

Next time, I take the Red Dragon—fatter tires and more power: 500 cubes!

Best regards,
Ed Abbey

Jack Shoemaker, Editor in Chief, North Point Press, San Francisco, California (29 JUNE 1988)

Dear Mr Shoemaker:

A writer I know named Charles Bowden tells me he has just completed another book. I suggested to him that he show the typescript to you before sending it off to New York.

Bowden has published three books of non-fiction so far—*Killing the Hidden Waters, Blue Desert,* and *Frog Mountain Blues,* all published by the University of Arizona Press. I have read all three and admire them very much. They are chiefly about the American Southwest, treated from an environmentalist point of view.

At present, Bowden works as editor of *City Magazine,* a Tucson monthly. Before that and for many years he was a reporter for the *Tucson Daily Citizen.*

I think he is a very good writer, with a shrewd eye for human folly and a sympathetic heart for the used and abused, both human and other. He writes in a laconic, highly compressed, indirect style, laced with irony, humor and a wholesome dash of cyanide. I.e., he regards the human race with less than total admiration. He deserves, in my opinion, a better publisher and a much larger audience than he has had to date.

If he brings his new book to you, I urge you to read it with full consideration. (But I don't imagine you bother reading anything with less.) Sorry that this letter is beginning to sound like a publisher's blurb. So I'll end it here.

Sincerely, Edward Abbey—Tucson

Arizona Daily Star (29 JUNE 1988)

Dear Editor:

The Growth Mania in southern Arizona seems to be completely out of control. The developers and instant slum-builders are running amuck, apparently with the full and willing cooperation of our elected officials, from local city councilmen all the way down to our U. S. Congressmen and U. S. Senators.

The U. S. Forest Service, probably the most corrupt of all Federal agencies (with the possible exception of the CIA and the Pentagon), is now engaged in a devastating road project on Mount Lemmon. The Pima County Transportation Department is doubling the width of Sweetwater Street, in the process destroying some of the biggest, oldest and loveliest palo verde trees in the city. (Our state tree, by the way.)

Star Pass is being turned into a wasteland of condo-mania and golf courses. Oracle Highway, Pusch Ridge, Bear Canyon, Ventana Canyon, the Tortolitas and the Catalina-Oracle area are going under in the usual smog of dust, diesel soot, bellowing earth-destroyers and the smoke from cremated trees.

"Our tax dollars at work." And why? For what purpose? All to enrich or further enrich a tiny group of greedy, insatiable and mostly absentee land speculators. We are witnessing every day acts of criminal vandalism that would cost an ordinary citizen at least six months in jail. But these developers are allowed to profit from their crimes because it contributes to the sacred and holy God of Almighty G-R-O-W-T-H.

When and how can we stop these scoundrels? They are destroying our city, our beautiful valley, a whole and once enjoyable way of life. Enough, I say, enough! Tucson is ugly enough already. Tucson is far more than big enough already. No more groveling before Hughes Aircraft, Mayor Volgy; now that we're getting rid of part of IBM, let's get rid of these other polluters, land rapers, water poisoners. Let's start thinking more about the quality of life around here instead of the quantity of dollars.

Sincerely yours, Clarke Cartwright [E.A.], Tucson

David Petersen, Durango, Colorado   (25 JULY 1988)

Dear Dave,

Thanks for your letter of July 19th.

Yes, rec'd the *American Country* magazines (stupid title) and the article and art look good. Several good pieces in there, which I intend to read. Someday.

Right now I'm preoccupied with *Hayduke Lives!* On page 135 today and typing right along. If I can keep up this pace, I should have a first draft of 450 pp or so by October. Which would be a load off my mind. (I hate commitments, obligations and working under pressure. But on the other hand, I like getting paid in advance and I only work under pressure.)

As you can imagine, I'm heartily sick of interviews and being photographed. But for you, old buddy, I might do it, one more time. But let's have *Mother Earth News* do something for me too: like buy a chapter of the book for publication in their manure-spreader magazine. Tell them that's my condition: publish a chapter of the book, for $1500, (No, $2500!) at least, and I'll submit to one more phukking interview. They could run it in *Am Country* if that seemed more appropriate.

Anyhow, no rush. This book will certainly not be published until sometime next Fall. 1989 I mean. If your boss agrees to my deal, I'll send you a copy of the first draft as soon as it's completed and you or he or them or it can choose a chapter. As for the interview, we could do that by mail. Send me a few questions and I'll think of some more, make it a self-interview perhaps. You can always fake the locale, say we met in Tuba City or Española, and I could easily supply you with a choice of recent photos.

Sorry to hear your Guthrie book is being ignored. Am not surprised, but I am offended by it. Those bastards back East should have the decency to give the old man at least one more review. I'll try to help. *EF!* wants me to review it, so I'll write up a review, try to sell it to the *NY Times* or *LA Times* and when they turn it down (as they probably will; I'm not in favor at either place) I'll pass it on to the *EF!* At least there the review would have interested readers and likely buyers of the book. Is there, or will there be, a paperback edition?

Sorry about old Amigo. Our dog is sick too but hanging on, as she's been doing for three years now. I look forward to seeing your elk book. Bumper

sticker: DID THE COWS GET YOUR ELK? Where'd I see that? Or THEM
COWS IS EATIN' GRASS THAT BELONGS TO OUR PHUKKIN' ELK!

Good luck. Best regards. Maybe see you sometime this fall.

Ed

Hon. Wayne Owens   (25 JULY 1988)

Dear Congressman Owens:

Thank you for your letter of June 22nd, re the latest antics of Cal Black
and the San Juan BLM.

I thank you also for your postscript to the letter inviting me to join you
in a look at some of the proposed BLM wilderness in Utah. I certainly wish
I could join you—might even be able to show you a few places you're not
already familiar with—but I won't be able to do it. Not this August. I'm halfway through another novel this summer, one that requires some research
at the Amerind Foundation here in Dragoon, Arizona, and I won't be free
to travel anywhere for at least another two or three months.

I do hope to return to Moab sometime in October and to spend a few
days in Salt Lake in late October or November. If you're in town at the
time, perhaps we could get together for a lunch or breakfast and talk about
a wilderness bill. As a longtime fan of yours, I'd be honored to meet you in
person.

Sorry about the delay in answering your letter; didn't get it until a few
days ago. Enclosed is a contribution to your re-election campaign. Good
luck and my best regards,

Edward Abbey—Amerind Foundation, Dragoon, AZ

New York Times Book Review   (2 AUGUST 1988)

Dear Editor:

Peter Baida is mistaken in saying that Wolfe's *Bonfire of the Vanities* lacks
heart and that his protagonist Sherman McCoy lacks an inner life. Tolstoy's
great story, to which Mr Baida compares *Bonfire*, is a story about dying—with
honor. Mr Wolfe's story is about living—and the achievement of honor.

Sherman McCoy is an empty character who becomes, through perse-
cution and injustice, a man. (A rare creature in contemporary American
fiction.) Forced to defend himself and his family, striking back directly
at his tormentors, McCoy the mere trader in bonds—good pun there—
acquires manhood, becomes the real McCoy. A heartwarming moment in
any novel, and almost extinct in contemporary American fiction.

McCoy confronts for all of us the rising tide of human muck (Mark
Twain's phrase) that is drowning our cities, rolling, flowing over our borders, threatening everything good and clean and free and spacious that
still remains in American life. The worst of our culture is greedily aped
and sought after everywhere; the best is under attack. Tom Wolfe's novel
reminds us, in the end, that defiance and resistance, manhood and honor,
are still possible. Few among our literati would agree, I acknowledge; but a
million anonymous readers and I call that possibility heartwarming.

Edward Abbey—Oracle

John Macrae, Henry Holt & Co. (20 AUGUST 1988)

Dear Jack . . .

Thanks for the news concerning *The Fool's Progress*. Sounds good, I
guess. I am certainly happy to learn that Holt plans to throw considerable
effort into the promotion of this book. I hope you are not disappointed. As
you know, I will do what I can to help, having submitted to most of Sarah
McFall's outrageous propositions. Trapped again in a gentleman's agreement!—and I'm not even a gentleman. And neither is she.

Well, expect to see me this fall, sometime in November I guess. I hope
that we have much to celebrate. Or even a little, what the hell. Whatever
happens, it's a good novel, an unusual good novel, and the House of Holt
and Clan Macrae honor both themselves and me in the publication of it.

In October, eh? No Kidding?

My best regards to you and Amy and Sarah et al.,
Edward Abbey—Tucson

Tucson Daily Citizen   (7 SEPTEMBER 1988)

Dear Editors:

In the land of bleating sheep and braying jackasses, one brave and honest man is bound to create a scandal. This accounts, I believe, for the childish, almost hysterical reaction to Dave Foreman's remarks on the Mt Graham controversy. Our two local newspapers, the dauntless *Daily Estrellita* ("*La Voz de Alta Mejico*") and the amazing *Daily Citizen* ("*La Voz de* South Tucson"), are accustomed to dealing only with politicians, bureaucrats and other reps of organized crime businessmen—i.e., The Suits. Confronted by a man like Foreman, who speaks plainly, consistently, they are thrown into a conniption of confusion, panic, outrage and fear. "What? Defend our public lands through direct citizen resistance? by possibly illegal acts? Unspeakable!"

But what alternative is available? The respectable conservation organizations (to which I've contributed my tithe for many years) have failed to stop or even slow down the advance of the Greed-and-Growth Machine. And the so-called "political process" is a fraud: Our elected officials, like our bureaucratic functionaries, like even our judges, are largely the indentured servants of the commercial interests. (The fate of the buffer-zone petition supplies a good, recent and typical instance; the conspiracy by DeConcini and Kolbe to violate the Endangered Species Act provides another.) "America's business is business," said Cool Hand Coolidge; he was never more right than now.

By the way, though I appreciate the kind attention, I must point out that my novel *The Monkey Wrench Gang* is a comedy, not a melodrama. If your editorial writer would read the book he'd discover the difference. That is, if he can understand the difference. And if he can read a book.

Edward Abbey—Oracle

***High Country News*, Paonia, Colorado**   (30 SEPTEMBER 1988)

Dear Editors:

Your recent issues on the "Reopening of the American West" are very good, quite timely, much needed. I especially like the series by Ray Wheeler on Boom & Bust in the Colorado Plateau area, and the article by Tom Wolf on the "real Wyoming."

The most powerful, reactionary and destructive little group in the western states are still the public-lands livestock ranchers; and they survive by hiding behind the cheap mythology of the "Cowboy": literally, a boy who looks after cows, which is exactly what the word means in Australia, for example. Gifted but innocent writers like Gretel Ehrlich in Wyoming and Thomas McGuane in Montana (to name only two) help keep the welfare ranchers in business by sentimentalizing the obvious and failing or refusing to perceive the significant. ("Instant rednecks" I call them, these *arrivistes nouveaux* from the Trust Fund World; with the true instinct of the sycophant (a common literary type), they follow their moist noses straight to the feet of the most powerful element in whatever social setting they find themselves.)

Edward Abbey—Oracle

PS: Check enclosed. Please renew my sub for two years. Keep the change.

Industrial Worker (1 OCTOBER 1988)

Dear Editors:

I thank you for the kind words about my books in your September 1988 issue. As a life-long admirer of the IWW and its traditions, I am honored to be mentioned in your publication. However—please let me clarify what your columnist "Lobo X99" calls my "peculiar views" on immigration.

As I have said and written many times, in many places, I am opposed to all further mass immigration, legal or illegal, from any source, and my reasons for this position are quite conventional. Like all Earth First!ers, almost all environmentalists, most union members and even (according to polls) the majority of blacks and Hispanics, I think we should seal our borders for the following good, clear and obvious reasons:

(1) the USA is overcrowded already;

(2) a large influx of cheap labor—docile, uneducated and desperate foreigners—will put bona fide native-born (or naturalized) American working

people at further disadvantage in their struggle with big business and big government;

(3) a growing population means greater pressure on all resources, including clean air, clean water, clean soil, open space, schools, medical facilities, wildlife, wilderness and our public lands in general;

(4) a growing population leads inevitably to more government, more laws, regulations, police, centralized control, authoritarian policies and a generalized stifling of personal freedom for all but the very rich.

Yours fraternally, Edward Abbey
Oracle

PS: Check enclosed; renew my sub and keep the change.

Norah (6 OCTOBER 1988)

Dear Norah,

As promised, some notes for your article:

The Fool's Progress is the fourth book I've had published in 1988. The first was *One Life At A Time, Please*, a collection of essays (Holt, NY). The second was a new edition of *Desert Solitaire*, in March, from the Univ of Arizona Press. The third was *The Best of Edward Abbey: A Reader* (Sierra Club Books, San Francisco), published in May. And the fourth, *The Fool's Progress* (Holt, NY) [will be] officially released, as they say, two weeks from today, tho' already in the bookstores.

The Fool's Progress is a novel, 485 pages long, based, as his introductory note says, upon the author's "experience, understanding and vision of human life." But it's also a comedy. In other words, it's a slapstick farce about love and marriage, work and play, life and death, etc. It's a good novel, in the author's opinion, but suffers from two major faults:

1) There's too much sex in it; and (2) there are too many jokes in it. People who think that love, sex, marriage, work, play, life and death are serious matters are urged NOT to read this book. Buy it, yes, but don't read it.

I should also warn readers that the sex in *Fool's Progress* is of a queer perverse kinky sort: it's about a hairy, greasy, rednecked, macho-type male animal who loves to make love to beautiful women, and only to beautiful women. What's wrong with this man? How did he get that way? Is there any hope for him? Read the book and find out; it's a tragic tale.

Now, you ask about my son Benjamin Cartwright Abbey, age one and a half, and his role in the composition of this latest novel. To that I can only say that Ben did his best to help. The first draft, about nine hundred pages, was writ in longhand, my usual practice, and many of those pages are decorated with Ben's drawings. The second (and penultimate) draft was typed on my 1955 Royal upright manual, a marvelous invention. I too believe in the latest in high tech. Anyhow, much of the typing was done with Ben sitting on my lap, assisting. He and he alone, I'm sorry to say, is responsible for any and all misprints, solecisms and errors of fact which the reader may find in the book.

For further details, read the novel. Good luck, Norah, and best regards,

Edward Abbey

Enclosures: two photos

Roger Donald, Little, Brown & Co,
New York City (26 OCTOBER 1988)

Dear Mr Donald:

Herewith, via Don Congdon, are the first 381 pages of *Hayduke Lives!*

I had hoped to have the whole thing finished by this time but, as you see, I failed my own deadline, and because of prior agreements with Holt, I'll not be able to get back to it until December. (Book tour.)

Three chapters remain to be written. They are (will go) as follows:

Chapter 27: "Goliath Falls"

Here we have the direct and final confrontation with the Super G.E.M., first by Erika and her Earth First! group, then by Hayduke and his little Gang of Four. Exactly as Hayduke predicts, the EF! group make a valiant public effort to stop the "Walking Dragline" at the choke point called "The Neck," get themselves martyrized, beaten up, arrested, and fail.

Then at twilight, while the crew of G O L I A T H celebrate their apparent victory, no doubt with booze and women, and after the police and rangers have left the scene, Hayduke, Abbzug, Sarvis & Smith succeed in hijacking the giant machine and begin walking it to the edge of the nearby thousand-foot cliff. (Make that 2500'.)

Not without attracting attention, of course. The police come swarming back in full techno-array, helicopters, searchlights etc, some kind of stand-off takes place (perhaps Bonnie & Doc pretending to be helpless hostages) and Hayduke wins again, as usual, pilots the machine over the brink and, naturally, vanishes with it.

Doc, Bonnie and Smith are captured, arrested, hustled off to the Landfill Co Jail.

Chapter 28: "The Trial"

Here I'm going to attempt a full-dress courtroom scene, with Doc, Bonnie and Smith on trial on a variety of felonious charges, including perhaps even the alleged murder of Hayduke. (We'll see.) Unable to get any decent lawyer to undertake their defense, Doc acts as attorney for himself and friends, basing his defense on the ancient Anglo-American doctrine of "preventing a greater harm." I.e., he argues that he and friends committed an admitted crime (destruction of private property) in order to prevent a far greater crime (destruction of a wilderness treasure, watersheds, wildlife habitats, etc etc). Such a defense has many historical precedents, and has been used most recently—and successfully—by Amy Carter and friends, I believe, before a jury in—Boston?

Anyhow, Doc attempts the same maneuver but is over-ruled, again and again, by the courtroom judge, a strict young Jimmy Carter appointee named . . . Darlene Strawberry? . . . eager to prove herself a hardnosed upholder of the most conservative interpretations of the law.

Nevertheless, Doc [succeeds], with help from Bonnie and Seldom Seen Smith, in somehow getting his point across to the jury, twelve good men/ women and true from the Phoenix Arizona area. (The trial takes place in a Federal court in Phoenix.)

After final summations by defense and prosecution, the intense young judge instructs the jury, in no uncertain terms, exactly what their duty is, what arguments are acceptable and what are not.

Judge's mistake, of course. The jury, consisting mostly of geriatric retirees from the upper Midwest, far more conservative by instinct than the judge herself, return a verdict of not guilty on all counts. Sensation! Furthermore (further sensation), the jury attempts to cite the judge for Contempt of Court. (Sensational uproar!)

While the judge defends herself, the defendants creep quietly out, acquitted and free.

Chapter 29: "The Manhunt"

Hoyle, Boyle and the Colonel, meanwhile, are hot on the tracks of George Hayduke, and their orders are to finish him once and for all. Terminate With Extreme Prejudice. George is well aware of this and is attempting to flee the country.

Somewhere on the San Francisco waterfront—or maybe on the shore of the Sea of Cortez—he has a final encounter with the three pursuers, defeats them (somehow) and swims out to sea, where he is picked up by the flagship of the Earth First! navy (Paul Watson's *Sea Shepherd*, an actual person and ship) and taken onto the broad bosom of the Pacific for a journey Down Under, where they all have important business.

Chapter 30: Brief epilogue:

The desert tortoise emerges from his grave and waddles off into the sunrise of the Arizona wilderness. (Lone Ranger watching from rim.)

The above will make more sense to you, of course, after you read the 381 pages now completed.

You will notice many loose ends in the book, mainly the result of ideas evolving in the course of the writing. Editorial suggestions will be much appreciated.

Sorry we can't meet this Fall. Maybe you could come out to Tucson sometime later this winter, if you'd like a conference on the book.

Best regards, Edward Abbey

Copy to Don Congdon

Robert Redford, Sundance, Utah (7 DECEMBER 1988)

Dear Robert,

Thanks for the note from Santa Fe. Good to hear from you now and then.

Sorry I didn't send you a copy of my latest book. (You mean *The Fool's Progress*?) But you didn't send me a copy of your latest movie. I had to buy a ticket to see *Milagro* [*Beanfield War*]—and then spend another four or five bucks to rent the video so my wife and kids could see it.

Milagro is a charming, even delightful movie, by the way. We all enjoyed it. That Ruben Blades is a wizard. And I especially loved the old men and women in the movie—they upstaged everybody else, it seemed to me.

I hear you're making a film of *A River Runs Through It* next. A marvelous story, which I've read three or four times so far. Don't forget my son the actor when you set about casting the thing; like most actors, he always needs work. I don't have his agent's name here, but you can talk to Joshua's answering machine. Yes, he's living in L.A. now, poor devil. Finally gave up on Avenue C in Lower East Side.

We're still living in Tucson, but spend the summers and autumns in Moab. Plan to build a log cabin at Pack Crick next summer.

Me, I'm scribbling another novel, as usual. Almost finished with *Hayduke Lives!*, a sequel to *The Monkey Wrench Gang*. The book should be out by March 1990. I promise to send you an advance copy this time.

I trust that all is well with you. If you ever come to Tucson, give me a call, we'll have a desert cookout with Doug "Hayduke" Peacock (the Grizzly Bear Man) and Dave "Earth First!" Foreman (the Wolf Man). I think you'd like them.

Best regards, Ed A.—Tucson

Miss D'Angelo, Editor, M.I.T. Student Newspaper (12 DECEMBER 1988)

Dear Miss D'Angelo:

Tough and interesting questions. I'll try to answer some of them as best I can, quickly, in order to get this back to you today.

Q.#1: To the Technocrats: Have mercy on us. Relax a bit, take time out for simple pleasures. For example, the luxuries of electricity, indoor plumbing, central heating, instant electronic communication and such, have taught me to relearn and enjoy the basic human satisfactions of dipping water from a cold clear mountain stream; of building a wood fire in a cast-iron stove; of using long winter nights for making music, making things, making love; of writing long letters, in longhand with a fountain pen, to the few people on this earth I truly care about.

Q.#2: Yes.

Q.#3: The ugliest thing in America is greed, the lust for power and domination, the lunatic ideology of perpetual Growth—with a capital G. "Progress" in our nation has for too long been confused with "Growth"; I see the two as different, almost incompatible, since progress means, or should mean, change for the better—toward social justice, a livable and open world, equal. opportunity and affirmative action for all forms of life. And I mean all forms, not merely the human. The grizzly, the wolf, the rattlesnake, the condor, the coyote, the crocodile, whatever, each and every species has as much right to be here as we do.

Therefore, we must limit and then reduce human population (by humane means, for Christ's sake, birth control, etc.) so as to allow time for our fellow living beings to recover their fair share of living space. A world without huge regions of total wilderness would be a cage; a world without lions and tigers and vultures and snakes and elk and bison would be—will be—a human zoo. A high-tech slum.

Q.#4: Most of human history consists of tribal warfare. In this recent North American incident the Indians lost to the invading Europeans. What do you want me to do about it? I'll go back to Europe if the Indians will all go back to Siberia. The best thing we can do for the American Indians is to stop feeling sorry for them; the best thing they can do for themselves is to stop wallowing in self-pity, display some grit and gumption, begin facing up to their problems (too many babies, too much alcohol, too much welfare, too much self-hatred) and stop waiting for the Federal government to solve everything for them.

In one way at least, the Indians are better off than most of the rest of us: they have their inalienable reservations, a land base, a true home. Let them begin from there.

Q.#5: *The Fool's Progress* is a picaresque comedy about life and death, work and play, love and marriage—with a happy ending. I mention these obvious points only because a few reviewers (a simple and literal-minded lot, generally speaking) seem unable to grasp them. Other than that, the novel speaks for itself. It's the best work I've been able to do so far and perhaps the best I'll ever do.

Q.#6: What is my favorite among my books? They are all my children; but I will confess to a special fondness for the novels *Good News* and *Black Sun*, i.e., the futuristic fantasy and the wilderness love story.

Q.#7: Whom do I nominate, among American writers, for the Nobel Prize? Easy: Lewis Mumford for literature (*The City in History, The Myth of the Machine, The Pentagon of Power,* etc.), David Brower for peace (he has devoted his life in the attempt to stop humankind's savage war against the natural world) and Noam Chomsky for science—and political truth.

Q.#8: What is the essence of the art of writing? Part One: Have something to say. Part Two: Say it well.

Q.#9: How do I feel about The War Between The Sexes? I love it. I'm in favor of it. Women and men must share everything eventually, including a common fate; but meanwhile, it is the poignant difference between them which creates the tension and the delight. There is nothing that bores me so much as androgyny—manlike women and womanlike men.

Q.#10: Does the human race deserve a final chance? Considering what we've done to each other and to life in general during the past five thousand years, I'm tempted to say that we do not. But I am the father of two small children. The children are innocent until proven guilty. For their sake, not ours, we must soldier on, muddling our way toward frugality, simplicity, liberty, community, until some kind of sane and rational balance is achieved between our ability to love and our cockeyed ambition to conquer and dominate everything in sight. No wonder the galaxies recede from us in every direction, fleeing at velocities that approach the speed of light. They are frightened. We humans are the Terror of the Universe.

Meanwhile, good luck to all of you. (Within reason.)

Edward Abbey—Oracle

Ed Marston, Publisher, *High Country News*,
Paonia, Colorado (14 DECEMBER 1988)

Dear Ed:

How come you and C. L. Rawlins sayin' all them mean and nasty things about me? I thought we were friends and allies. To say that people like Foreman and I regard monkey-wrenching as an end in itself is plain silly. Dumb. Stupid. Eco-sabotage is a last resort, desperation, balls-to-the-wall defense strategy and you know it. Nothing else has worked. This probly won't work either, but at least we've got to try it.

Your interpretation of that brief quote from my "Life & Death of the American West" article in *Mother Earth* [*News*] makes no sense. Where do you get such cockeyed notions? My friends and I live in the American SW because we love it, and love it for its own sake—not merely because it's the last region of the forty-eight states to be buried under asphalt and greed. My whole life, everything I've written, has been an expression of that belief. Nor do I want to see the small towns of the West disappear; where'd you get that idea? I certainly don't have any respect for the greedheads who tend to dominate them, but I like most of the people I've known here, including the cowboys (not ranchers), miners and loggers—even a few realtors.

And why does Rawlins accuse me of "rant and rave"? Humor is my style, in the old Mark Twain tradition, and that's probly why none of my books ever go out of print. When I made that speech in Missoula attacking "The Cowboy & His Cow," a few cattlepersons got mad and stormed out, but the majority of the audience laughed, and laughed with me, all the way through. As an essay, it's proved to be one of the most popular pieces I've ever done, appearing and reappearing so far in about forty newspapers and half a dozen anthologies.

And who are these "recreational elitists" Rawlins imagines I speak for? The Winnebago tourists? The safari-type trophy hunters? The O.ff R.oad V.ermin? The Ivy-League fly fishermen? I doubt if he likes them, as types, any more than I do. The main reason I want to get the stinking cattle out of our public forests and those four-leg range maggots [sheep] off our public rangelands is to make room for elk, pronghorn, bighorn, mule deer, javelina, desert turtle, wolf, grizzly, black bear, mountain lion etc etc—and I've said so a hundred times. By what warp of the imagination does that make me a "recreational elitist"? Enclosed is another $100 for your lousy little rag and don't print this letter neither.

Edward Abbey

1989

ALTHOUGH ABBEY REMAINED outwardly vital to all who did not know—and very few knew—his health continued to fail. Just as he was preparing to depart on a weeklong desert camping trip with Jack Loeffler and me, Ed suffered a severe "bleed" that returned him to the hospital. When it became clear that there was no help for him, he had himself kidnapped and returned home. About daylight on the morning of March 14, surrounded by family and friends who had been keeping vigil, Ed passed peacefully in his sleep, on a fold-out couch bed in his little writing cabin. From that point on, all went as he had requested. Friends buried his body in a secret desert location with a grand wild view. A raucous wake was held at Saguaro National Park, Tucson. A joker to the end, Ed asked that the epitaph "No Comment" be engraved on the unobtrusive volcanic-rock headstone marking his grave, and it was. In May, a memorial service, organized by "Seldom Seen" Ken Sleight, was held along the old entrance road to Arches, at one of Abbey's favorite campsites.

Don Congdon, New York City   (11 JANUARY 1989)

Dear Don,

Got your letter regarding Holt and Avon paperback reprint deal. If you think you can make a better deal somewhere, let me know and I'll refuse to sign the agreement with Avon. Otherwise, I don't see that any of it makes much difference.

What really exasperates me and should annoy you too is the rotten treatment my novel received from the NYC reviewers. I mean those utterly perfunctory, silly, stupid, superficial, fake reviews that *Time, Newsday* and the *NY Times Book Review* gave *The Fool's Progress*. Not one of them, for example, even mentioned that the book is a comedy. None except the *NYTBR* even quoted a sample of the book—and that quote was a sidebar, not part of the review. Why do those sonsabitches do that to me?

I've been writing books now for thirty-five years ([*Jonathan*] *Troy* was published in 1954), and it's about time the goddamn NY literati gave my work a fair shake. My books should at least be reviewed by my peers, that is, by other novelists and essayists, not by embittered feminists (male and female) from the rubyfruit jungles of Manhattan and Connecticut. John Skow, Dan Cryer, the fellow in the *Times*—who the hell are they? I never heard of any of them.

They tried to bury *Monkey Wrench* too, the same way back in 1975, but the book got away from them, and here it is, fourteen years later, and that "unacceptable" novel is still very much alive, now in its eighteenth printing and third American edition. Those bastards. Swine. *The Fool* will do the same thing—outlive the scum. Piss on their graves.

(What, am I peeved? Me? Well, maybe a little bit.)

Have you tried to sell anything from *Hayduke Lives!* yet? As you know, I sold the opening chapter to *Mother Earth News*. It might be possible to sell other parts to *Playboy, Penthouse, Outside, Rolling Stone, Atlantic*, etc. I hope you feel it's worth a try.

Please send me Frederick Exley's address if you know it. Or that of his publisher, Random House. I meant to write Fred a fan letter. *Last Notes from Home* is a delightful book.

Best, Ed A.—Tucson

**Howard Coale, c/o *New York Times Book Review*,
New York City** (12 JANUARY 1989)

Dear Mr Howard Coale:

I am puzzled by your review of my *Fool's Progress* novel. You accuse me, for example, of "slightly malevolent" and "self-indulgent" writing, but fail to cite any examples of either or to even explain what those vague phrases mean to you. The truth is, that novel was written line by line with great care and deliberation; there is not a single "self-indulgent" sentence in the whole 485 pages.

You fret at great length about Dostoyevski and "Mishkin" while completely failing to notice the Congreve epigraph, the repeated references to the Villon poem, and what should be obvious, the influence of Charles Ives upon the structure, tone and general character of the novel. Ives in fact was my model throughout, as a few reviewers (and many readers) have already noticed.

Strangest of all, you don't even mention the fact that *The Fool's Progress* is a comedy—with a happy ending. I have read many sections of the book to many live audiences during the past four years, and never failed to get a satisfactory response: jubilant laughter. The first chapter in particular, the satire on doctrinaire feminism and gourmet cooking, is always a big hit. (Oh yes, a few hardcore fem-libbers, male & female, glare at me in sullen silence, but everywhere I go I find those types a decided minority among college audiences.) If you actually read the book—which I doubt—how could you have failed to see what is actually there?

Not that your dislike of the book matters to anyone but the author. *The Monkey Wrench Gang, Desert Solitaire, Down the River*, etc, received the same sort of ill-tempered response when they first appeared. But twenty years later, all three are still in print, still being bought and read, still bringing in a constant stream of letters. And in the long run that's what matters. Readers, not critics, are the people who determine a book's eventual fate. Twenty years from now, *The Fool's Progress*, like almost all of my dozen or so other books, will still be in print, will still be read and enjoyed.

So what am I complaining about? Who's complaining; I do this for fun.

Sincerely, Edward Abbey

PS: Your review is dishonest. There is no "narcissistic" "facing mirrors" "explanation of explanations" in *Fool's Progress*. Show me. Where? Cite pp numbers. *Tout aux contraire*, I ridicule that kind of self-obsession in Chapter 1, the group-encounter therapy episode.

Brigitte Barkley, U.S. Editor, *Geo* Magazine,
New York City (13 JANUARY 1989)

Dear Miss Barkley:

Herewith, as requested, an extra final sentence or two for the "Hard Times in Santa Fe" story:

". . . Any town that could withstand the cruelty of the Spanish, the comic misrule of the Mexicans, the misguided ministry of a misplaced French archbishop (the famous Lamy) and the vulgar and rapacious domination of us Americans, will not succumb for long to mere techno-industrial turismo. Santa Fe is built of finer, firmer stuff than money or plastic or sheet metal; I mean that Santa Fe is built of and upon—earth. The earth itself. The best of its people arose from and partake of that fundamental substance. They and their city will endure. Will perdure. For sure."

As for a bio-sketch of the author, you may write as follows: "Edward Abbey, novelist and essayist, is the author of many books, including *The Fool's Progress, One Life at a Time, Good News, Desert Solitaire*, and *The Monkey Wrench Gang* (published in Germany as *Die Universalschrauben-schlussel Bande*). He lives near Tucson, Arizona with his wife and two small children."

Okay? By the way, I've still not received payment for this piece.

Sincerely, Edward Abbey—Tucson

Malcolm Brown, Taos, New Mexico (13 JANUARY 1989)

Dear Malcolm—

Thanks for the card. I'm delighted to learn that you've enjoyed reading *The Fool*—there was much in it, I feared, that might seem fake to you. (Of course, one could like the book despite that.) Who is Morton Bildad? And Van Hoss? et al? All of them—even Myra Mishkin & Henry Lightcap—are mostly fictional creations. The portrait of actual people is a task far beyond my powers. I would not even attempt it. I am a cartoonist, not a portraitist.

Love, Ed—Tucson

Gerald Freund, Giles Whiting Foundation   (2 FEBRUARY 1989)

Dear Mr Freund:

Thank you for your letter of January 6th. I am honored by the request to act as a nominator for awards in your writing program and am happy to accept such a pleasant task.

My nomination (and nominee) for one of the awards this year is Mr Charles Bowden of Tucson, Arizona. (See enclosed resume for details of his career and publications.) Of his five books published so far, I would find it difficult to name one as my favorite, for they are all remarkably even in literary quality (high) and in significance of subject matter (both important and *au courant*). He has not yet attempted to write fiction and I don't know if he intends to; his work thus far deals mostly with contemporary American life as enjoyed—or endured—mostly among people in the lower and lower middleclass. About half of his writing is concerned with environmental issues in the USA in general and in the American Southwest in particular. His style is highly personal—laconic, idiosyncratic, extremely graphic, clear, direct, often funny, always sardonic.

Aside from the distinctive merits of Mr Bowden's writing, I think he deserves the award also on the basis of financial need, if that is a consideration in your choice of awardees. He has no independent income and therefore has been forced to work full time, mainly as a journalist, in order to support himself, his wife and their one child. The award of $25,000 would enable him to devote at least a full year to full-time work on his next book.

Sincerely, Edward Abbey
Tucson

Edward Hoagland (5 FEBRUARY 1989)

Dear Hoagland,

Thanks for your note of December 17th. I too felt a surge of affection for you, that strange evening, at Jack Macrae's party. If only you were willing to be a true correspondent, that is, to write letters, we could probably become actual friends rather than mere literary acquaintances—trade associates.

You mention Gretel Erhlich. I'm afraid that I've lost all respect for that woman. Her childish idolatry of cowboys and cowboyism is forgivable, perhaps, since most newcomers to the West are guilty of it for a while. But two or three years should be time enough to outgrow that silliness.

Not forgivable is the way she reacts to criticism of the Kowboy Kult, rather than attempt a rational defense of the public-lands beef industry— i.e., because I have criticized the welfare ranchers as a class and urged the removal of cows and sheep from our national forests and parks. The fact that I've always qualified that position by agreeing in advance that ranchers as individuals are no worse and no better than any other occupational group makes no difference to Mizz Erhlich.

Worst of all, however, is her successful effort at ingratiating herself with the rich and powerful in the Rocky Mt West by her defense of cowboyism. She's only a Ralph Lauren cowperson herself, like most of our contemporary hobby ranchers, but the grazing industry in Wyoming has adopted her as a kind of pet or mascot—their writer. The only quality I despise more than any other is sycophancy; toadyism; this groveling before the powerful.

All of which reminds me of Paul Horgan. I skimmed through his *Encounters With Stravinsky* last night. What a servile, pompous, *Uriah Heep* sort of book!

Write me a real letter, goddamnit! And send me an autographed copy of *Seven Rivers West* and I'll review it for *Earth First!*

Regards, Ed

David Petersen, Durango, Colorado (19 FEBRUARY 1989)

Dear Dave—

As you probly noticed, the *High Country News* has printed a really malicious and dishonest review of *Fool's Progress*: grotesque distortions, personal attacks, absurd accusations—all without any evidence whatsoever. They hate my guts—but why? (When are you coming to Tucson?)

Best, Ed A.—Tucson

American Hunter Magazine, National Rifle Association, Fairfax, Virginia (22 FEBRUARY 1989)

Dear Editor:

As a long-time member of the NRA, and as a hunter all of my life so far (sixty-two years), I would like to bring up a problem that most of your eastern and Midwestern readers are not aware of: I mean the running of domestic cattle and sheep on the public lands of our western states.

All of our national forests, BLM (Bureau of Land Management) lands, most of our wildlife refuges and even a few of our national parks are presently infested with these privately owned livestock that now eat up the forage that should and could be supporting a much greater population of elk, antelope, deer, bighorn sheep, black bear and bison.

The public lands are supposed to be the property of all Americans. Both as citizens and as hunters, we must begin to bring political pressure on the government agencies that allow this subsidized grazing to continue. I urge all hunters to think about this question and to get involved in the effort to remove cattle and sheep from our national hunting grounds.

Yours, Ed C. Cartwright [E.A.]—Tucson

DeWitt Daggett, Paonia, Colorado (25 FEBRUARY 1989)

Dear DeWitt:

Thanks for the Stegner tape.

Stegner hardly needs praise from me, but if you wish, you may quote me as follows re that old gent:

"There are only two living American authors fully deserving of the Nobel Prize. One is Lewis Mumford. The other is Wallace Stegner, whose novels and essays provide us a comprehensive portrait of industrial society in all its glittering corruption and radiant evil."

By the way, thinking of good old Wally, I'd sure appreciate it if you'd delete his quote about me from future editions of your catalogue. I've always resented that crap about a "gadfly with a stinger" etc. It typifies the most narrow kind of view of my work and I'm certain Stegner himself would retract it now. After all, he wrote it more than twenty years ago, when I was just getting started as a writer.

If you want a blurb for my tape, my favorite is this from Wendell Berry, as quoted on the jacket of *The Fool's Progress*:

> "We are living . . . among punishments and ruins. For those who know this, Edward Abbey's books remain an indispensable solace. His essays, and his novels too, are antidotes to despair."

I'd like to suggest two other western authors for your tape library: Charles Bowden, author of *Blue Desert, Mescal, Red Line* (Norton) and other books. . . . The other writer I especially admire is Cormac McCarthy, author of *Blood Meridian* and five other fine novels.

Good luck and best regards, Ed A.

Condé Nast Traveler, New York City   (27 FEBRUARY 1989)

Dear Editor:

We much enjoyed Jim Harrison's amusing piece in *Traveler* (March 1989), but were amazed by this one amazing statement near the end:

". . . the worst stewards of the land are not the so-called (sic!) greedy ranchers, but our careless sprawling government itself."

Obviously Harrison, like most tourists in the West, is not aware that such Federal agencies as the BLM, the Forest Service and the (so-called) [U.S. Fish and] Wildlife Service are completely dominated by the grazing interests. Any government range manager who dared attempt to free our public lands from private livestock would be putting his job—and sometimes even the physical safety of his wife and children—in serious jeopardy. As a result, through natural selection, these agencies are run by men who rarely question the beef ranchers' priorities.

Thus, the ranchers profit—but the land, the water, the wildlife and we the public, all lose. Contrary to Harrison, the abuse of the West most

certainly is due to the greed of the cow farmers, a tiny but powerful group
of businessmen who hide behind the sentimental myth of the "cowboy."

Sincerely, Edward Abbey

John Nichols, Taos, New Mexico (27 FEBRUARY 1989)

Dear John,

My friend Jack [Loeffler] tells me you've suffered another heart attack
recently. Sorry to hear that. You take care of yourself; we're all expecting at
least six more fat novels and a dozen screenplays out of you. DON'T CHOP
WOOD; GET YOUR NEW WIFE A NEW AXE. Etc.

Me, I'm living under a sword too, as Jack may have told you. An old
wino's disease, which could lay me in the grave most anytime. Not that I
mind too much; I've done everything I ever wanted to do. But . . . as you
know, one would like to continue doing the good things over and over
again, so long as there's pleasure in it.

We saw your movie *Milagro*. A charming, delightful film: that Ruben
Blades is a lovable guy. And the old folks in the show, they upstaged everyone else.

What're you doing now? Another book? Another film? Sure wish I could
get back in that Screenwriter's Guild again: I need the medical insurance.
Any ideas?

Me, I finished *Hayduke Lives!* a couple of weeks ago; should be out a year
from now. Only a potboiler but easy and fun to write. A sequel to *Monkey
Wrench*, of course. What next? Maybe an exposé of the public lands ranching swindle . . . or a book on Mexico before Mexico erupts: call it . . . *On
the Edge of the Volcano*. Or a book on Australia, my favorite land and favorite people (next to Sweden and Norway and Ireland and Italy); call that
one . . . *The Last Good Country*. Or a book on music; I've always wanted to
write a book on music from the layman-listener's point of view; music has
played a bigger part in my life than anything else except love, nature, sex,
poetry and philosophy.

Give my regards to old Malcolm Brown next time you see him—a friend
of mine from long long ago—and the only person I know, aside from yourself, still living in bleak grim cold picturesque Taos. Poor Malcolm: He

thinks that Morton Bildad, in my *Fool* novel, is a parody of him. Not so of course; as I told him, reality and real people are too subtle and complicated for anybody's typewriter, even Tolstoy's, even yours, even mine.

Enuf of this maundering. You be careful. Best regards,

Ed—Fort Llatikcuf

David Petersen   (CIRCA MARCH 1989)

Dear Friend:

Perhaps you have heard of me and my nationwide campaign in the cause of temperance. Each year, for the past fourteen years, I have made a tour of Arizona, Colorado, Utah, Nevada and Texas and have delivered a series of lectures on the evils of drinking.

On this tour I have been accompanied by my young friend and assistant, Clyde Lindstone. Clyde, a young man of good family and excellent background, was a pathetic example of life ruined by excessive indulgence in whisky and women.

Clyde would appear with me at the lectures and sit on the platform, wheezing and staring at the audience through bleary, bloodshot eyes, sweating profusely, picking his nose, passing gas and making obscene gestures to the ladies present, while I would point him out as a perfect example of what over-indulgence can do to a good man.

Last fall, unfortunately, Clyde died.

A mutual acquaintance, Dr. Stan Silberman, has given me your name and suggested that you may be seeking employment in the near future. I wonder if you would be available to take Clyde's place in my forthcoming lecture tour?

Yours in Faith, Rev. Edwin P. Abbott

NOTES

6 Family, Home, Pennsylvania: Ed's parents, Paul and Mildred Abbey.

7 Billy: Abbey's brother.

7 Bud: Bud Adams was a fellow student at the University of New Mexico. He appears in Abbey's essay "Desert Places" and in his lecture "The Cowboy and His Cow," under the pseudonym "Mack." An antithetical cowboy, Adams debunked Abbey's romantic idealization of the American West.

8 Gilbert Neiman, Professor, Clarion State College: Neiman and Abbey were classmates and friends at the University of New Mexico.

8 Newcomb: Ralph Newcomb was a friend from the University of New Mexico. Newcomb countered Bud Adams' postmodern cowboy and would eventually serve as the model for *The Brave Cowboy*. Abbey wrote fondly of Newcomb as "an anachronism in the modern commercial-atomic America."

12 Judy Pepper (8 September 1965): A few weeks after this letter was written, Judy Pepper became Abbey's third wife. The mother of Ed's first daughter, Susannah (August 28, 1968), Judy would die of leukemia on July 4, 1970.

12 Tukuhnikivats: The highest peak in the La Sal Range, southeast of Moab, Utah.

12 Al Sarvis: Alva "Al" Sarvis was an artist friend from the University of New Mexico days, when he, Ed, and other student pals "monkeywrenched" highway billboards because they blocked the scenery and littered the landscape. In his journal entry for November 28, 1964 (*Confessions of a Barbarian*), Abbey notes: "And the great Al Sarvis, most beautiful of friends but also, in his way, absurd and desperate." Sarvis contributed inspiration for both Art Ballantine in *Black Sun* and Doc Sarvis in *The Monkey Wrench Gang*. In an almost ethereal coincidence, Sarvis and Abbey would die on the same day: March 14, 1989.

18 wildlife conservation and trophy hunting: Abbey's views of "blood sport" were complex, sophisticated, and generally right on. While he endorsed fair-chase hunting when the meat is consumed by the hunter, he decried trophy or "head" hunting, hounding, baiting, "varmint" shooting, and the often woefully uninformed politics of hunters and hunters' groups.

18 Senator Dodd: Thomas J. Dodd, a Connecticut Democrat, championed stricter gun control legislation. His efforts led to the passage of the Gun Control Act of 1968. Opponents to the GCA claimed that Senator Dodd adapted the law from Germany's Nazi-era National Weapons Law. .

22 Wendell Berry: The author of more than forty books of essays, poetry, and novels, Berry has worked a farm in Henry County, Kentucky, since 1965.

23 Senator Frank E. Moss: Frank E. Moss, a Utah Democrat, facilitated the creation of Arches, Canyonlands, and Capitol Reef National Parks, among Abbey's favorite places.

23 the Lake Powell-Rainbow Bridge: Glen Canyon Dam was authorized by Congress to fill the Lake Powell Reservoir in 1956. Though Congress initially stipulated that the water not reach Rainbow Bridge National Monument, by 1971 Lake Powell's rising water level had not only reached the monument, but engulfed the Colorado River and flooded its surrounding canyons. Many sacred Navajo sites were likewise inundated by the reservoir.

25 Art Greene and his tour boat business: Art Greene ran a lodge, restaurant, and trading post near Lees Ferry. Greene offered tourists trips up through Glen Canyon to Rainbow Bridge on his airboats.

27 Leadbelly: Huddie William Ledbetter, later known as Leadbelly, was an African American folk and blues musician, active during the 1930s and 1940s. His legendary pugnacity frequently landed him in prison, where he earned both his moniker and his entrée into the music industry.

27 Big Bill Broonzy: William Lee Conley Broonzy was a Mississippi-born blues artist. After his relocation to Chicago in 1924, Broonzy became a leading figure in the Chicago blues scene.

27 Satchel Paige: After playing for two decades in the Negro Leagues, Leroy Robert "Satchel" Paige signed with the Cleveland Indians in 1948 to become the first black pitcher in the American League.

27 Richard Alpert: Dr. Richard Alpert was a professor of psychology at Harvard University whose controversial research on the effects of LSD established him as a countercultural icon in the early 1960s. He was dismissed from Harvard in 1963 for his involvement in the Harvard Psilocybin Project. Alpert assumed the name Baba Ram Dass ("servant of God") after a trip to India in 1967.

28 Victoria McCabe: Author of a cookbook, *John Keats's Porridge: Favorite Recipes of American Poets* (1975), which included Abbey's recipe.

29 John Davis: A friend of Abbey's and the editor of *Earth First! Journal.*

29 William J. Briggle: As the Superintendent of Glacier National Park, he drew criticism from environmentalists during the early 1970s for his interest in exploiting Glacier's potential for development.

30 Jack Macrae: Over many years, John "Jack" Macrae III, in the service of various major publishing houses, was Abbey's primary editor in New York.

33 Chief McGuire: John R. McGuire served as chief of the Forest Service from 1972 until 1979. McGuire's tenure as chief coincided with the public's heightened concern with environmental issues.

34 Alan Harrington: The author of *The Immortalist* and other books, Harrington was a friend of Abbey's in Tuscon.

35 Gaddis: William Gaddis's first novel, *The Recognitions*, was published in 1955. His second novel, *JR*, would be published in 1975.

35 Ed Burlingame: Editor at Lippincott (see below).

36 Lockridge: Ross Lockridge, Jr., was a novelist best known for *Raintree County*, an expansive evocation of nineteenth-century Midwestern life. Shortly after the novel's publication in 1948, Lockridge committed suicide.

37 *Indiana* [Pennsylvania] *Gazette*: The newspaper of Abbey's birthplace.

37 *Love and Evil*: *Love and Evil, From a Probation Officer's Casebook*, published in 1974, was a collaborative effort by Dan Sakall and Alan Harrington.

38 William Eastlake: The author of *Castle Keep* and other books, Eastlake was a good friend of Abbey's.

41 Seldom Seen Smith: A fictional character in Abbey's novel *The Monkey Wrench Gang*.

41 Lippincott: J.B. Lippincott Company sprung from a bookstall that was established in Philadelphia in 1792. In 1975 Lippincott published *The Monkey Wrench Gang*.

44 *Rolling Stone*: Abbey's disdain for pop music and the musicians who made it—his stubborn unwillingness to recognize anything artful in even the best of it—struck many of his friends as ironic, given his abiding love of music. As a young man, Ed had aspired to become a composer, and he enjoyed a lifelong passion for live classical music, which he requested, and received, at his memorial service.

44 *Scalpdancers*: A novel later renamed *Dancers in the Scalp House*.

44 beat it into print: That is, with *The Monkey Wrench Gang*.

46 Painful subject: The elder Abbey did, in fact, outlive Ed, who died exactly fourteen years from the day this letter was written.

46 someone I love: Judy, Ed's third wife.

47 Don Congdon: Abbey's long-time literary agent, whom he would fire and subsequently rehire over the years.

49 Euell Gibbons: Euell Gibbons became famous during the 1960s as an advocate for organic diets and a spokesman for Grape Nuts cereal. Gibbons was credited with the much-jibed line "Ever eat a pine tree?" for a Grape Nuts advertisement. In uncanny accordance with Abbey's prediction, Gibbons died later that year (1975) from a heart attack.

49 My book: *The Monkey Wrench Gang.*

50 Suzi: Abbey's daughter. He used a variety of spellings for her name: Susanna, Susannah, Susi, etc.

50 Doug Peacock: Abbey first met Doug Peacock at William Eastlake's home in Tucson in the spring of 1970. A Vietnam Veteran and eco-warrior, Peacock served as a model for George Washington Hayduke in *The Monkey Wrench Gang.* Though their friendship was characterized by fraternal friction, Peacock would be present at Abbey's deathbed.

50 NAU: Northern Arizona University.

51 Dianitia: A publicist at Lippincott.

51 *PW*: *Publishers Weekly.*

52 Walter Clemons: An editor at McGraw-Hill, Clemons inherited the manuscript of *Desert Solitaire* from his predecessor, Bob Gutwillig.

54 Joshua Abbey: Ed's first son.

54 that old Cowboy movie: *Lonely Are the Brave*, which was based on Abbey's novel, *The Lonely Cowboy.*

55 Aaron: Ed's second son.

57 *The Good Life*: A fictionalized autobiographical account, never finished, about growing up on the farm. Themes from this would subsequently reemerge in *The Fool's Progress.*

58 the head is full of books: Like most working writers, Abbey conceived and played with many ideas that never came to be. Moreover, in Abbey's case this habit proved to be particularly frustrating to scholars and confusing to readers, as he often played with titles for years, trying them out on various works-in-progress before finally dropping them altogether or appending them to works that had little or no thematic relation to their litany of nominal predecessors.

60 "Telluride Blues": Abbey's article "Telluride Blues: A Hatchet Job" would be printed in November of 1976 by *Mountain Gazette*, and later revised and reprinted elsewhere, but never in *The Atlantic.*

61 Edward Hoagland: An East Coast friend and writer.

64 Paul W. Allen: President of Cyprus Pima Mining Company and Executive VP of Cyprus Mines Corp., which owned and operated the Pima and Bagdad copper mines in Arizona.

65 Martin Litton: Legendary Grand Canyon boatman.

65 Blaustein's book: Abbey published *The Hidden Canyon: A River Journey*, a collaboration with photographer John Blaustein, in 1977. The book documents Abbey's trip through the Grand Canyon with Litton, Blaustein, and Renée.

67 Mike Di Leo: Author of "Turkey Vulture" and other wild poems.

68 *The Imperial Animal*: Written by Rutgers University professors Lionel Tiger and Robin Fox, the book discusses the relationship between biology and culture.

69 *Malice Aforethought*: Published as *Abbey's Road: Take the Other*, in 1979

70 Florence Krall: Florence Krall Shepard is the author of the memoir *Ecotone: Wayfaring on the Margins* (1994), and posthumous editor of the works of her late husband, Paul Shepard, "the father of human ecology." Laughing with the memory, Flo tells of once having loaned her VW bug to Abbey for a couple of days, only to have him return it "late and trashed."

71 Luna Leopold: A geomorphologist renowned for his work in hydrology, Leopold advocated for enlightened water management that considered environmental as well as political factors.

71 Stewart Udall: A Democrat, Udall served as a Representative from Arizona (1955–1961) and was the Secretary of the Interior during the Kennedy and Johnson Administrations. Published in 1963, Udall's bestselling *The Quiet Crisis* established him as a champion for environmentalism.

71 Elvis Stahr: President of the National Audubon Society from 1968 to 1979.

71 Barry Commoner: A biologist, professor, and activist who rose to prominence as an opponent of nuclear testing. In 1980, Commoner founded the Citizens Party, turning his ecological message into a political platform on which he would run for President.

71 David Brower: The founder of myriad environmentalist organizations, perhaps most notably the Sierra Club Foundation, an organization that campaigned against the construction of dams in Grand Canyon National Park during the 1960s. Abbey and Brower both shared a profound concern with overpopulation and immigration.

71 Paul Ehrlich: A professor of biology at Stanford University. Ehrlich's *The Population Bomb* (1968), written at the behest of David Brower, affirmed Abbey's views that overpopulation posed an economic and environmental threat to the United States.

76 B. Traven: A mysterious author with a penchant for pseudonyms and alternate identities. Though Abbey praised him as America's greatest writer, Traven's origins remain unknown and the majority of his work was written in German. Like Abbey's, much of Traven's writing was rooted in the Southwest, though Traven's influence on Abbey was not limited to literature: similar to Abbey's desert internment, Traven's ashes were scattered over Rio Jataté.

77 Bruce Babbitt: A Democrat, Babbitt served as the Governor of Arizona from 1978 until 1987. He would go on to serve as Secretary of the Interior in the Clinton administration.

77 George Sessions: The author of *Deep Ecology for the Twenty-First Century* and a celebrated pioneer of the Deep Ecology movement in North America. The movement maintains, in sum, that all living things are equal and have innate value beyond their utility to humans, a worldview Abbey found largely in tune with his own.

81 Mr. Haslam's proposed introduction: Gerald Haslam, professor of English at Sonoma State College, California, wrote the afterword to the 1978 UNM Press edition of *Fire on the Mountain*.

86 this Alaska book: *Coming Into the Country.*

90 you're right about *Black Sun*: *Black Sun* would be reprinted in 1981 and 1982 by Capra and Avon, respectively.

92 *Eco-Philosophy*: An academic newsletter published by George Sessions.

92 Mark Dubois: An environmental activist in California.

93 Devall: Bill Devall, like George Sessions, was a proponent of deep ecology.

94 my favorite American poet: Robinson Jeffers.

97 *Mariah/Outside*: *Mariah* would soon be dropped from the magazine's name.

101 John G. Mitchell: An editor at Sierra Club Books, Mitchell worked with Abbey on *Slickrock: The Canyon Country of Southeastern Utah*, a coffee-table book that memorialized the title region. Mitchell would later grace Abbey's classroom at the University of Arizona as a guest lecturer.

102 book about Neal Cassady & Friends: *Holy Goof: A Biography of Neal Cassady.*

104 *Rocky Mountain* Magazine: Once the premiere photographic, literary, and cultural periodical of the Intermountain West, *Rocky Mountain* was bought up by strong-arm competition and killed.

106 Morton Kamins: Freelance writer and reviewer.

107 my wife Clarke: In fact, Ed and Clarke were not yet married at this writing.

116 Howie Wolke: A co-founder of Earth First! Earth First! was founded in 1979 by a group of individuals who had become frustrated at the inability of more modest, compromising environmental groups to preserve wildness and wilderness in North America.

116 Dave Foreman: A co-founder and polemical leader of Earth First! Like other members of the organization, Foreman was profoundly influenced by Abbey's writings, as is evidenced by the title of his 1985 book *Ecodefense: A Field Guide to Monkeywrenching*.

117 Dick Estelle, KUAT Radio: Abbey was referring to Dick Estelle's public radio program *The Radio Reader*, which featured Estelle reading from contemporary novels.

120 Aaron Abbey: Abbey's second son with Rita Deanin, Aaron was born in 1959 in Albuquerque.

121 Howard: Howard Abbey, born in 1928, was Edward's younger brother, and closest to him in age. Abbey partially modelled the character of Will Lightcap in *The Fool's Progress* on Howard.

134 Joe Kanon, Dutton Books: Joseph Kanon spent the early part of his career in publishing, working as editor-in-chief, president, and CEO of both E.P. Dutton and Houghton Mifflin, before launching his own literary career in 1995 with *Los Alamos*.

137 the C.A.P.: the Central Arizona Project was an elaborate and costly surface canal system designed to transport water to Tucson from the Colorado River.

153 Smith in SLC: Gibbs M. Smith founded the publishing company that bears his name in Santa Barbara in 1969 and relocated to Utah in 1973.

155 Mr. Woodworth: Since the 1970s, Fred Woodworth has been the editor of *The Match*, an Arizona-based anarchist magazine.

156 Karen Evans: Abbey had met Ms. Evans at a Solstice party, and agreed to be interviewed. The fate of said interview is unknown.

160 David Petersen: At the time, Western Editor for *Mother Earth News* magazine.

161 the blurb from Larry McMurtry: The blurb to which Abbey referred ("the Thoreau of the American West") is actually a paraphrase from McMurtry's 1975 *Washington Post* review of *The Monkey Wrench Gang*, in which he wrote: "Eastlake is the Kafka of the American desert; Abbey is its Thoreau."

164 Carroll Ballard: Ballard had directed the film version of Farley Mowat's *Never Cry Wolf*, which was among Abbey's favorite books and films.

164 that screenplay: for a movie based on *The Monkey Wrench Gang*.

165 the GEM: Giant Earth Mover, which Abbey would subsequently enlist as the archenemy in *Hayduke Lives!*

169 *Confessions of the Barbarian*: This was later renamed *The Fool's Progress*.

171 R. Crumb: Robert Crumb, the iconic cartoon illustrator.

172 Poor old Alan H.: Alan Harrington.

173 S&S: Simon & Schuster.

181 Ken Sleight: An old friend and the model for Seldom Seen Smith in *The Monkey Wrench Gang*.

181 Cal Black: A Utah businessman and politician who appears as Bishop Love in both *The Monkey Wrench Gang* and *Hayduke Lives!*

182 my goddamn novel: *The Fool's Progress.*

183 Cliff Woods and Family: Clarke Abbey recalls Cliff Woods as "a kind and generous man" who ranched in Aravaipa Canyon, Arizona.

189 I saw the stone horse once: In the August 1986 issue of *Antaeus*, Lopez had written of his visit to and concern for a fragile prehistoric "ground glyph" depiction of a horse, located on remote Bureau of Land Management land.

189 Daniel Halpern: Daniel Halpern was an editor and the co-founder (with Paul Bowles) of the quarterly literary magazine *Antaeus.*

189 Gretel: Gretel Ehrlich is the author of *The Solace of Open Spaces*, a book that was praised by Annie Dillard.

196 the Abbey Reader: The collection would later appear as *Slumgullion Stew.*

196 *A Writer's Credo and Other Essays: 1984–87*: This was later published as *One Life at a Time, Please.*

198 one of Krutch's books: Joseph Wood Krutch was a prolific writer, critic, and biographer. After teaching at Columbia University from 1937 until 1953, Krutch moved to Arizona, where his writing began to address environmental issues. Abbey made Krutch's acquaintance in Arizona, shortly before Krutch's death in 1970.

198 Horgan's book about Gregg: Abbey was referring to Paul Horgan's *Josiah Gregg and His Vision of the Early West.*

199 Jon Krakauer: As a freelance writer, Krakauer solicited similar views from several well-known writers in the pursuit of an article assignment. His best-selling books, *Into the Wild* and *Into Thin Air* would come later, in 1996 and 1997, respectively.

200 new book of essays: *One Life at a Time, Please.*

202 Hoots and Iva: Ed's brother Howard and his wife.

205 the Abos: Australian Aborigines.

209 A.B. Guthrie: Guthrie's *The Way West* won the 1951 Pulitzer Prize for distinguished fiction.

213 *Die Universalschraubenschlussel Bande*: *The Monkey Wrench Gang.*

215 A.B. Guthrie: Abbey is referring here to *Big Sky, Fair Land: The Environmental Essays of A. B. Guthrie, Jr.*, ed. David Petersen, 1988.

216 Charles Bowden: An author, an editor for *City Magazine*, and a friend of Abbey's, Bowden shared his dedication to the conservation of the Arizona desert.

220 Donn Rawlings: A friend of Abbey's and a professor at Yavapai College, Prescott, Arizona.

222 at the U: University of Arizona, Tucson.

223 Johnny: Abbey's brother.

223 Nancy: Abbey's sister.

223 Paul: Abbey's father.

223 poor old Rini Templeton: Templeton worked with Abbey when he edited *El Crepúscolo de la Libertad*, a Taos newspaper.

223 John DePuy: DePuy, a.k.a. Debris, worked with Abbey and Rini Templeton at *El Crepúscolo de la Libertad*. Templeton was gorgeous and the two men competed for her "insatiable" affections. DePuy won and married her.

226 Jim Carrico: Ed met Carrico at Organ Pipe National Monument, where the two worked together.

226 Bill Hoy: A mutual friend and Park Service naturalist.

226 Big Bend: The National Park in Texas.

229 Ann Zwinger: Abbey had written a favorable review of Zwinger's *Run, River, Run* for *The New York Times*. Gratitude for that review compelled Zwinger to attend Abbey's Moab wake nearly fifteen years later.

229 WC Wms: William Carlos Williams.

231 the bright, clever story by young Aaron Abbey: Aaron Abbey's publication in *Playboy* marked the height of his short-lived literary career.

235 Robert Houston: Friend, writer, and director of the creative writing program at the University of Arizona, where Abbey briefly taught.

238 Mike Roselle: A co-founder of Earth First!

243 Dear Iggie: Charles Bowden.

244 Jim Fergus: Fergus would eventually publish his first novel, *One Thousand White Women: The Journals of May Dodd*, in 1998.

245 the Red Dragon: Abbey had recently purchased a bright red 1975 Cadillac El Dorado convertible.

245 Jack Shoemaker: The founder of and editor-in-chief at North Point Press. Shoemaker would later found Counterpoint Press.

247 your Guthrie book: *Big Sky, Fair Land: The Environmental Essays of A. B. Guthrie, Jr.*

248 Honorable Wayne Owens: A Democrat Representative from Utah, Owens served multiple terms in Congress: from 1973 until 1975 and again from 1987 until 1993.

248 the San Juan BLM: The San Juan Bureau of Land Management.

250 the Mt. Graham controversy: Home to native pine forests and an endangered tree squirrel species, Mt. Graham was being pursued as a site for the construction of yet another Arizona space observatory.

250 the conspiracy by DeConcini and Kolbe: Democratic Senator Dennis DeConcini and Republican Representative Jim Kolbe both supported the University of Arizona's observatory proposition. In 1988, DeConcini secured an exemption from the Endangered Species Act that would facilitate the observatory's construction.

258 C. L. Rawlins: *High Country News* poetry editor and essayist.

264 Malcolm Brown: Among Abbey's closest friends when they attended UNM together, Brown inspired the comedic "goo-roo" character Morton Bildad in *The Fool's Progress*.

267 DeWitt Daggett: A books-on-tape entrepreneur.

269 John Nichols, Taos, New Mexico (27 February 1989): Less than three weeks after typing this note to Nichols, on the morning of March 14, 1989, Abbey would die of "esophageal hysteria"—uncontrollable internal bleeding, bouts of which had plagued him for years. The "wino" joke arises from the fact that his disease, varices, is often associated with scleroses of the liver. Abbey had never been an alcoholic, was exceedingly parsimonious in his drinking in later years, and a biopsy not long before his death proved that his liver was healthy.

270 David Petersen (circa March 1989): This is a form letter that Abbey had sent to many friends over many years—a family joke, as it were.

INDEX

Edward Abbey was born in 1927 in western Pennsylvania. At the age of seventeen, he traveled west and fell in love with the desert country. After a stint in the army, during which he was stationed in Italy, he studied at the University of New Mexico and the University of Edinburgh. After returning to the U.S., he worked for a summer as a seasonal ranger at Arches National Monument in the late 1950s. The journals he kept that summer would eventually become one of his most famous works of nonfiction, *Desert Solitaire*. Abbey was also known for his fiction, most notably *The Monkey Wrench Gang*, in which a group of friends commits acts of sabotage against industrial development projects. Abbey spent nearly his entire adult life in the Southwest, and died in 1989 near Tucson, Arizona.

David Petersen is the author of nine books, including *On the Wild Edge: In Search of a Natural Life*, and the editor of four more, including *Confessions of a Barbarian: Selections from the Journals of Edward Abbey*. David and his wife, Caroline, live in a small cabin on a big mountain in the San Juan Mountains of Colorado.

MORE NONFICTION BOOKS
FROM MILKWEED EDITIONS

Brown Dog of the Yaak:
Essays on Art and Activism
Rick Bass

Wild Earth: Wild Ideas for a
World Out of Balance
Edited by Tom Butler

The Book of the Everglades
Edited by Susan Cerulean

Winter Creek: One Writer's
Natural History
John Daniel

The Colors of Nature: Culture,
Identity, and the Natural World
Edited by Alison H. Deming
and Lauret E. Savoy

Grass Roots: The Universe of Home
Paul Gruchow

Taking Care: Thoughts on
Storytelling and Belief
William Kittredge

Arctic Refuge: A Circle of Testimony
Compiled by Hank Lentfer
and Carolyn Servid

An American Child Supreme:
The Education of a Liberation Ecologist
John Nichols

Ecology of a Cracker Childhood
Janisse Ray

The Dream of the Marsh Wren:
Writing As Reciprocal Creation
Pattiann Rogers

Testimony: Writers of the West Speak
On Behalf of Utah Wilderness
Compiled by Stephen Trimble
and Terry Tempest Williams

Shaped by Wind and Water:
Reflections of a Naturalist
Ann Haymond Zwinger

To order books or for more information, contact Milkweed at (800) 520-6455
or visit our Web site (www.milkweed.org).

MILKWEED EDITIONS

Founded in 1979, Milkweed Editions is one of the largest independent, nonprofit literary publishers in the United States. Milkweed publishes with the intention of making a humane impact on society, in the belief that literature can transform the human heart and spirit. Within this mission, Milkweed publishes in four areas: fiction, nonfiction, poetry, and children's literature for middle-grade readers.

JOIN US

Milkweed depends on the generosity of foundations and individuals like you, in addition to the sales of its books. In an increasingly consolidated and bottom-line-driven publishing world, your support allows us to select and publish books on the basis of their literary quality and the depth of their message. Please visit our Web site (www.milkweed.org) or contact us at (800) 520-6455 to learn more about our donor program.

Interior design and typesetting by Percolator

Reformatting for paperback edition by
Prism Publishing Center

Typeset in Whitman and Univers

Printed on Rolland Enviro 100
(100% post consumer waste)
by Friesens Corporation